Allyson Shaw has worked a[...]
thirty years. Her writing on [...]
in numerous journals and an[...]
Poems Human and Inhuma[...]
Poets series, *Rituals & Dec[...] and The Bottle Imp*. She
spent her formative years in California and now lives in Orkney.

~

'*Ashes & Stones* is its own reminder of a dark
period in Scotland's past, but also carries a warning
for the present day . . . This is not the book you
think it is, and it is all the better for it'
Alistair Braidwood, *Snack*

'Profound, personal, and tragically timely, this is more than an
important book – it's a requiem that rises to a rallying cry'
Jesse Bullington, author of *The Folly of the World*

'[Shaw] gives life to many of the women burned as witches in
Scotland. Shocking and important – it made me realise this
hasn't been done before, nor have I questioned why until now'
Laline Paull, author of *Pod*

'The book is a fascinating exploration of the search for
personal identity, the ever-present dangers of religious
and political extremism, and how we examine and
process the murderous injustices from our past'
Helen Callaghan, author of *Dear Amy*

'Shaw's writing is utterly compelling and her perspective is
vital . . . *Ashes & Stones* is a work of devotion. This is what it
means to write with care and with candour. *Ashes & Stones* is
both genuine memorial and galvanising activism in book form'
Sally Huband, author of *Sea Bean*

Ashes & Stones

A Scottish Journey in Search
of Witches and Witness

ALLYSON SHAW

sceptre

First published in Great Britain in 2023 by Sceptre
An imprint of Hodder & Stoughton
An Hachette UK company

This paperback edition published in 2023

1

A CIP catalogue record for this title is available from the British Library

Paperback ISBN 9781529395495
ebook ISBN 9781529395471

Typeset in Sabon MT by Hewer Text UK Ltd, Edinburgh
Printed and bound in Great Britain by Clays Ltd, Elcograf S.p.A.

Hodder & Stoughton policy is to use papers that are natural, renewable
and recyclable products and made from wood grown in sustainable
forests. The logging and manufacturing processes are expected to
conform to the environmental regulations of the country of origin.

Hodder & Stoughton Ltd
Carmelite House
50 Victoria Embankment
London EC4Y 0DZ

www.sceptrebooks.co.uk

To Michael

Contents

Orkney

Highlands

16

Moray Coast

3   2

Cairngorms

Aberdeen

6

Dundee

7

7

8

9   Fife Coast

15

1

Glasgow

10

4

12

5   13

11

Edinburgh

N.

Introduction
Pipe Song

In the midst of a pandemic, I sit at my writing desk, an old side table, looking out of the bay window at the grey slate rooftops where gulls cackle, vigilant over their chimney-pot nests. I live in Banff on the north-east coast of Scotland. In 'My Father's House', Angela Carter writes of 'ancient and graceful' Banff, 'a small, granite seventeenth-century town so obscure that letters directed to it are sometimes sent to Banff, Alberta, in error'. Carter, that extraordinary writer of feminist fairy tales, knew Banff well. Her 'ain folk' were from MacDuff, the rival village across the river Deveron. If you try to google Banff, you will probably get the Canadian tourist hotspot, with its resorts and film festivals. Scotland's Banff, the original, has none of those things. Banff, its name a one-syllable bark, was once a royal burgh; now, it is a place where nothing much happens. The apocalyptic angels of the medieval graveyard face off with a garage. These memento mori brandish their scythes as you pass them on the way to the local shop. Low cliffs by the pebbled beach, upholstered with scurvy grass and the pink of sea thrift, were once called the Elf Kirk, or Elf Church. Many here feel trapped and wish they were somewhere else. Some young people leave for jobs and schools in the city; others never leave. Here, you keep your head down, you don't call attention to yourself. The tacit, neighbourly agreement is one of deep privacy.

But Carter felt at home here, saying, 'You don't choose your landscapes. They choose you.' Banff is a bit like cats, then. Undoubtedly, this same north-east coast has chosen me. It's been a fraught race just to arrive at what feels like the end of the world. I've been on the run from gentrification and hardship. This house came without a proper kitchen, and its bathroom had leaky pipes. The cottage garden is large and untamed, with a giant ash, sycamores, and an apple tree grown into the drystone walls. In a dark corner, stagnant rainwater collects in an old metal washtub where midges swarm in the summer. A willow, coppiced and bent, grows sideways instead of up. Holed up in my stone cottage, it is as good a place as any to write about witches – maybe better.

Four months have passed since the start of the pandemic. The hospital across the street is half empty and underfunded. Its Gothic presence of stone and iron is wedded to an unsympathetic addition of metal siding. The pavement floodlights seep through my windows, mixing with the blue light of a SAD lamp. Spring comes, but the days remain dark and cold. It's April, that cruellest month. The *haar*, the freezing mist from the North Sea, rolls through the streets, bringing with it the first keening notes of a pipe song. I go out to see. A woman in full piper's uniform plays outside the hospital doors, honouring those working inside, the frontline workers of the NHS putting their lives at risk during the pandemic.

Bagpipe music makes me cry; I well up at even a happy tune. It's homesickness, but for which home? I am an immigrant from California, a vast paved desert, a place with no seasons. Though I have been in the UK over fifteen years, I'm often asked why I would leave the presumed paradise of California for this wet, dreary island. There is no simple way to tell the tedious story of displacement. Yet, here I am, a daughter returned to Scotland. Like many Americans with a Scottish surname and a story of ancestry, Scotland is also a metaphorical home, a place where I seed dreams of belonging.

When I was a girl in the United States, there was a catalogue that came to the house filled with different kinds of plaids. It was an extensive booklet sent to anyone with a Scottish last name. Inside, one could find the tartan and crest of one's clan. In Scotland, this is considered the tat of the 'cultural cringe'. As a girl, I knew none of this. Scotland was a fairy-tale place to me, one I could only just find on the pastel-coloured globe at school, a pink wedge blurred into the United Kingdom. Scotland was remote and filled with imaginings. In this catalogue of clan paraphernalia, the name Shaw appeared alongside a disappointingly garish red-and-turquoise tartan. The crest was a hand holding a dagger, framed with a belt. It said *Fide et Fortitude* – faith and courage. The crest looked like the ace of swords in the iconic Rider–Waite–Smith tarot cards. I had a set of these as a girl, a spooky child fascinated by the occult. Witches and magic were tied to Scotland from the very start.

As a teenager, I had run from Southern California to San Francisco, trying to escape sexual trauma and the PTSD that followed in its wake. My life was marked by departures. I survived suffering by trading one geography for another. I found myself in the Sunset District of San Francisco, where the thick fog of the Pacific oozed in from the west. There is very little sun in the Sunset. The perpetual marine layer shrouded the tiny house I lived in, and black mould crept up the walls. I was working three jobs and trying to go to school. I shelved books in two different libraries, and cleaned the houses of the wealthy on Nob Hill. I was often hungry, and my existence was precarious.

The Piper came to the house in the Sunset. He stood at my door like a fairy lover appearing from nowhere. Somehow, he'd found me, this man from my old life as a college student in Southern California. We had both volunteered for Amnesty International, and we'd gone on dates. I think he might have been seeing someone else at the same time, juggling us both. He was a bagpipe player by profession and made his living playing at weddings and funerals. He claimed bragging rights for playing on a Rod Stewart album, but this was confessed with chagrin. Looking back, it was probably another lie. He had the full regalia hanging at the ready in his little Honda – the kilt, the brogues and hose with garter flashes, the short jacket and sporran. He was proud, and wanted me to see it. It got my blood going; he didn't even have to be wearing it. He was handsome, with a strong jaw and bright blue eyes, and a mane of tawny hair cascading over his shoulders. He asked me to dinner and I went. In an upmarket restaurant at the edge of Chinatown, he conjured a dream of Scottishness: I had a surname and a clan, perhaps even a castle. I didn't know at the time that this is the stuff of 'ancestral tourism', a story of tribal inclusion that Scotland exports and the Scottish diaspora embraces. It was as if The Piper had discovered some secret part of me filled with thistles. His proposal was like a bargain from the Fair Folk. He would take me to Scotland, for good. He said we had something called *right of return* – Scotland would have us.

I said no. It sounded too good to be true and, without researching immigration policy in the late 1980s, it probably was. I trusted the dream; I just didn't trust the man. Decades later, I paid the tithe to hell a few times over to get here. I have known for most of my adult life that nationhood is more than the trinkets and trappings of ancestral tourism, the kilt pins and plaids sold to Americans in lieu of authentic identity. By now, I understand Virginia Woolf's assertion that: 'as a woman I have no country. As a woman I want no country. As a woman, my country is the whole world.' It became my motto throughout the flag-waving, warmongering years I lived in the USA, and I understood Woolf's rejection of nationalism as I crossed my fingers behind my back and pledged to the Queen. This bargain meant I could stay in the UK as a citizen. My heart was saying, 'I want no country.' But what if I did? What if I do?

Before I became Scottish, I was legally British. Would that this transformation had been of the alchemical kind, with epic blessings from ladies in lakes, land spirits or the like. It was bloodless, expensive and full of bureaucracy, which is perhaps appropriate. Expense and bureaucracy have marked my life on this island since I arrived. When I took the oath to become British, I sat together with twenty other immigrants in a beautiful gilded room in a Georgian mansion house, the residence of the Lord Mayor of York. There was handshaking and commemorative gold-plated coins. A patient civil servant oversaw the ceremony with an admirable degree of sincerity. We were here now, she said, to share our talents and cultures with our new home. A brass band drowned her out. For a moment, I thought, *They really do it right up here in York, though the timing could be better*. But the fanfare wasn't for us; it was for the sixty-second anniversary of the Queen's coronation. The Queen was there, too, in the form of a gigantic, gold sceptre laid on the table before us, looking like some blinged-out cudgel. We said the oath. The faithful went first, swearing on their various holy books, and then the rest of us, the godless, affirmed the oath of loyalty to the Queen. There were no other options. You couldn't swear to, say, Quentin Crisp playing Queen Elizabeth I in the film version of *Orlando*, or the Scottish unicorn, or the Cailleach. After the ritual, there was a mean portion of tea, inexcusably tepid and too strong.

In Scotland, this oath is tested by reality and political complexities. Scotland is a crash course that I'm still taking. The people of the Celtic diaspora might have ideas about Scotland. Curious tourists come looking for an integral Scottish land-scape, and then they leave, back to their far-flung homes across the world. I am here among people to whom I'm a stranger. I am suspect, a perennial outsider. In rural Scotland, everyone knows everyone else and has for generations. If they don't know you, you are an *incomer*. While there may be civility or even kindness, there will never be inclusion. Perhaps in a city like Glasgow or Edinburgh, I could have imagined that I now had a Scottish iden-tity, but living in this insular place, I knew I had no claim to any of it. The strife and beauty didn't belong to me, and yet it was still mine.

The paradox is present in the cliffs, bens and ancient recumbent stone circles. The land embraces me on my treks. I have no doubt I am Scottish, even though I have no genealogy on my father's side, the Scottish side. There are no known ancestors, though centuries ago someone in the family left Scotland for the United States. I will never know any more than this; my family's secrets and the furious silence of my father's death guarantee it. I feel this lack of ancestry acutely. I consider adopting ancestors who were unclaimed, unloved and forsaken – the women ostracised by their communities and accused as witches. I would claim them as my own.

When I arrived at this little house by the sea, the whole garden was littered with decades of detritus. I doggedly cleared away the fly-tipped mysteries: a broken shed, bags of hardened concrete, mangled lawn furniture, rusted golf clubs and a suitcase. It became home. Now, a riot of wild-seeded flowers blooms in the spring. The garden is sheltered from the extreme weather of gale-force winds, horizontal hail, and freezing mist – it's a place to write. Storm clouds sulk past the bay window. Incandescent pink sunrises herald each day.

I wake early and compile notes I've made over years of visiting monuments to accused witches – the stones, fountains and even hedge mazes dedicated to people who were accused during the witch-hunts of the sixteenth and seventeenth centuries. Secreted away outside a village here, beside a suburban lawn there, each has its own story. Some are called 'The Witches Stone' or are menhirs marked with a date. Many are unremarked by archaeological records or heritage signs; they are merely big rocks with stories that have been told over hundreds of years. Sorting through my field notes is a bit like clearing junk from the garden: historical refuse and lies obscure the reality of the place, the country where I find myself. There's a lot to shift before I get to fertile ground. I see evidence of the witch-hunts everywhere – the 'witches' rings' where people were chained to the walls of churches; lonely Carlin stones and memorial plaques that show themselves to me wherever I go. I want an authentic glimpse of these women accused of witchcraft, and I go out into the landscape to meet them. My research accumulates, and the scope of atrocity deepens. Everywhere, it seems, is evidence of these mass, state-sanctioned killings. The hunts terrorised generations, and the overwhelming majority of the victims were women.

Witch-hunts raged across Europe, and tens of thousands of people were killed. The European hunts peaked in the sixteenth century. The witch-hunts in Scotland began later that century, and continued into the eighteenth. An estimated 4,000 people were formally accused and over 2,000 were executed. These numbers do not represent the whole. Some names were not recorded, many records were lost, and some extrajudicial persecutions were never written down. Considering the small population of Scotland in the seventeenth century (approximately 800,000 people), these numbers are sobering. There was once a time when people, the overwhelming majority of them women, were hunted all over Scotland. Although we don't know the full extent of the horror, it remains in the collective memory and the landscape.

Witch-hunting was, in the words of historian Christina Larner, 'a synonym for woman-hunting'. The most powerful institutions in the land – the Crown, landowning men, and the Church – persecuted the most helpless of the souls in their care as if they were evil incarnate. The ministers of church meetings, or kirk sessions, worked with the governing body of the Privy Council and landowners to orchestrate the interrogation, trial and execution of thousands. This was not a populace gripped by panic; this extermination was a deliberate and systematic application of the law. Today, King James VI and I is best known for commissioning a poetic translation of the Bible, but his most enduring legacy is forgotten: his instigation of the murder of thousands as state policy, a sweeping attempt to force the entire populace to conform to the mores of a strict godly society. The evidence given in these trials was made up of hearsay, circumstance, and confessions extracted under torture.

Many of the accused speak of ghosts, of *cantrips*, of strange workings with even stranger results. There are fragments in the confessions, seen through the veil of pain and suffering, that seem authentic and real enough to the woman saying them, even if they are unconvincing to a modern reader. Theirs was a world where animals could communicate, where ghosts could walk out from a hill and offer you advice, where the land was alive with spiritual presence. This folk animism has been reduced to fairy lore. I map out the landscape we share with the accused and plan my routes. What will I find in these places, and could they offer clues to the lost lives of those who died during the witch-hunts? Much evidence about these sites and their history has been destroyed, or was never written down in the first place, but I search for fragments of a forgotten whole.

Witchcraft confessions are my primary source for this history, but they are hostile documents, written down by demonologists, witch-hunters and judges. The voices of the accused arrive *wirried* – strangled. They are demonised or erased completely. Sometimes the only mention of a woman is found in a treasury record itemising the cost of her execution. During the witch-hunts, learned men believed a treasonous conspiracy of women were in league with Satan. This is not so difficult to grasp, given those in power will always find justification for their own violence, no matter how implausible the scapegoat. What is harder to understand is that after the Enlightenment, the genocides of the nineteenth and twentieth centuries, and with all our understanding of modes of oppression, we have not yet paid full witness to this history. Much traditional lore has vanished. Ways of working with the spirits of the land, of knowing its rhythms and wants, are dismissed as the fallacies of superstitious and credulous people. These beliefs were demonised during the witch trials, and those who kept them alive through oral history were snuffed out. These women's stories are little known. They are rarely taught and have only recently started to be seriously discussed.

The people who died during the witch-hunts in Scotland were not witches. They did not have special powers to change the weather or bring death with a glance. They were women, often poor, old and isolated. If those who died were women and not witches, what drove this misogyny? Though men in Scotland were also executed for the crime of witchcraft, eighty-five per cent of those who died were women. Many voices and ideas created this hostility. The Scottish Reformation was part of the wider European Protestant separation from the Catholic Church. Scotland became a Calvinist nation with new spiritual ideas: faith alone could redeem the soul, regardless of one's behaviour. In Calvinist belief, certain souls were predestined to be saved and others were damned. John Knox, the architect of the Scottish Reformation, wrote the tract *The First Blast of the Trumpet Against the Monstrous Regiment of Women* in 1558. It was a diatribe against female monarchs, written in reaction to Mary I of Scotland and Elizabeth I's rule. It railed against women holding any sort of power and was nothing less than a declaration of war on an entire gender.

#WomenNotWitches is now a rallying cry for online discussions around justice and witness to this history. For centuries, the thousands killed during the hunts were forgotten or imagined as cartoonish hags or demonic seductresses. If we were to start remembering them as human beings, would this change anything for modern women? A growing number of women self-identify as witches, and this is happening alongside a movement of oppressed people telling their own stories in their own voices. Who has told the story of these women called witches – and who will tell it in the future?

As I delve deeper into this dark history, I wonder about the collateral damage of this four-hundred-year-old campaign of terror against women that lasted for over a century. What have we lost, and what ghosts do we live with now? Those unmourned souls of this near-forgotten history still deserve justice, and warn of the centuries of shameful silence. In seventeenth-century Scotland, witches were thought to be people who made a deal with the Christian devil. They signed away their souls in return for secret knowledge, but more often for food or a coin. Some of the accused were wise women, diviners and healers – called *spaewives* by the communities they served, from the Scots verb *spae*, meaning to see into the future. These women wouldn't have identified themselves as witches, or pawns of the devil, though many of their beliefs about fairies, ghosts, healing charms and herbal remedies would be demonised during the witch-hunts. The confessions talk of the accused working weather magic and healing spells, but these documents are also full of women *stravaiging* or rambling, giving birth, herding cows, brewing beer and praying.

Modern self-identified witches borrow concepts of spellcraft, herb lore and second sight from the myths and legends of witch-craft folklore and the evidence presented in the witch trials, yet it is anachronistic to impose this modern idea of a witch on the women executed for witchcraft in Scotland. Could modern witches – women such as myself – really reclaim the moniker without thoroughly understanding the stories of the women who died accused of its fictions? The idea of the witch eclipses the reality of the lives of those executed for witchcraft. The witch is the embodiment of a powerful myth, an archetype embraced by feminists, radical thinkers and spiritual seekers. Witches are a strange company. The more closely you peer at them, the less you'll see. They are in-between beings, best looked at sidelong. When I first saw Albrecht Dürer's *Witch Riding Backwards on a Goat* at the British Museum, my back was raw with a fresh tattoo of a fox and badger dancing under the moon, drawn into me the day before. I'd just emerged from the cellophane, having cared for the tattoo as best I could at the sink of a Soho hostel. It was starting to prickle. Part of a tattoo's appeal is this sensation of healing, the magic of the body mending itself, a reminder that one is alive. This tattoo was tucked between my shoulder blades. I couldn't reach it, and I definitely couldn't see it, but I could feel it was there. Such is my life with witches.

Dürer's witch gallops furiously through the centuries, as if drawn just for me. She is beautiful in her absolute agency. Is the goat riding forwards, and the witch looking backwards out of hell? Or is the goat riding backwards into the future? She is going both ways at once. Dürer has signed this print with his monogram in reverse, and in this place of the backwards, the reversal, there is freedom. The witch hollers her naked song directly at me, at us, the future who will know her. We are in the middle of a witch-wave, newly anarchic and feminist. I claim the denomination *hedge witch* and all the unbounded mysteries that implies: a liminal thinker, someone open to the edges where other ways of knowing seep in. Those of us who identify as witches are feminist tricksters, myth-makers and storytellers in search of a history.

The cunning folkways and ancestral knowing embraced by modern neopagans has roots in the much-maligned studies of Margaret Murray, the first scholar to approach the witch-hunts systematically. *The Witch-Cult in Western Europe*, her study from 1921, uses witch-trial confessions, many of them Scottish, to argue there was once an ancient goddess cult wiped out by the witch-hunts. Her methods have been called into question by numerous scholars, but her ideas persist in modern Wicca and neopagan thought. Murray may have been wrong in an empirical sense, but she was the first to list the names. We lost something during those traumatic centuries of the witch-hunts. We feel it in our bones, this missing thing: power, wisdom, and a connection to the land, our ancestral birthright. The truth exists between the rhymes of a lost spell. To reclaim it, we must heal – and, in healing, face the horror of our past.

In Britain, stories of accused witches are dusted off in newspapers at Halloween. Special-interest pieces include salacious details of sex with the devil, along with stock photos of green-faced hags with warts on their chins. This clichéd image of the witch is fantastical, but like any myth, there is some truth in it. Most of the women accused would have been stripped, shaved and searched for the telltale mole or 'devil's mark'. Those dragged to the stake to be strangled and burned may have had greenish bruises over their faces from beatings. I look for these women, trekking across muddy fields, dodging bulls and barbed wire, reading marker stones obscured with lichen, poring over old Presbytery session records written in Scots, searching for these ancestors burned as witches.

'We are the granddaughters of the witches you couldn't burn' – such is the rallying cry of modern witches. It isn't historically accurate, but it's useful, as so many fantasies are. It's more likely that many of us are descended from those who tortured and killed women accused as witches. How many thousands were also complicit in their accusations? If we are looking for ancestry, those men in power left a much better paper trail. The accusers wrote the records of the trials. Of the women who died, almost nothing remains. The secrets and revelations of their lives went to the fire with them.

When I tell people that I'm writing about this history, they ask, 'Were they really witches?' When I say, 'No,' I can see they've lost interest. These women were not Glendas, Geillises nor Willows; there was not a Prue, Piper nor Phoebe among these dead, our dead. We watch Hermione Granger and Nancy Downs for a glimpse of power, something real and lost. Before Geillis was a time-traveller, carried writhing to her death on the show *Outlander*, Geillis Duncan was a Scottish healer tortured in front of King James VI and I, and later killed for the crime of witchcraft. All that is left of her is a distorted version of her life and death in a sixteenth-century witch-hunting propaganda pamphlet, *Newes from Scotland*.

Between reality and the imagined versions of this history, there is something like memorial. All over Scotland, artists, writers and musicians give shape to this remembrance. It is a movement that gains momentum as I write my own contribution to this creative outpouring. Perhaps in the future, genuine memorial and healing will be possible. When we turn to listen to this witness, might it sound like a pipe song played at dusk on a lonely hill where the pyres once burned? Composer Karen McCrindle Warren's formal mourning tune 'Lament for the Accused' remembers the nine women killed in Dumfries in 1659. The composition is also a memorial for all those for whom there is no physical monument. Steve Rooklidge of the Shasta Piping Society of California commissioned Karen to create the piece. He had seen the Interactive Witchcraft Map published by the University of Edinburgh, which offers a visual representation of the recorded trials and deaths of the accused. The map was produced by a student intern, Emma Carroll, and it makes a visual argument no statistics can match. The emotional impact of the map informed Karen's composition, written in a dissonant key with high notes symbolising the torment of torture and public executions. Her song is a *piobaireachd*, an ancient, traditional music for the Highland bagpipe, played for formal occasions of lament. When I interviewed her, Warren explained to me that the piece grows in intensity, 'like waves of grief coursing through the body and soul'. The repetitions intertwine, becoming cyclical and grounding. The pipe's staid procession repeats like an incantation. The plaintive, questioning melody turns back to its quiet advance. There's a call, like birdsong, urging others to listen. The notes, the mourners, gather and the meditative drone breaks open in a keening wail.

While the song is played, there is anguish but also dignity and peace.

My research begins with a computer-generated portrait of a woman, vivid and familiar. She could be a neighbour, an auntie or older sister, but hers is the face of a woman killed in 1704. Her image was created by a forensic artist, Christopher Rynn, using a photo of her skull. Her features are clear; her sad eyes stare back at me from my iPhone. She is certain I'll find some truth, even if I'm not. I keep this image on my laptop, the tutelary spirit of my work. Her grave is the first sojourn on this grim pilgrimage, which I begin in Torryburn, looking for a woman named Lillias Adie.

I

Seamark

Lillias Adie, Torryburn, 1704

'I am in compact with the devil, and have been so since before the second burning of the witches in this place.'

– Lillias Adie's first confession

It's high summer when I travel to see her grave, over 150 miles south from my home in Banff. Torryburn lies between Stirling and Edinburgh on Torry Bay. The intertidal mudflats of the bay, exposed at low tide, are a mixture of silt and clay filled with eel grass, laver spire snails and rag worms, all food for wintering birds. Rain spits down in fat drops, and the low, grey sky reflects the mudflats and the water of the Forth like a dirty mirror.

The Fife Coastal Path runs beside a green space with a play area framed by a trimmed lawn. Young families with children play together. Their gay laughter creates a dissonance. I've come here alone to visit a murdered woman's grave. But the survivors of this history live, work and play here; I am only passing through. There's an informational plinth illustrating local flora and fauna as well as a 'Witches Rock'. It explains that the large rock, visible in the shallows of Torry Bay, was used in the witch trials. According to the heritage sign, a suspect was tied to the stone and, as the tide rose, they were sentenced. If they drowned, they were innocent; if they survived, they were guilty, and were then strangled and burned. There is nothing to this claim; it is fiction. 'Dunking' or the water trial, was not used in Scotland, and there is no evidence it ever occurred in Torryburn. It is one of many myths about women accused as witches that heritage signs in the landscape make into official history.

I set off down the coastal path, going the wrong way, not realising Lillias's grave is behind me. I walk the length of Torryburn before I turn around. As the tide slowly creeps in, I wonder if I will find it. Wading in is an impossibility. It's dangerous, the mud deep in places, and one can easily sink. I retrace my steps. Back beside the car park, I see her grave at the foreshore, much closer than I'd imagined it would be. Lillias's grave is doorstop-sized, wreathed with frills of black bladderwrack. It is a stone trapdoor to some unkind realm. I stand before it and wonder why the sea hasn't taken it away, swallowed it up entirely. The water comes and goes gently, rises almost without movement. A deep patience resides in this place. Perhaps it has something to teach me about justice – changes in attitudes and ideas are made in tenuous increments. At the high shore, just as I'm leaving, I spot a cluster of *Cirsium heterophyllum*, a flower with the common name 'melancholy thistle'. One fluffy flowerhead nods with the weight of a bee rumbling through its petals. It was once thought that this flower could cure melancholy. Maybe Lillias knew of it. It strikes me – she is not here. She's not beneath the mud; her coffin and bones were robbed from her grave over a century ago. Nor is she in the heritage signs or ghost stories. She's gone, and it's the living that must wrestle with the truth of her death.

The location of Lillias's grave was recorded in the transcription of her trial record, published in 1820. The editor states in a footnote that her grave was still visible at the 'west end of town'. Her remains were dug up by hired hands in 1852. The phrenologist Joseph Neil Paton exhumed her body for his private collection. The wood from her coffin was made into walking sticks, one of which was sent to Andrew Carnegie. I wonder at this ghoulish prop, smooth from use and unassuming in a glass case at the Carnegie Library in Dunfermline. The atrocity of her death is reduced in this object to a curio. Joseph Neil Paton kept her skull in his personal museum and proclaimed her 'animal-like', as all witches before her. Paton's son, Joseph Noel Paton, renowned Scottish painter of fairies, perhaps depicted her skull as a memento mori in his 1861 work *Dawn: Luther at Erfurt*. Paton also sketched an imagined scene of Lillias dancing with the devil. His brother, landscape painter Waller Hugh Paton, rendered the surreal stone of her grave in a painting of Torry Bay.

In the years I spend writing this book, I will repeatedly return to Torryburn, a kind of sister revenant to Lillias. In 2019, I make my way down again at Samhain, the Celtic New Year, when it's said the veil between the worlds of the living and the dead is thin. I meet West Fife Councillor Kate Stewart, one of the people behind the call to return Lillias's bones. The sea is rising as we walk out to Lillias's stone in between the low and high tides. A wall of cold, white humidity sinks into my bones. Kate, in floral wellies and a pink mac, kneels over the stone and smiles as I take a picture with my phone. We talk about Lillias, and Kate tells me of the preparations for community wreath-making. People come together, weave greenery from the high shore and talk about bringing her home. Kate asks me what I would do with Lillias if we find her: 'Would you put her back in the mud?' No, I would not. Surely, there is space alongside others in the kirkyard, safe in the earth beneath a stone carved with her name. The sea grave was expensive and time-consuming for the eighteenth-century town council to build. Those in power were terrified of Lillias and had to keep her down, keep her soul from rising up again to seek justice. They buried her in unconsecrated ground at a distance from the place of her ordeal. A slab of sandstone sealed her there. But we can imagine something different for Lillias – a peaceful and respectful site for her memory.

Before the ghost of Lillias became my muse, she inspired Scottish artists and writers of the nineteenth century. The story of Lillias's bones, of a skull gone missing from a revenant grave, became a curiosity. Robert Louis Stevenson perhaps heard the legend from his beloved nanny, Alison Cunningham, or 'Cunny', who was born in Torryburn in 1822. She no doubt knew about Lillias's grave. Stevenson would have been two years old when Lillias's body was exhumed. Alison Cunningham's strict Christian convictions and knowledge of folklore found their way into Stevenson's work, including his story 'Thrawn Janet', about a woman who may or may not be a dead minion of Satan. In 'Thrawn Janet', an old woman ostracised by her community becomes a reanimated witch corpse, a pathetic and increasingly uncanny figure as the story progresses.

Paton's phrenologist museum is no more, its memory flattened beneath a Tesco car park. Lillias's skull isn't there. It isn't in the anatomical collections at the University of St Andrews, where it was photographed in 1910, posed in a flattering three-quarters profile. The photo documents Lillias's prominent cheekbones and the high bridge of her nose, the white teeth pronounced and singular as a thumbprint. In 1938, people queued at the Empire Exhibition to see the witch, her skull displayed as part of the History of Scotland exhibit. Her last appearance was at this exhibition hall in Glasgow. Then war began. Decades went by, and her memory was buried under the rubble of a new collective trauma, sunk deep like her grave in the tidal mudflats of Torryburn.

Fife, where Torryburn is located, was once a hotbed of witch-hunting. Violent witch-hunting began in the 1590s and peaked in 1649–50, but continued into the eighteenth century in places where religious leaders were committed to stamping out witchcraft in their parishes. The minister who oversaw Lillias's interrogation and death was the Reverend Allan Logan, a man who claimed he knew how to detect witches. During Communion, he would single out a woman and declare, 'You, witch-wife, get up from the table of the Lord.' His approach did not go unchallenged. In 1709, five years after Lillias's death, Reverend Logan was delivering one of his diatribes against witches when Helen

Key took up her stool and stormed out, later telling a neighbour she thought him 'daft'.

Lillias Adie was arrested in 1704, when witch-hunting in the rest of Europe had died down. Thirty years later, it would be abolished in Scotland. There were moments in the seventeenth century when witch-hunts were carried out on a mass scale, with hundreds arrested across the country, but individuals were accused and executed into the eighteenth century. The pattern of arrest and execution was the same whether part of a mass hunt or singular arrest. Cursing or quarrels, suspected healing, or associating with a reputed witch could result in accusation. The accused were summoned to the kirk session, or church court, and evidence was collected against them. The accused would then be arrested, tortured, interrogated and pricked for the 'devil's mark'. During this inquisition, others could be named, and the process would begin again. A commission for a trial was required from the central government, and the evidence gathered through interrogation and witness statements would be used to petition for this. Many died in prison from neglect and torture while waiting for a trial, and others died by suicide. Only after a formal trial could the accused be legally executed. Accusation and arrest could be based on 'repute', or a bad reputation built up over the course of years of neighbourly arguments and sexual reprimand by the Protestant Kirk, but a formal accusation could also happen suddenly, when one person, usually under torture, named another as an accomplice. If a reverend was inclined to seek out witches in his parish, rumour was enough to doom anyone.

Lillias's accuser was a woman named Jean Bizet. Neighbours could come forward with accusations during a kirk session. In the session minutes, Jean Bizet describes going from house to house in the village one night, drinking. Near the end of the evening, she was seized with terror, convinced that Lillias was coming for her. Other witnesses heard Jean Bizet cry out, 'O

Lilly with her blew doublet! O Mary, Mary Wilson! Christ keep me,' while wringing her hands and then passing out. According to the minutes, Jean Bizet was at a friend's house late into the evening and was in a state of drunken distemper. She accused Lillias Adie of acting with Janet Whyte and Mary Wilson in a conspiracy. When Jean Bizet's husband, James Tanochie, heard of this business, he said he would 'ding the devil out' of his wife.

Lillias was perhaps vulnerable as an elderly, single woman. The victims of the Scottish witch-hunts were overwhelmingly poor, older women. Lillias had an unusual appearance that perhaps marked her out from her neighbours. We know from the dimensions of Lillias's coffin before it was destroyed that she was uncommonly tall. Her teeth were very prominent. Jean Bizet fixates on Lillias's blue doublet, and from the scant statements at the trial, it's impossible to know why this troubled Bizet. Was Lillias's doublet brighter or finer than most? While this detail is seemingly inconsequential, it forms a fragment of Lillias as an individual woman, part of a time, a place and a people, and it helps us picture her. A blue doublet would have been a common garment at the time. The clothing of the poor was often dyed with woad, a yellow-flowered plant with tall stems and pale leaves. Woad blue is the blue of the sky reflected in the sea on a sunny day. That blue was the colour of much modest clothing, and had been for a millennia, and it was the blue Lillias wore.

Following the accusations of Jean Bizet, Lillias Adie was arrested by Bailie Williamson at 10 p.m. on 28 July 1704. Modern readers marvel at the confessions wrung from the accused during the witch-hunts, perhaps imagining women on a witness stand, confessing bizarre, sordid behaviour. This is often the way witch trials are portrayed in fiction. The reality is that, after arrest, the church needed evidence to take to the Privy Council in Edinburgh. The bulk of the evidence was the confession, extracted over months, during which the accused was often tortured, starved and sleep-deprived. There was no limit on how long the Kirk could hold someone before producing this 'evidence'. The interrogators would ask leading questions: 'When did you sleep with the devil?' 'Where did you meet other witches?' and, crucially, 'What are their names?' These interrogations would have been intense. A room of powerful men questioning a terrified, tortured woman.

During Lillias's initial interrogation, she swore, 'What I am to say shall be as true as the sun is in the firmament.' She confessed to a flurry of demonic meetings. Between interrogations, she was possibly held in the garret of the Townhouse of Culross – the seat of government and also a prison, where women accused as witches were confined and 'watched'. The loft space where she was held had no fire for warmth, and what little light there was came up through the slats of the floor. A man would have been paid to watch her and keep her awake. Sleep deprivation was the most common form of torture used to extract confessions from the accused. It was effective. Lack of sleep for one or two nights created a docile suggestibility in the prisoner's mindset. Longer periods of sleep deprivation resulted in hallucinations and deeper confusion.

Between Lillias's trial record and everything that went unsaid and unrecorded, we must read her sufferings. The interrogators only wrote down what they thought they needed to convict her. Perhaps she was led, in her exhaustion, to believe what was being asked of her. The crime of witchcraft involved merry-making with the devil, renunciation of Christian baptism, and the sex crime of 'meeting with the devil carnally'. The ministers pointedly asked accused women if they'd had sex with Satan, and the churchmen wanted details.

Lillias was interrogated by the minister and church elders four times during the course of her month-long incarceration, which ended only because she died, perhaps of suicide or the effects of imprisonment on her aged body. The trial record states that Lillias had been meeting the devil since the previous witch-hunt in Torryburn in 1666. She would have seen these earlier public executions as a young woman. Over the course of their lives, almost everyone in early modern Scotland would have witnessed the spectacle of women strangled and burned at the stake. It was an event, and often ale was given to the spectators. The bonfire would have been seen for miles and the smoke would have lingered for days, a signal to other women. No one was safe; none were immune to accusation. This is how terror works.

Lillias's interrogation went on; she met with a coven of 'twenty or thirty' witches, all now dead. She stated that she could not name the others, as they were 'masked like gentle-women'. As with all confessions extracted under torture, one must read beyond what is written. In this detail of others being dead or masked, we glimpse Lillias's courage. Her interrogators wanted names, and she initially provided none. In her further confessions, she said that the devil had come to her hundreds of times and 'lay with her carnally'. When he first trysted with her, it was at the hour just before sunset on Lammas, or the first of August, a transitional hour on the cross-quarter day in the harvest calendar. Lammas, or 'Loaf Mass', marked the midpoint between the summer solstice and the autumn equinox. At this pivotal moment, at an hour that was not quite night nor day, Lillias said she met the devil behind a stook, or bundled sheaf, set up in the field to dry. He was both pale and black, and his flesh was cold. Lillias added details: the devil wore a hat and arrived at their dances on a pony. Though he promised her much, she said he gave her only poverty and misery.

In many of the confessions, the devil is free of any supernatural menace. His appearance and broken promises are those of a human man. Repeatedly, women under interrogation describe Satan as a man, perhaps drawing on memories of sexual violence they had endured, details of other partners, or even the men who stood in judgement before them. Hours before she died, Lillias affirmed that her confession was 'as true as the sun shines on that floor, and dim as my eyes are, I see that'.

The cause of her death is not recorded, but here we glimpse that she was losing her sight, and that perhaps she was dying as a result of torture and imprisonment. Her last recorded words, that ray of sun on the floor with its promise of truth-telling, haunt me. Much can be made of the more fantastical things she said under duress. The confessions that survive were often written down in collections many years later, repeated as curiosities or evidence of superstitious belief. Some interrogation records reveal fragments of folk magic echoed in other sources. Methods of guarding against fairy wrath or ways to bring luck appear in the confessions, and are also seen in nineteenth-century collections of folklore, like John Gregorson Campbell's *The Gaelic Otherworld* and Walter Gregor's *Notes on the Folk-Lore of the North-East of Scotland*. Lillias's confessions of sex with the devil are nothing more than the words of a woman who wished to hasten death, while naming as few others as possible. Her strange stories, with their uncanny details, confound a modern reader. Why would she say such things if they weren't true, if they would surely lead to her death? Interrogators promised women mercy and freedom if they confessed and named others. But the yarns the accused spun for their torturers might have a deeper significance, too. Scholars like Diane Purkiss have argued that the accused fought for their lives and sense of self in these narrative confessions. In the face of intimidation, torture and the dehumanising process of interrogation, they tried to retain a sense of their own humanity through telling stories, bizarre and strange as they might seem.

The Kirk justice system was a product of the Protestant Reformation. In 1578, the founder of the Presbyterian Church in Scotland, John Knox, drew up *The Second Book of Discipline*. This document established the governing process of Presbyterianism, with a system of church courts extending from the parish kirk sessions to presbyteries, synods and the general assembly. This structure oversaw witch trials. The pattern of interrogation at kirk sessions was laborious. Simply saying, 'Yes, I made a pact with the devil,' wasn't enough. The interrogators wanted the confession to be personal, to ring true. The accused were repeatedly questioned. In Lillias's case, no verdict was reached because she died before the session acquired a commission for a trial. She could not be strangled and burned as was customary for those found guilty, and yet her guilt was assumed. I revisit the abrupt end to her interrogation record, looking for some other detail. How exactly did she die? Lillias's interrogation ends with a brief note from 3 September 1704: 'Lillias Adie was buried within the seamark at Torryburn.' The end of her life is an afterthought, her body a curio for collectors, and her grave a tourist site.

*

In September 2020, West Fife Heritage erected the Fife Witches Trail. Three bronze discs, the size of manhole covers, tell a grotesque version of Lillias's story. The discs are not easy to find. The first is set in the ground, beneath a community bulletin board, across from where Lillias was imprisoned in Culross. It shows a woman carrying a bundle of herbs surrounded by crosses. This disc is a general memorial for the women who died in Culross accused of witchcraft. The second disc is harder to find, but, as I return to her grave, I see it located near the sea wall. It's a lurid tourist sign, essentially pointing to her stone. What was once a melancholy, mysterious site is now an attraction. The disc depicts Lillias surrounded by the flames of hell, with the devil playing pan pipes in her ear. The drunken words of Jean Bizet are misquoted over her: 'Oh keep me, there she is coming.' The third plaque is almost impossible to find. I search for hours, walking footpaths around Culross and Torryburn, until I find it beneath the wildlife interpretation sign at Valleyfield

Woods, where Lillias claimed she met with the devil. Joseph Noel Paton's sketch of Lillias appears on the plaque: a naked devil holds a tiny woman aloft in a dance. The disc reads 'an innocent victim of unenlightened times'. I stand before this recent monument to an accused woman in Scotland, and wonder who, exactly, is this devil's doll? It isn't Lillias. All my hopes for more sensitive signage fade in that moment. The only thing worse than no public recognition of this history is a monument to the satanic fantasy used to condemn countless people during the witch-hunts. Those who accused and killed Lillias Adie, who desecrated her grave and put her on display, are still the ones telling her official story. Heritage signs like these discs record a version of history in the landscape. The word 'heritage' conjures a hegemonic body of conservators, the purveyors of 'days out', a certain cosiness. Succinct versions of events are presented on child-friendly signs, designed to be digested between a picnic and a meander. Historical fact seems optional. The three bronze discs of the Witches Trail are an ellipsis of everything that has not yet been said about the accused, the truth of their lives. These discs are set in the ground, at a child's eye level. When children ask, 'What is that woman doing with the devil?', what story will we tell them?

As I write this, a battle over monuments rages. Statues of slave-traders and Confederate generals in the USA are defaced, toppled, dumped. All over the world, Black Lives Matter activists have insisted we ask which version of history should occupy shared public space. Monuments play an essential role in mobilising public opinion and dictating the stories we tell about our landscapes and history. Do the sensational, sentimental aspects of the Witches Trail represent a temptation to turn Fife into a 'Scottish Salem', a place well known for its witch tourism? Might we see this historic suffering exploited for profit?

Lillias's story has gone viral. Global news coverage of the search for her bones has captured the attention of journalists and podcasters, and even gets a mention in Jenni Fagan's novel *Luckenbooth*. If Lillias's skull is found, Torryburn would need to decide what it wants to do with this object that was once a person – and in that decision rests a larger question. What will we do with this history of atrocity and ancestral trauma? Do we keep it in a dusty case, ushering it out at Halloween to exploit the suffering it represents, or do we finally remember and pardon these souls, giving them the dignity and peace they deserve?

The village of Torryburn has called for Lillias's remains to be returned. Her bones might be in a private collection or mislabelled on the shelf of a museum. Her skull is somewhere. It could be anywhere, like behind the bar of a pub. The Saracen Head pub in Glasgow has a woman's skull on display in a case. The pub's legend has it that this is the 'skull of the last witch burned at the stake', and that it belongs to a woman named Maggie Wall. Maggie Wall's memorial in the village of Dunning is perhaps the best-known monument to a woman in Scotland. No remains have been excavated from this site, and some historians say Maggie Wall never existed. One thing is certain: the 'witch's skull' in the Saracen Head pub can't belong to a woman who was burned at the stake. There are no remains left from those burned. Still, I wonder, what if the skull did not belong to Maggie Wall, but to Lillias Adie? The evidence of her skull ends in Glasgow, and it would be distinct enough that I could recognise it from my research. I make plans to travel down to Glasgow to try and find out for myself if it is indeed Lillias's.

The Saracen Head is a football pub in Glasgow's East End, known to locals as the Sarry Heid. I walk to the pub from the Mercat Cross in the centre of the busy crossroads. It is said witches danced here at their sabbats, or nocturnal group meetings. I follow Gallowgate, deeper east, out of my depth in a city I don't know. It's a straight shot; I find it easily. At 4 p.m. on a Thursday, the pub is locked up tight. A sun-bleached flyer flutters by the door. If it is open, as its Facebook page seemed to suggest, it appears to be in a kind of secret speakeasy capacity, and I do not have the passcode. I have come a long way, and for what? I'm determined to find someone who can help me figure this out.

After returning home, I email Douglas Speirs, who has written to every anatomical collection in the UK searching for Lillias's bones. He has no leads. I forward a photo I've found online of the skull in the pub. He says that its dark colouring is typical of skulls that have been in numerous anatomical collections. The bone of the skull has taken on a deep brown colour with a sheen, as if it has been varnished. Speirs explains this is the result of repeated handling, and that the skull shows some similarity to Lillias's. He also cautions that it might be 'too good to be true'. It is. An archaeologist working with Speirs manages to get into the pub and examine the skull. It isn't Lillias's, but it is a woman's skull, probably from a medical school.

I imagine this woman in the pub; the shadowed sockets of her frail bones stare out above the crowd of men gathered to drink and roar. Other tiny men run and kick a ball on a bright screen. After the place closes and empties out, it's dark. Like a trophy from a forgotten war, whoever is in that case waits.

2

Fatal Sisters

Issobell Monro, Forres, 1661

'Fair is foul, and foul is fair.'

— Witches, *Macbeth*, Act 1 Scene 1

Across Scotland, enigmatic megaliths – large standing stones or slabs – mark the landscape. Some are lone survivors from destroyed Neolithic circles, while others were dragged across the country by Ice Age glaciers, deposited at random. Today they stand in fields, in suburban cul-de-sacs and on the edges of country roads and wide streets. Churchyards, graves and housing estates have sprung up around them. Some are marked with exquisite Pictish carvings from between the sixth and ninth centuries. Many of the early stones are sculptural masterpieces that depict totemic animals and symbols. Later stones incorporate mesmeric, twisting designs into early Christian crosses, battle scenes and coronations.

Other singular stones are Carlin stones. In Scots, *carlin* is an old woman, but this word can also mean a witch. Carlin stones evoke the Cailleach, an old woman – or *the* old woman. The Cailleach is the old Celtic goddess of winter, and her myths tell us she created the landscape of Scotland. Carlin stones are rich in folklore, and some are said to have been dropped by a giantess from her apron, while others are witches turned to stone by the devil. Some Carlin stones have been adopted as folk memorials to women who were killed during the witch-hunts.

As I have visited these stones across Scotland, they have become more than markers: they are living things. Perhaps this is how our ancestors saw these stones, as beings who were there before they were born and who would outlive them. Weather-beaten, dressed in ragged moss and lichen, they embody the old woman whose power is her survival – both pathetic and mighty. She has seen much and, in her freedom, perceives of even more: the gaze she returns cuts through all posturing. She sees you as you are, and this makes her dangerous.

I first encountered a stone of this kind in the town of Forres on the Moray coast. The Witches Stone in Forres is a survivor – fractured, removed, replaced and put back together. In it, I also see myself, a survivor of illness and violence, poverty and displacement, put back together against the odds. Every Hogmanay, I come to the Witches Stone in Forres with a dram of whisky to warm it. Each New Year, my understanding of this stone and the women it marks has grown, yet it remains a knot of legend and near-forgotten histories. It is one of a group of three local Carlin stones, said to mark the deaths of the three witches who bewitched King Duncan in 960, the legendary weird sisters immortalised in Shakespeare's *Macbeth* seen gathering at a 'heath near Forres' in the first act of the play. The stones are now separated. One is in a private garden nearby, and another has been destroyed completely. The last of the three sits unassumingly in a green verge beside the police station, the pavement poured around it. The police station, with its ornamental sandstone surrounds at the windows, looks like a grand cottage, yet there are yellow-and-blue checked cars parked in front. Standing at the stone, in front of this building, is unnerving. Am I being surveilled while paying homage to ancient outlaws?

The Witches Stone crouches low to the ground, seamed in three parts. Leaf mould fills its crevices. Two iron bars, rusted and warped, are bolted into it like staples in a giant suture. Many self-identified contemporary witches speak of a 'witch wound': the inheritance of ancestral trauma from persecution during the witch-hunts. Our adopted ancestors grew up knowing the pyre, even if they did not face it themselves. This concept of ancestral memory is real for many, and the hardhanded repair job is a fitting embodiment of that pain.

The brae of Cluny Hill rises high beyond the Witches Stone and, on this bright day in January, it is brown with bracken. A tower built to commemorate the Battle of Trafalgar sits on the hilltop, looking like Rapunzel's fairy-tale prison. This hill was supposedly the site of executions. A macabre heritage sign from the 1930s marking the Witches Stone declares: 'From Cluny Hill witches were rolled in stout barrels through which spikes were driven. Where the barrels stopped they were burned with their mangled contents. This stone marks the site of one such burning.' No one is sure these killings really took place, and certainly there is no evidence for this form of execution. In Scotland, the accused were strangled and burned at the stake. This is not the stone's original home and the claims made on the plaque, like so much of the 'official' history of those killed during the witch-hunts in Scotland, are untrue.

If there is no evidence in the witch-trial records of death by spiked, flaming barrel, where did this gory detail come from? These Forres witches share this mode of execution with Scotland's Nostradamus, *Coinneach Odhar*, or Sallow Kenneth. Better known as the Brahan Seer, he was supposedly killed in this manner by the wife of the Earl of Sutherland in the late seventeenth century. In Scottish folk traditions, witches and seers were two different kinds of magical practitioners. Seers were most often men, burdened with the terrible gift of second sight, a curse bestowed on them by the Fair Folk. Scottish witches were thought to be women who gained power by making a deal with the devil, often involving sex.

Scottish witch lore influenced Shakespeare. Ten years before *Macbeth* was written, King James VI and I published his tome on witchcraft, *Daemonologie*. He wrote this philosophical treatise on sorcery and demons in the form of a Socratic dialogue, and the text justifies the moral imperative of witch-hunting in a

Christian society. The influence this work had on Shakespeare is clear. The witches in *Macbeth* plot shipwrecks, storms and a 'deed without a name'. In one of the witches' scenes, they promise to meet when the 'hurly burly's done; when the battle's lost and won'. They revel in their singularity. Their uncanny appearance disturbs Banquo, Macbeth's friend and military commander. He thinks they are not of this world, yet here they are. He famously says, 'You should be women, and yet your beards forbid me to interpret that you are so.' The hair on their faces marks them as something other than women. Witches, often depicted in art, literature and fairy tales as menopausal and perimenopausal women past childbearing age, are *other* in the eyes of the dominant culture. The archetype of the witch and her dark glee, as rendered by Shakespeare, persists as an autonomous agent of power. These sensational witches are archetypal; they are the three fates, *fatal sisters*, determining the destiny of kings and warlords.

Forres has another stone monument called Sueno's Stone, a giant Pictish stone over six metres high, the tallest in Scotland. Local legend claims it marks a place where *Macbeth*'s witches gathered, and that the weird sisters are trapped inside it. Should the stone break, the three witches would be freed. Like the Norse Norns, these fictional witches wove the strands of destiny, the pattern of human lives, and they had the power to make or destroy kings. Perhaps this mythic fate-weaving might look like the Celtic knots depicted on the sides of Sueno's Stone. The stone is named after Sweyn Forkbeard, or Suanus Rex, son of Harald Bluetooth, a Norse king from the tenth century. His relationship to this stone is debated, and no one really knows what violence and triumph it depicts. Sueno's Stone is encased in a large glass and steel box, and standing in the glare of its glass case, squinting past the angles reflecting off the surface, you can see the details of a battle depicted in phases, demarcated like panels in a graphic novel. Vanquished soldiers lie decapitated, their heads in a pile. Down the sides of the stone, the web of wyrd, or fate, intertwines, eroded to winter vines.

This stone celebrates male military prowess, yet it also holds the legend of the weird sisters within it. I stand in this unquiet space between myth and history, in search of consolation. I lean back, small in the shadow of Sueno's Stone, and I think of a sensational poem about three valkyries. The eighteenth-century poet Thomas Gray wrote a version of this poem set in Scotland, calling it 'The Fatal Sisters: an Ode', based on a Latin translation of the Old Norse original. In it, a group of Valkyries weave the 'crimson web of war' on the 'great loom of hell', which is made of lances. The shuttles of their loom are spears, the warp is made of entrails, and the weft is weighted with the heads of slain warriors. The Fatal Sisters order the chaos of battle and arrange destinies in a bloody tapestry. This poem and its horrific imagery, like something from a Frank Frazetta painting, thrill me. The quiet, methodical, women's craft of weaving takes on an epic scale, ominous with violence and portent. The sisters proclaim their brutal song will be heard throughout Scotland:

> *Horror covers all the heath,*
> *Clouds of carnage blot the sun.*
> *Sisters, weave the web of death;*
> *Sisters cease, the work is done.*

This is certain. If you stay long enough, you'll hear it, too – myths twined with the land, running up the sides of old stone giants, in the caterwauling gales off the North Sea, and in the gallop of freezing rain. Yet these Valkyries bear little resemblance to the real women, marginalised, hunted and killed as witches.

*

The puzzle pieces of the Witches Stone, squat beside a pavement, bound together and crowned with a heritage plaque, don't fit. Who, exactly, does it memorialise? The archaeological record mentions legendary tenth-century witches as well as the fictional witches in Shakespeare's *Macbeth*. The sign suggests actual women died here. The recently published online Interactive Witchcraft Map reveals the death locations of thousands of people accused of witchcraft in Scotland in the seventeenth century, and there are Forres women on this map, and many more in the outlying area, which was a hotbed of accusations in 1661–2. Some were tried together, like Isabel Simson and Isobel Elder of Forres, who were imprisoned together in 1662. They confessed but later denied their statements, explaining they had only given their confessions under torture. Alexander Brodie, a landowner living at Brodie Castle, four miles outside of Forres, was a witch-hunter who investigated many accused women, including Isabel and Isobel. Their cases were controversial, and other landowners involved in the trial dissented or voted to spare them. In his diaries, Brodie mentioned he hoped they would not be tortured, yet he believed their recantations to be the work of Satan who had 'hardened them to denie'. There could be no truth but his own. Brodie noted that on the afternoon of 4 May 1662 the two women were burned at Forres and 'died obstinat'. He was not there to watch them die as he 'desired not to be looked on as the pursuer of these "poor creatures".' This execution was held a few days after May Day, or Beltane, in the agrarian calendar. Happier fires would have been lit to herald the start of summer, yet this pyre devoured not only Isabel and Isobel but also joy in the old ways.

The vagabonds Mary Burges, from Inverness, and Issobell Monro were also tried together in Forres. Vagabondage was a vague term used in the historical records to refer to souls completely outside the system of governance, unrecognised by a particular parish. A 'vagabond' could be an itinerant labourer, a

Gypsy, a Traveller, or a wandering musician or entertainer. Many vagabonds were those banished from the place of their birth or driven, starving and war-ravaged, from their homes and forced to survive by begging. We don't know what kind of vagabonds Mary Burges and Issobell Monro were. They faced a local trial, and the only record we have is in the family papers of the Clan Grant.

Documentation of torture is usually omitted from the trial record but, in this instance, a mention of the torture used on Issobell Monro survives. While being held for trial in 1656, Issobell sent a petition to the Commission for Criminal Justice in Edinburgh describing her maltreatment as torture and a drawn-out form of execution. She was an illiterate Gaelic speaker, so someone else wrote to the Commission on her behalf: she had been imprisoned for years awaiting a formal trial, and for much of the time she was held in the stocks, wearing only a salted sack. She was kept so long in this position that she developed pressure sores, and was starved and denied water so that 'she was many times constrained to drink her piss'. At one point she managed to escape but was re-arrested. The Clan Grant submitted a formal request for a local trial on 3 October 1661 – five years after Isobel's petition. There is no record of her sentence. Of Mary Burges, I could find even less, save that her trial was also petitioned by the Laird Grant, or landowner belonging to the Clan Grant, at the same time.

Much is missing from the witch-trial records in Scotland. I guess at lives, and patterns emerge. These were not solitary executions, a woman led alone through a howling crowd to her death at the stake. Women were tried together and killed together, in groups or pairs. During episodes of witch-hunting, women's interconnected lives were demonised. In early modern Scotland, alliances and friendships between women were practical, deep and ever present. Women worked together and cooperated in group tasks like waulking, the cleaning, shrinking and softening of cloth by hand. They assisted each other in child-birth and met at market days. They exchanged information and debated ideas. In this century-long hunting of women, these friendship bonds were attacked and broken down. All women would have witnessed the horrific deaths of the accused at some point in their lives, and the accused were forced to betray each other during witchcraft interrogations under the threat of such a horrific death.

I return to the Witches Stone on a bleak February morning. The grass is still frozen all around, with spring hiding some-where in the west. It's Imbolc, or Bride's Day. As I stand in front of the Witches Stone, I think about the Gaelic vagabond Issobell Monro, imprisoned and tortured by the Laird Grant. How might Issobell have celebrated? How might she have marked this day? The agrarian year of early modern *Gàidhealtachd*, or the Gaelic-speaking area of Scotland, turned in quarters and shifting moons. I imagine a life for her beyond the pain that defines her in the written record. Issobell's February was *Faoilleach*, or the Wolf Month, with its hail shot and flying winds. Perhaps she would have made a soup of whelks and dulse, as it's said the shellfish are at their best just after New Year. She might have walked the sand dunes at the neap tide at Nairn Beach. The seals would have been swimming there, watching her curiously.

I wonder at the shared traditions Issobell might have kept with her mother, sister or friends before she became a wanderer without a home. Might she have celebrated this day belonging to Bride, the Celtic goddess of poetry, healing and smithcraft? Bride is the daughter of the Dagda and kin to the dreadful goddesses of war, the Celtic Fatal Sisters: Bahb, the goddess of battle; Macha, who fed on the heads of the slain as if they were nuts dropped from trees; and Morrigu, the crow, who consumed and comforted the dying. Bride alone of this lineage migrated with people who came in war and peace from Ireland to the Scottish Highlands, bringing with them their Celtic language and myths. Historically, in Gaelic culture, the last sheaf of corn was used to fashion a straw doll. On Bride's Day, women would celebrate Bride embodied in this doll, perhaps like the corn dolly I had as a child, with a little kerchief, apron and skirts made of husks, her head a small nut, her face blank. The memory of this beloved object from my childhood is a tentative link, a relic I share with Issobell. I imagine her taking a sheaf of oats and putting it in a little dress, tucked inside a bed of birch twigs with a wooden club beside it. With her neighbours and kin, she calls out three times, *Bride come in, your bed is ready*. If they were lucky, the oat-sheaf Bride would be enticed by the hospitality, by the promise of a home. She might stay the night and trace her blessings in the ashes of the hearth with her little distaff. I imagine her, the finely dressed oat sheaf, flying up and out the chimney on her staff, like the carlin, the Cailleach, and all good witches to the sabbat before her.

It's said that at the spindle of winter and spring, the Cailleach and Bride do battle, but I prefer to think of them dancing together in the hare's gloom of late winter. The Cailleach's last hurrah in the Gaelic calendar, between the last of winter and early spring, was called the *Feadag*, or the whistle. This whistle is a cold, fierce wind, but it is also a signal. Lady Augusta Gregory wrote of Bride, 'it was she first made the whistle for calling another through the night'.

The Witches Stone is slick with rain. Someone has been here before me and left a jar of flowers, curled and brown with frost. An onyx stone sits beside the mistaken history of the heritage sign. There is another sign hung with red thread over the old one. Engraved like a desk name plate, it says: 'To All the Girls and Women Sacrificed to Patriarchy.' It's a whistle in the dark. This work is not solitary. I write it down; I whistle back.

3
Kirkyard and Hollow Hill
Isobel Gowdie, Auldearn, 1662

'Alas, I deserve not to be sitting here, for I have done so many
evil deeds, especially killing of men . . . I deserve to be riven
upon iron harrows and worse if it could be devised.'
— Isobel Gowdie's third confession

Years ago, when I first heard the song 'Isobel Goudie' by the
Sensational Alex Harvey Band, I didn't know who the 'witch
queen' of Britain was, this woman who 'didn't do the things she
should'. Now, I see this glam-rock anthem as a compelling
memorial to her. I wonder if she would have liked the song, and
if she might recognise Harvey's voice — crooning, histrionic and
carnivalesque — as her devil, the sinister, ribald gang-leader at
the centre of her fable. *Glamour* is a Scots word meaning to
dazzle or enamour. Isobel's confessions after her arrest for
witchcraft are lengthy and bizarre, and they've glamoured me.
Though she has no physical monument, she lives on in music —
neofolk ballads, as well as an orchestral requiem, *The Confession
of Isobel Gowdie* by composer James MacMillan.

Isobel Gowdie was tried for witchcraft in 1662, during what
historians call 'The Great Scottish Witch-hunt', due to the
unprecedented scale of suffering and death during that spate of
mass hunts. In these turbulent years, the Scottish judicial system
was changing after the dissolution of the Cromwellian union. It
was a time of political and economic crisis, where influential
members of the ruling elite felt the threat of witchcraft was
urgent. This led the central government to issue an unprecedented
number of trial commissions. These years saw an increase in

professional witch-finders or 'prickers', who were paid by the number of witches they claimed to discover. The hunt grew exponentially as those arrested named others. Isobel was one of at least 664 people accused across Scotland between the spring of 1661 and the autumn of 1662, and she may have been one of the 300 or more executed. The Privy Council in Edinburgh granted a commission to try her, but there is no record of her death.

Isobel's famous confessions are the most extensive of any witch-trial interrogation. She was questioned four times between 13 April and 27 May 1662. John Innes, the *notar* (notary), was barely able to keep up with her. He wrote down her words as best he could, adding 'etc.' at points where he just wouldn't get it all down. An unlikely amanuensis, Innes transcribed her confessions in the first person, giving her voice an immediate subjectivity. Though she speaks in seventeenth-century Scots and much of the document is damaged, her words are intimate. They spin outrageous fictions, weaving in ballads and rhyming charms that teem with bad magic, mystery and folk practices. In them, we see a woman who was at once angry and charming – a self-styled agent of fate, a threat to those in power around her. She knew the laird, the minister and others were listening to her every word, so she said more and more. Her last words were a death rattle of a swan song – gleeful and damning. This was her final spell, and it is a masterful literary work in its own right. She describes the uncanny beings of her world in evocative detail. Her fairy queen is '*brawlie*' or beautiful, clothed in white linens. Elf boys speak '*gowstie-like*' (ghostly) as they '*whytts and dightis*', creating fatal arrowheads. The poetry of her shape-changing chant is haunting.

> I shall go into a hare
> with sorrow and *syt* [sigh] and *meikle* [great] care
> and I shall go in the devil's name
> Aye, while I come home

Witchcraft scholar Emma Wilby recently found the full confessions tucked away in a box of uncatalogued papers at the National Archives. Her massive study, which grew from this finding, is nuanced and extensively detailed. She argues that Isobel Gowdie may have been a shamanistic practitioner. European witchcraft scholars Carlo Ginzburg and Éva Pócs present similar interpretations of ecstatic experience presented in the witch trials. Other scholars remain sceptical about the possibility of genuine spiritual experience in these documents. Contemporary shaman Jonathan Horwitz of the Scandinavian Centre of Shamanic Studies told me, 'Paradox is the logic of the shaman.' The rational mind might ask what is true. To that question, the soul might say, 'Let me tell you a story.'

Isobel was undoubtedly a storyteller. Some of the surviving confessions from the witch-hunts – as enigmatic as Isobel's – leave us with an impossible task, a riddle for any and all who listen, and a dare. Can we see the speaker not simply as an innocent victim or madwoman, but as an individual thrumming with creative power and a lust for life? Isobel speaks to us through centuries in a voice filled with rage at the powers that be, peppered with sorrowful remorse. Her words are those of a woman preserving her identity, and her stories are a refrain against a loss of self. When I recount the things Isobel did, I am speaking of the character she created in the narrative of her confession. In mining these records, I have come to understand that what is real might not be what is true, and vice versa. One thing is certain: Isobel's agile intelligence could hold two contradictory truths simultaneously, and I can only hope to be as clever.

Isobel's confessions also reference myriad ballads and folk tales, all repurposed for the fevered story she told her interrogators. One ballad, 'The Elfin Knight,' sometimes called 'The Devil's Courtship,' has countless versions: the first was recorded in 1610, though the story itself is much older. It's a kind of

Bluebeard tale, with the heroine outsmarting her serial-killer suitor. In the ballad, a lady named Isobel is seduced by the sound of an elfin horn. She dreams of an uncanny knight who comes and invites her to the 'greenwood'. There, she finds he has killed seven other women, and she is to be the eighth. She tricks him and kills him with his own dagger. In another version, Lady Isobel outsmarts the Elfin Knight by daring him to accomplish a series of impossible tasks; and in others, the two spar with a series of riddles. Cunning as a means of escape is the common thread in this cautionary tale that is woven through Isobel Gowdie's confessions. Such fairy-tale lessons might prepare a woman for encounters with a lone predator, but they could not equip her with the tools she would need to survive a witchcraft interrogation.

In the ballad, the Elfin Knight asks for a shirt made without needle or thread, and Lady Isobel says she'll make one as soon as he can find a piece of land between sea and strand, and then 'plow it with a ram's horn/ and sow it all over with one pepper corn'. In one of the infamous passages from Isobel Gowdie's confession, she yokes a plough made of a ram's horn to a team of frogs and leads them around a field widdershins so that 'thistles and briars might grow there' instead of corn.

The marginal landscapes of the ballad, both the greenwood and the place 'between salt sea and strand' were places Isobel Gowdie knew well. Nairn Beach, near where Isobel lived, has a spit of land subsumed daily by a treacherous incoming tide. Solid ground sinks into the sea quickly and fog descends, confusing walkers. I have seen children swept up from the shallows here, and have heard stories of others who have gone missing. Isobel knew a world that was two things at once, and could change with the shifting of a cloud. Her Elfin Knight was a devil, an animal, and a human man who danced and made merry, but also beat and raped her.

She describes the devil as:

a werie meikle blak roch man. He will lye als hewie upon ws . . .
lyk an malt-seck . . . He wold com to my hos-top in the shape
of a crow . . . now and then. I wold ken his woice, at the first
heiring of it, and wold goe forth to him . . .*

At times, she had 'carnall cowpulation' with him, noting he was
'werie cold; and I found his nature als cold within me as spring
well water'. She said she could not refuse him – he was irresisti-
ble and inexorable.

Isobel lived in Lochloy, a strip of land south of Nairn Beach,
now a newly planted forest, an equestrian training ground and
golf course. High, deer-proof fences and baby pines hem the
road, and on the day I was there, a lone detectorist wound their
way into Lochloy Wood. Downie Wood is to the east, a short
walk away, and it was there Isobel met the king and queen of
the fairies. She lived in a blackhouse on this land belonging to
the Laird of Park. It would have been a modest earthen house
that was dark inside and smoke-filled from the open fire, with
a hole in the ceiling for a chimney. In the Highlands, diarist
Dorothy Wordsworth noted that blackhouses looked like 'so
many black molehills'. Isobel's house was made of stones,
covered with sod and red clay, thatched with heather, broom
and branches of fir bound in ropes made of star moss. It had a
single room, divided by a partition woven of marram grass and
willow. In winter, the animals would be on one side; on the
other would be Isobel, her husband John Gilbert, any children
who survived and the ghosts of those who did not. The floor
was wet with rain that came in gusts through the door. In the
darkness, she tied up a pennant of fish stolen from the fishing

---

* 'The devil was a very big, dark, hairy man. He will lay all heavy upon us like
a malt sack. He would come to my house-top in the shape of a crow now and
then. I would know his voice at the first hearing of it and would go forth to
him.'

boats on the beach, tossing *durkins*, or pinecones, into the fire to scent and flavour the smoking meat.

I come to Nairn Beach to think about Isobel, picturing her wandering these glittering white sands. The wind is high and the grass-bristled dunes sift in little waves. She pulls her plaid around her, a long piece of wool, putty-coloured with dirt. The narrow spit of land past the shallows glimmers gold in the morning sun. The Black Isle is purple in the distance. Scattered mosaics of pulverised shells trace the high-water mark. She walks barefoot, the sand warm between her toes. A long-dead tree that had come down the Nairn River sinks into the wet sand; its tangled roots look like an eldritch thing, the remains of a sea beast, fuel for another story. And there's real fuel, too: black lumps of sea coal dropped into the makeshift pockets of her kilted plaid. She chants, 'The fishers gone to sea and they will bring home fish to me,' and they come in, their nets full. She says when she steals a fish or two, she takes their goodness and leaves the froth.

I walk the same long beach on a bright day in early spring. Shells litter the high shore, bleached white. The shattered nacre of razor clam shells crunches underfoot. I find a hinged cockle, a little box big enough for a secret. Three young women pass me with backpacks and bedrolls, their kit bright and functional. They've come to spend the night together by the sea. Would Isobel and Jonet Breidhead, her coven member, have slept on the dunes, on the shortest night of midsummer, with their besoms tucked in their beds beside their husbands?

*

Isobel went to church in the Kirk of Auldearn, now a picturesque pink sandstone ruin, a roofless shelter perched on a volcanic hill. Auldearn is a quiet, leafy village near the sea, hemmed in by the susurration of the A96. Green hills soften the landscape to the north. Here, she listened to the sermons of the zealous, Covenanting minister Harry Forbes, a man she hated so much that she cursed his children with wax poppets. She claimed she met the devil at the pulpit at night, the shadowed church turned upside down by her coven's sabbat. Nothing of the interior of the church is left. Gone is the lectern where the devil pantomimed a church service. He held a black book where all the coven's deeds were written. Perhaps she imagined it to be like the book where John Innes recorded her confessions. She said it was here in the kirk that Margaret Brodie lifted her up to be baptised by the devil, and she gave herself to him.

It's high summer now, the stones of the kirkyard dark with rain. Come winter, the moss-clotted corners of drystane will silver with hoarfrost. Here in the ruins, one day is no holier than another. A sundial marks the passing light, and time is a tugging of the moon. The kirkyard has long been landscaped with fey ivy and moss. Graves lean here and there like old blackened teeth, the names of the dead worn away by countless storms. Lichen-spotted cherubs and gurning skulls stare out from the stones. They are my only company, save a wee mole, quite dead. She's stranded in the grass, dropped from the claws of a raptor. I linger and see more faces, fragments of primitive angels salvaged from tombstones. The memento mori skulls still serve their purpose to watch and warn the living. They peer from the facade of the kirk and the wall of the graveyard, watching me. The warm drizzle is laced with tobacco, a human smell full of sensual delight.

Isobel's story leaves a strange grace in the ruined kirk. There is no record of her detention or sentence. A heritage sign at the gate of the kirkyard offers more fiction: she killed lairds with her magic and was hung on the hill. The illustration depicts her as a slovenly hag. Once again, these 'official' signs about witches can say anything, but they rarely offer any truth. What is left when the congregation is gone, the pews missing and the sermons have long gone silent? The uncanny move into the vacuum left by absented faith. It is a fairy place, now. The faces of the kirkyard follow me. Stone roses turn into dazed eyes. The painted white pupils of a skull are weirdly bright. A judgement-day angel with his trumpet turns into a pipe-smoking fairy. On another grave, a great wind spirit blows storms from its mouth.

Isobel's is also a story of shapes shifting. She had rhyming chants that enabled her to adopt the form of other animals. While in the shape of a hare, Isobel said she was chased by hounds. She could change back to her own form with the words, 'Haire, haire, God send thee caire. I am in a hare's likeness just now, bot I sal be in a woman's likeness ewin [now].' She found scratches and tears in her skin – 'werie sor [very sore]' – inflicted during the chase; the hunted woman accused of witchcraft is also the hunted hare praying for protection.

Isobel met with her coven and they changed into cats and crows. They snuck into the homes of neighbours who were better off, climbing down chimneys and flying through windows to feast. They drank beer and topped up the barrels with their piss, 'bot did no more harme'. The devil asked them to say grace: 'We eat this meat in the devil's name with sorrow and seething and much shame . . . little good shall come to the fore, of all the rest of the little store.' She claimed these parties were sad affairs, as if to say, *You didn't miss much, and there's nothing left*.

Isobel said that she 'covenanted' with the devil. She confessed to this compact, a satanic version of the Covenanters' agreement with the Presbyterian God. The Scots word *covin* – meaning both an agreement and a band or company – is the root of the word coven. Covenanters were the dominant political and religious movement in Scotland at the time of Isobel's interrogation. They believed in the Covenant of Grace – the faithful gave themselves soul and body to God in return for salvation. This deal could be a ceremonial, public promise of conformity to Covenanting doctrine, or it could be deeply private, spontaneous and ecstatic. Though the seventeenth-century Kirk disapproved of these passionate promises, they persisted. Isobel used the word meaning an agreement, as in *covenant*, but also a crew, a fellowship. Yet her wording, as with so many of her confessions, has a subversive ring.

Isobel Gowdie might have been kept in the church steeple in between her interrogations. She was held in solitary confinement from April to mid-May of 1662, and officially questioned four times. While John Innes comments that the confessions were 'voluntary', this must be qualified. Some forms of maltreatment – beating, sleep deprivation, and being shaved and pricked for the 'witch's mark' – were not considered torture. It is possible Isobel endured all of these during her imprisonment.

In 1662, a 'pricker' named Mr Paterson worked the forty-mile stretch of coast from Inverness to Elgin. Auldearn lies squarely between these two towns, making it almost certain Paterson would have examined Isobel Gowdie. Paterson's infamous method required that the accused, while blindfolded, find and remove the pin after it had been inserted 'to the head'. Paterson was later discounted as a fraud after it was discovered that they were a woman disguised in men's clothing. Pricking was a lucrative profession in 1662, and perhaps some thought it was safer to operate on the side of the hunters rather than potentially fall prey to them.

While Isobel was imprisoned, her interrogators built a case for a commission to try her as a witch. One of the investigators was Alexander Brodie, the man who condemned Isobel Elder and Isabel Simon in Forres. At the time of the second confession, John Innes records that several other witnesses were present, and there is a similar note in the third confession. Word had got out, and a crowd had gathered. Perhaps these folk came to hear Isobel the tale-teller say her piece. She warmed to the crowd, and the confessions grew more performative with each meeting. By the third confession, she gave her audience taunts of rhyming iambs and complex curses tinged with remorse. Emma Wilby argued some of the strangeness of her confessions can be attributed to

47

false memory created by the repeated interrogations and the psychological effects of isolation. By the fourth confession, all the vivid song and bravado were gone, as was the crowd. She was alone again with her interrogators, repeating by rote what they asked of her.

In the extensive record of her interrogation, information surrounding her execution is missing, and perhaps this is her last, vital trick. In the gaping silence where her fate should be, I resort to invention. Could she not have slipped out, in soul if not body, through the narrow window of the kirk's steeple, like a pigeon from a dovecote, escaping with *sorrow and sigh and much care*?

*

Isobel also met the devil in Inshoch – a field belonging to the Hays family, the hated Laird of Park in Isobel's confessions, marked by a crumbling castle. It was abandoned, its tower disintegrating, even in Isobel's day. In the shadow of this grand ruin, she said she lay with the devil, claiming his member was exceedingly great: 'no mans memberis ar so long and bigg as they are'. He kept his boots on.

She went on to tell her interrogators – the churchmen, the landowners and the gathered crowd – that the devil was like a wild stallion 'among mares'. She rendered him vividly and gave him the best lines. Her account is shocking, even now, and it is hard to imagine how this story was received by the sexually repressed audience who first heard it. 'Neither haid we nor he any kynd of shame, bot especially he hes no sham with him at all.'

Isobel offered a vision of the devil as an impossibly virile overlord, petty and paranoid. When he thought the coven was talking behind his back, he said, 'I ken well enough what ye were saying of me.' The devil was a cheat and counterfeiter; his money and word were no good. He gave her 'the brawest lyk [finest] money that ever was coined; within four and twantie houris it wold be horse-muke [muck]'. He beat them, turned into an animal and ravaged them. He held up his tail as they kissed his ass, and then he expected them to curtsey and say, 'Ye ar welcom owr lord, and how do ye my lord.'

Perhaps Isobel's version of the devil is a satire of the men who investigated her – the witch-hunter Alexander Brodie, or the Laird of Park, a man on the verge of financial ruin who believed that he and his family had been hunted by witches. Or it could be a bawdy caricature of the Reverend Harry Forbes, a minister saddled with a sex scandal, un-payable debts, and a witch obsession. Isobel turns the tables on her interrogators. Her hatred of their hypocrisy is palpable. She reminds me that in the face of the overwhelming cruelty of this history, rage is an option.

There is another possibility. This story of sexual aggression may be drawn from her lived experience. Sixteen years before her trial, in May 1645, the royalist general James Graham, the Marquis of Montrose, invaded Auldearn. He raised his banner on Dooket Hill and led troops of mercenaries into Auldearn, overrunning the small village with soldiers preparing for battle. Later, the surrounding fields were soaked in blood and crowded with the dead and dying. Montrose was merciless, known for his use of gang rape as a weapon. Isobel would have been a girl or young woman at the time. The violence of that day no doubt marked her. Perhaps Isobel's devil is a distorted memory not only of the predatory Elf Knight of song, but of the very real men who came to Auldearn, bringing death, terror, and violation.

*

Though some scholars have diagnosed Gowdie as insane, I choose to read her as an anti-hero, an all-black everything. In her confessions, she travelled in the shape of a jackdaw. She worked with her coven to taint dye baths, taking a thread of each colour from Alexander Cumming's dye vats and knotting them. When they returned them to the vats, the dye turned black.

Her coven flew in a wild hunt, a fairy raid. Like a posse of outlaws in a western, they rode the gusting winds on straw horses, and if you saw them, you had to sanctify yourself, or you were, as the saying goes, a 'dead man'. They shot fairy arrows, or elf-shot, by flicking them from their thumbs like marbles. When coven member Margaret Brodie aimed at and missed the minister Harry Forbes, Isobel begged the devil to give her another shot. The arrows could supposedly penetrate even the best armour, and those who were shot were doomed. Their soul went to heaven, but their body joined the hunt.

When I moved to the north-east, other 'incomers' who had settled here told me that I was now in 'bandit country'. Local legend has it this is the 'lawless frontier' of Scotland. The road beside Auldearn and Lochloy, linking Aberdeen to Inverness through Moray, was infamous for banditry and highwaymen. Isobel cast herself as a fairy highway-woman. Her helper spirit was called 'The Read Reiver' – The Red Reiver. Isobel expressed some regret about killing many people with elf-shot: a 'woman at the plewgh landis [arable lands]', and another in the east of Moray; a man named 'James Dick', and another named 'William Bower'. The lists grew longer, as she included others killed by her coven mates, and became hyperbolic, a kind of brag.

Her other claims to magic were gleeful. Isobel's bridle-cry, 'Horse and haddock in the devil's name', has become a catch-phrase, attributed over the centuries to fairies and repeated in neopagan spells. She cursed on her knees with her hair loose of its headscarf, strands falling over her face – a transgression in seventeenth-century Scotland, where married women kept their hair covered. Isobel was a master storyteller, embellishing her narrative with lively details. I imagine that in other circum-stances, were she not tortured, imprisoned and intimidated by possible execution, her tales would be captivating and even humorous. Like a criminal gang, her coven had nicknames for each other, like Pickle Nearest the Wind, Through the Corn Yard, and Bessie Bauld [Bold]. The whole coven had helping spirits with compelling names like 'Thomas a Fearie' [Fairy]. Another was called 'Thief of Hell'. Perhaps Isobel was familiar with the legendary Belgian 'thief of hell' called *Dulle Griet*, or 'Mad Meg', another legendary plunderer who led an army of women on a hell-raid and lived to brag about it.

'Better to reign in hell than serve in heaven' – Milton's devil famously gets the best lines. Isobel understood this sentiment. But despite her bravado, she also expressed contrition and even torment. Perhaps she hoped for mercy, either from her interrogators, or the distant God of the Psalms. Her final confession begins with a statement of self-reproach. After months of solitary confinement and certain torture, she told her interrogators she would 'aknowledg[e] to my great grieff and sham[e]' that she had denied her baptism. Like a girl on the outskirts of the battlefield, she chanced allegiances with two mercenary armies. This time, one was in the kirk and the other in the greenwood, and it was too late to go unnoticed.

*

Downie Wood once stretched for miles in either direction before gradually being sheared away for pasture over the last hundred years. Today, it's early winter and everything is golden, dying. Gates of rattling broom announce my presence as I walk through them on the path: their percussive black seedpods hiss and shiver. There's horse-muck everywhere. The path is a makeshift bridle-way, and horseshoe tracks turn up mud in great gushing crests. I wonder – have those on horses come to illegally hunt foxes? They do this in Scotland, still, though not to the same degree as in England. I look for hunting dogs' prints in the sucking mud, walking in that familiar dread and sadness. To be hunted, run down without mercy, as my sister ancestors were, is a certain kind of hell.

The narrow wood in the cold sun seems inviting, traversable. The tall, bare trees let in light, and I think I will easily see where I am going with barren fields on both sides. The hillock is in there; I've found it on an Ordnance Survey map. It is still light out, early yet, but getting darker fast. I find something matted and tangled in the grass, looking like the hide of a tiny lamb, deflated, desiccated. I stare at it. With a Pandora's impulse, I turn it over with my walking stick. As I bend down to get a good look, I realise it's a mask with four holes – for eyes and nostrils – and a slit for a mouth. The woolly curls of an uncombed roller set hang off the moss-furred latex: an abandoned granny mask. The wood has transformed the joke-shop witch-skin into a grotesque green woman. I tell myself not to make a story out of this find. I move on, heart beating in my ears, footsteps sucking loudly, giving me away. *No stories.*

The path of crushed cider cans and stubbed-out cigarettes leads the way to a small fire pit in a clearing, with larger logs pulled up for benches. I have a weird longing to be young again, and bad; to be the kind of girl who would come to the wood at night to drink and dare you, playing with menace and power. Might Isobel's 'coven' have met in the wood, around a fire, with ale, songs and stories? They met at quarter days, solstices and equinoxes. They danced to '*gillatrypes*' or mouth music – vocalisation in place of instruments. The youngest woman in the coven had the nickname 'Over the Dyke with It', because this is what she would call out as she danced with the devil. I see them leaping, laughing, and calling out, *Over the dyke with it!* as they reel in the night.

I have a good hour or so of light left to find the hillock. I'm a slow walker; I rely on a stick and sometimes can't walk at all. It is a disease Isobel would have understood – chronic and causeless, a curse without a cure. Inside the wood, the shadows interlace and the light dapples and fades, seeming to go on forever. I keep on and smell the hillock before I see it, dense with fox funk. It looms, covered in coppery bracken as tall as I am. I'm alone with the hillock and its foxes. Their holes riddle the hill, an earthwork that was once an Iron Age hill fort. We know now that not all hill forts were military in purpose. I take a guess that beneath the bracken, this would resemble a hill-slope enclosure that may have been used for livestock or ceremonial purposes. The archaeologists can't tell us these things with any certainty. We must feel them in our bones and in the old stories; here is the Green Knight's Chapel that Gawain finds so evil.

Something brushes against me. The *seelie wights*, those fairy-ghosts and spirit helpers of my ancestors, are here. The acrid smell of phantom-fire mixes with generations of nesting things and all their hoarded stuff. Foxes – red reivers – can make it to the chip shop in the next village and come home to feast and brag. There might be half a Pukka pie, a crab claw, part of a doll, or another mask hidden within.

Isobel Gowdie said she turned her neighbours into cats and they all went into the hillock. The hill opened, and inside it was lovely, large and bright as daylight. They dined with the fairy court, the queen dressed in white and brown – fox colours. Isobel said, 'There were elf bulls crowtting and skoylling [rumbling and shrieking] up and down, and they afrighted me.'

I stand at the ditch surrounding the hillfort, and consider how I might walk around it, stick and all. I smell something else now, ripe and seductive. Fresh tobacco and leather, like a heady offering. This hill is a cosmopolis of tunnels, well worn, the sides smoothed by generations of creatures – foxes, definitely, and maybe badgers, too. The tunnels are almost sculptural in the way of a badger set. It's said that foxes often share nests with badgers. I get halfway up, pushing aside the bracken, stepping over nettle and bramble before I panic and a feeling of obtrusion sets in. I stumble down while I can, but that feral musk follows me. It isn't until I am well away, nearly out of the wood, that I imagine I can see them: the party of cats, crows, foxes – and the badgers, those *skoylling* elf bulls. There at my feet, I meet the mask again, its laughing mouth open, dark and silent.

4

Climbing the Law

Gelie Duncan and Agnes Sampson, North Berwick, 1590

> 'All kinds of ills that ever may be, in Christ's name, I conjure
>   ye:
> I conjure ye, both mair and les, With all the virtues if the
>   mass,
> And right so, the nails so, that nailed Jesus and no more;
> And right so, the same blood, that rake'd over the ruethful
>   rood;
> forth from the flesh and from the bane, and into the earth and
>   into the stane.
> I conjure thee, in God's name.'
>
> – Agnes Sampson's healing charm

King James VI and I believed a manifold conspiracy of the devil's minions were hell-bent on undermining his power. Under his reign, the call to exterminate accused witches became royal protocol. His translation of Exodus commands, 'Thou shalt not suffer a witch to live'. This persecution demonised folk belief and practice. Ideas that for centuries had been passed down from older women through the oral tradition were now seen as a direct threat to royal power. Visiting holy wells, the use of charms to cure animals and people, and even celebrating harvest days were outlawed. Simply knowing a curative charm, even one that called on the Christian God, was seen as treason, punishable by death.

In 1597, King James wrote *Daemonologie*, his tome on the thought-crime of witchcraft, to justify his interest in hunting witches. James believed this work was central to his political career; he perceived his reign to be in the throes of an apocalyptic crisis of good and evil. His subjects and their 'greate wickednesse' were to blame, and he was God's champion. In 1589, Queen Anne of Denmark married King James in a ceremony where neither were present. She attempted to sail to Scotland to meet him, but severe storms prevented her, and she had to return to Norway. James sailed to meet her there, and they travelled to Oslo and around Denmark together. When they attempted to return from Denmark to Scotland, the King and his new bride were caught in a storm at sea. They sheltered in Norway, where King James heard news of the Copenhagen witch trials. The accused confessed to raising a storm to prevent Queen Anne – the sister of the King of Denmark and Norway, Christian IV – from reaching Scotland. James suspected the Danish witches were in a conspiracy with Scottish covens, and began his own witch-hunt in Scotland. In this war on poor, isolated and older women, landowners and churchmen sought to curry favour with the King. They looked for witches among the women who lived with and worked for them.

Gelie Duncan worked for a man named David Seaton. He had some power as the bailie, or civic officer, in Tranent. He believed his dire financial situation was a result of witchcraft waged against him. In the autumn of 1590, he imprisoned Gelie in his own home and interrogated her for witchcraft. Gelie was a suspect because she was a healer and liked to go on night wanders. I imagine Gelie on her crepuscular walks in the long gloom of early winter. Strolling in darkness, perhaps without purpose, alone with her thoughts and the shifting moon, must have felt like a freedom none could begrudge – whose business is it where one walks or when? Yet these walks, as well as her abilities as a 'most miraculous' healer and a musician, made her guilty of witchcraft in the eyes of her violent, paranoid employer. Under torture, Gelie confessed to plotting against the King with witches in faraway Copenhagen. If we are to believe contemporary accounts, she flew over the sea in a boat shaped like a chimney and met the devil in the form of a rick of hay.

Gelie is repeatedly mentioned in the network of interconnected confessions of the North Berwick trials. What I know of her is cobbled together from these trial records and the unreliable *Newes from Scotland*, a pamphlet about the North Berwick trials published in London for an English audience. Written anonymously in 1591 by Haddington minister James Carmichael, it records what he had witnessed at the formal trials, conducted after Seaton's preliminary interrogations. This trial was a royal event; the King was present, and all sought to appease him and gain his favour.

Gelie Duncan was interrogated as the first foot soldier in Satan's mighty army. It was likely she appeared before the King with her head shaved and her body marked by torture. James demanded she perform the same tune she had played for the devil. If we are to believe the account from *Newes*, she played the mouth harp with broken thumbs. The King 'took great delight to be present at [the accused's] examinations'.

After her audience with the King, she was held for another six months and interrogated further. She named other collaborators. Before Gelie Duncan's execution on 4 December 1591, she made a statement retracting her confession, claiming it to all have been a lie extracted under torture: the others she had named were innocent. The courage of this is remarkable. In speaking her truth, Gelie defied not only the minister and bailie set on killing her, but the King himself.

*

There is no memorial in North Berwick, but there's a landscape steeped in myth. The Law is a majestic conical hill, a dramatic crag overseeing this flat land and temperamental coastline. 'Law' is a Scots word for a rounded hill. As I wrestle with the force of law that led to the deaths of thousands, I become fascinated by this *other* Law – the grand, ancient overseer of North Berwick, unmistakably breast-shaped. It survived the glacial scouring of the Ice Age. The interpretation sign for the Law is written like a recipe:

> *How to Make a North Berwick Law:*
> 1. *Bring to a boil of 700 degrees.*
> 2. *Leave to bubble and simmer for about 80 million years.*
> 3. *Put to one side and allow to cool for 300 million years.*
>   *Knead occasionally . . .*

I love the tongue-in-cheek kitchen wisdom of this sign, and its suggestion of a creation myth. It's the kind of recipe only a Cailleach could follow – or, perhaps, a Gyre Carling. The Gyre Carling is a legendary giant, an elemental being with a taste for Christian men. *Gyre* has Norse roots, meaning a giantess or earth being. In my search for witches and women, I read ballads and folktales, finding clues that guide me through the landscape. 'The Ballad of the Gyre Carlin', written by an anonymous medieval Makar or poet, describes the creation of the Law. The ballad is a surreal, scatological tale of revenge. In the poem, a man named Blasour falls in love with the sound of the Gyre Carlin's laughter. He attempts to woo her by gathering an army of moles to bring down her tower. Surprisingly, this gesture doesn't win her over. She beats him with an iron club, and as she flies away, she farts out the Law.

Places in the North Berwick landscape suggest the curved silhouette of a reclining woman's body – a giant or goddess made visible in the land. If a giant earth goddess reclines here, then North Berwick, with its breast-like Law, nestles at her heart. To see her is to understand glacial time – millennia – and the spirits of the land spanning it. I long to traverse this landscape and know it intimately, but my disability prevents me. I return to Nan Shepherd's book *The Living Mountain* to live vicariously through her words. She did not go up the Cairngorms, but entered into them, encompassed by 'the elementals', climbing mountains 'older than thought'. The Law is as old as these peaks, give or take a few hundred million years.

I've come to North Berwick to climb the Law. I sit in the Scottish Seabird Centre. I'm warm and snug, drinking black tea and looking out the wide windows. The sea is choppy, a churning, frothy white, and the sky is dense with pent-up rain. In the distance, the Bass Rock is a black heap of stone, empty of gannets. In February, they will return en masse to their colony here to riot and nest. If you dream of the Scottish seaside, you dream of North Berwick, a stately town lined up along the shore of the Firth of Forth. The old kirk, an infamous site of witches' sabbats, is just off the path to the Seabird Centre. According to *Newes from Scotland*, it was here that the devil arranged himself over the pulpit to receive kisses. Now it is hollowed out, abandoned, over half of it swept into the sea. The white building that remains is the porch, more like a large garden shed than a place where hundreds of witches met, intent on overthrowing a king.

I cannot go up the Law today; it isn't possible. I'd be climbing into wind and stinging rain, and I have other challenges. My body has its own weather – a sub-dermal hail strikes me at whim. I feel other toes bent under my own. I'm pricked by phantom pins through the soles of my feet, like an endless search for the devil's mark, but I feel it all; the spot is never found. It's the alarm my body sounds before a return of my fibromyalgia, ushering in other symptoms that can't be soldiered through: the brain fog, exhaustion and paralysing depression. I will have to return to North Berwick another day. But I am here now, warm and dry, as I watch the gale swell in earnest and the waves boom on the shore: a tempest worthy of a vast coven.

*

During Gelie Duncan's interrogations, she named the healer and midwife Agnes Sampson as an accomplice. The witchcraft confessions from Agnes recorded at the North Berwick trials are extensive, with much folk belief detailed along with the standard demonic pact. This spaewife from Haddington near Edinburgh lives on, despite the best attempts of King, Kirk and history. One version of her story keeps ghost tours in business: 'Bald Agnes' is said to haunt the location of her interrogation and sentencing, the Palace of Holyroodhouse, the residence of the royal family in Scotland. She has also been a muse to feminist installation artist Judy Chicago. In the Brooklyn Museum in New York, Agnes's name appears in gold on lustred tiles, along with the names of 999 other women, both mythical and historical, set in the floor of *The Dinner Party*, a monumental feminist sculpture consisting of a large banquet table set for great women and goddesses.

The interrogation records claim Agnes was a midwife and healer. When we look at the thousands of accused, healers are only a small minority. Many of the women I have chosen to write about knew healing charms and herbal cures. Their confessions are fascinating and provide more information about who they were as people. It is easy to focus on this small cross section and assume that all those executed for witchcraft had similar knowledge. Perhaps this is at the heart of the persecuted healer myth, yet the overwhelming majority of the accused were targeted simply because they were women.

Agnes used a witches' stone to ease birth pains. The folklore of a witches' stone or 'holey' stone suggests it's a multipurpose talisman. Through sympathetic magic, the holed stone would help the baby through the birth canal. The natural hole through the middle was made by running water. A stone like this is sometimes called an Odin stone, because Odin had only one eye, and looking through it, you see as the one-eyed god sees. Sometimes it's also called a fairy stone. I have a witches' stone that I found

on a beach. Through its narrow lens, I like to think someday I
might see Agnes the *grace wyff*, the Wise Wife of Keith. I imagine her offering a steady hand to a woman in the agony of childbirth, her grip hard and certain. I can almost hear the urgent
whisper of her now-forgotten birth-prayer. Would that I could
use my own stone to birth this writing about her and the other
accused. *Let it be as true; let it live.*

A thread of otherworldly justice runs through Agnes's confessions. She was alone in a field at twilight, newly widowed and
grieving for her husband, when she met a being she called Elva.
This ghostly helper promised retribution for those who'd
wronged her. He appeared to her in different forms: a dark man
with a staff, a white stag or a haystack. Though painted as
demonic in the trial record, Agnes denied these manifestations
were the devil. In her role as a charmer, Agnes Sampson was an
intermediary for women who had been wronged. Women in the
sixteenth century had no judicial recourse, but their words had
power. Cursing could bring justice when the law could not. At
the request of one of her clients, she crafted a poppet in yellow
wax of a man called Archie. As the figure melted, the man would
pine away. Charming was a skill Agnes's father had taught her,
but foreknowledge was an innate ability – some clients could be
cured, but for others her prognosis was grim. Knowing the time
and nature of one's death was useful in fatalistic, early modern
Scotland. If one knew death was coming, one could prepare.
Agnes's trial records a long list of all the people she had healed
– and the many she had not.

The records are full of wild claims that make little sense to a
modern reader. In sorting through them, I apply what I know of
folk magic, healing, ballads and lore. Like sifting stones from
lentils, I pull the interrogator's devil out from everything else the
accused said. Sometimes it is just a feeling I have; this is what she
really said, this is a fragment of a life, and everything else is part
of the machine of a forced confession. Specific claims were

clearly extracted under torture. Agnes confessed she had premonitions of the great storm that threatened the King's new bride.
She said she rode out on to the sea at Halloween in 'riddles or
sieves' with two hundred other witches. They drank wine and
'made merry', baptised a cat and used the pulverised knuckles of
dead men to make curses. This christened cat was the cause of
the 'contrarie winde' that delayed the King's ship. The treasonous plotting was clearly invented in answer to leading questions
and intense pressure to say what her interrogators wanted to
hear. Agnes repeated the story she had been told of her own
guilt, perhaps embroidering it in a plea for mercy.

A version of this story is preserved in *Newes from Scotland*.
In his salacious account, the minister James Carmichael used the
North Berwick witch trials to illustrate the urgency of the holy
war against the devil and his minions. It is one of the only written records of the torture used to extract confessions, the details
of which were omitted from almost all church records of the
witch trials. Carmichael details the use of the bone-crushing
boots, thumbscrews, the winching of the neck or head with a
cord, and the search for the witch's mark, usually a mole or
other natural skin pigmentation. Though such marks were quite
common in appearance, witch-hunters thought they were 'insensible' to pain: supposedly, they were numb, a supernumerary
nipple for feeding a familiar. Carmichael said these marks
appeared after 'the devill doth lick them with his tong in some
privy [private] part of their bodie before he dooth recyve them to
bee his servauntes'. The pamphlet goes on to detail the torture
of the elderly Agnes, who was one of Carmichael's own parish-
ioners. She was completely shaved and tied in a chokehold in
front of an audience of the King and other noblemen. Carmichael
claimed her naked body was searched until the mark was found
on her 'privities', or genitals.

The actual trial records reveal the pamphlet's sensationalism.
The mark was not found on her genitals, as *Newes* proclaims,

but on her right knee. This discrepancy reveals a deliberately sexualised version of events. Carmichael embroidered the experience of one of the members of his congregation, a woman he would have known personally. The sexual, sadistic obsessions underlying the witch trials in Scotland are profoundly disturbing. These innocent women were caught up in the perverse fantasies of men in power.

The sexual nature of this torture is significant. Intercourse with the devil was central to the boilerplate confessions women were forced to reproduce, a script that was used repeatedly for over a hundred years. The story of the demonic pact as a sex act was read to thousands of accused women. They were often asked what the devil's penis felt like inside them. The interrogators wanted to know if they had performed the *osculum infame*, or kissing the devil's anus. The ministers and noblemen interrogating the accused wanted to know where the devil touched them. Satan used his servants 'carnally', yet, according to *Newes from Scotland*, the women did not enjoy this, as his member was too cold.

Finding the devil's mark was essential to a confession. *Newes from Scotland* details myriad modes of torture that the accused endured stoically, only to break down when the mark was found. Scottish women of the sixteenth century were modest. They would have rarely been fully naked in their lives, washing only their hands, feet and faces regularly, and wearing their shifts while bathing. The women being interrogated would probably have shared the conservative ideas about sexuality dictated by the Church. To stand naked, shaved and subjected to intimate examination in front of men of power would have been beyond endurance, and the impact of this psychological torture must have been overwhelming.

Elements of the accounts in the *Newes from Scotland* pamphlet may seem absurd to us today, but they would have had historical precedence. Oral history maintained gory stories of saints' martyrdoms and chieftains' feats of war, all with the superhuman ability to withstand suffering. In reality, the accused were powerless. Agnes Sampson was an aged midwife, but for the purpose of the new war on the devil, she was his mighty agent, a demonic version of a powerful saint as would befit the archenemy of an all-powerful king. She was burned on Castle Hill in Edinburgh on 28 January 1591.

*

I return to North Berwick in the summer, deciding to adopt the Law as a memorial in a place where there is none. Gelie and Agnes must have climbed this hill, perhaps under a full moon on a summer night when the way up was luminous and certain. A hill climb means I will have to sleep for days afterwards. I still attempt it, despite my disability. I have what Nan Shepherd called a hunger for height. Hill-climbing is the closest you can get to the sky without flying. I envy others who can out-walk families on a day out, and who can traverse longer distances and discover remote places. I have always been a walker; I walked everywhere, until I couldn't. Making peace with my chronic illnesses means I have had to see my world circumscribed, its diameter shrinking.

It's a bright, warm day and the hill is heaving. Despite the steep climb, groups clamber up and down the massive volcanic hill. The well-worn path up the Law is parched and crumbling, the colour of a shortbread biscuit. I have my stick, but at several points I crawl, using my hands to pull myself up. It's ungraceful, and perhaps looks desperate. I'm here now, at this massive hill made by an angry giant. I'll make it. Hill-climbing, or its macho cousin, mountain-climbing, is tinged with a conqueror's mentality. Climbers 'do' a hill or mountain, and tick it off their list. I can no longer look at the landscape this way. I'm in it, and it's in me. Today, the hill is busy, and I'm self-conscious about my walking stick, my measured pace. A couple stops and watches me, the woman muttering apologetic encouragement. The man, older than me and dressed in a crisp white polo shirt and shorts, frowns. I know that look. When I first began using a walking stick, almost ten years ago, there were stares of mild outrage from those who found me guilty of malingering in their field of vision.

The hilltop is full of families resting from their climb, taking pictures of themselves at the summit beside the fibreglass whale bone replica that marks the top. Nearby sits a stone ruin, once a signal post, built during the Napoleonic wars. Its ragged Gothic arch frames the view: the glassy cobalt sea surrounds the green tablet of Craiglieth. The horizon spreads around me in a great ring. Here is the laurel wreath of land and sea; my heart is crowned with this sacred vista.

Coming down is harder, as I knew it would be. It's the first summer of the pandemic, and there is no way to keep two metres apart. I stand off the path to let others overtake me. One woman carrying an infant ambles past with ease, thanking me breathlessly. The baby watches me over her shoulder, bright eyes new and unfocused, like little sapphires. The mother reaches the bottom of the Law and sighs loudly. She turns around and calls out to me in encouragement: 'You're almost there!'

I normally resist any gesture that singles me out, but I'm shattered by the climb, and I take it for what it is, a kindness. She's right – a few more stumbling steps and I'll be on flat ground.

And what of Gelie and Agnes? I carry their memories with me, as if in a creel on my back.

5

Athena of the

'Wherefore then layest thou a sna
die?'

5

Athena of the Saltpans

Keddie Liddell, Prestonpans, 1678

'Wherefore then layest thou a snare for my life, to cause me to die?'

— Witch of Endor, I Samuel, 28:9

I'm in Prestoungrange, a seaside village eight miles east of Edinburgh. Proportionate to its population, the surrounding area of Prestonpans convicted more accused witches than any other locality in Scotland, exceeding more populous places like Aberdeen. Many of the accused in the first witch-hunts of 1590, overseen by the King in North Berwick, were from Prestonpans. The hunts here continued for generations and ended late, with women seized and tortured illegally in 'extrajudicial trials'. I've come to see the garden memorial at the back of a pub called the Gothenburg. It's a lovely old Edwardian building with a wooden bar and a beautifully painted ceiling. Stained-glass windows look out to the sea, and a vinyl banner advertises a Sunday carvery. When I enquire about the garden, the man behind the bar clarifies, 'The witches?'

The manager takes me to the rear exit of the pub, apologising for the state of the 'garden'. 'We don't get many tourists this time of year. The bin men have destroyed it.' She leaves me alone with the gate unlocked. The concrete enclosure houses overflowing bins. The walls are lined with a loosely figurative, fresco-like mural. Shadowy faces loom out, partially obliterated, as if by acid. Pale hues of salmon pink, blues and lichen green swirl about in anthropomorphic shapes, suggesting a storm. Tiles bearing the names of people accused of witchcraft frame silhouettes on the wall above. One stray tile has fallen loose: it says 'Thou shalt not suffer a witch to live' – the infamous war cry from Exodus. This damage was not merely the work of careless bin collectors. This is years of neglect. A narrow wall of planters filled with weeds and stray garbage are all that remain of a memorial garden. Crisp packets, traffic cones and cigarette butts litter the space. Painted plywood panels lie splintered, stacked behind the bins. I pull out the images, painted in thick acrylics like a secondary school history display. Portraits of John Knox and Mary Queen of Scots with her eyes scratched out are left here to rot. The last one, tucked behind a traffic cone, is of Gelie Duncan.

This is the first of several modern 'memorials' I find vandalised, uncared for by the communities that built them. This garden was born of a celebratory moment in Prestoungrange, sixteen years ago, when a local ceremony pardoned eighty-one victims of the hunts. The 14th Baron of Prestoungrange issued the pardon, which came into force just before the Scottish government abolished the ancient baronial courts in 2005. The pardon included the witches' cats, but it was serious enough: the Baron appealed to Queen Elizabeth II for a royal pardon, and she sent the matter to her ministers. They replied that the amount of research necessary to even consider a decision was impossible and there was 'no precedent for a successful outcome'. Nonetheless, the community of Prestonpans gathered in this pub garden, once the Gestalt Garden, to celebrate the legal gesture of the baronial pardon and hold a festival at Halloween. A special beer was brewed for the occasion.

A legal campaign to pardon those accused of witchcraft during the witch-hunts began to gain momentum in Scotland in 2021. As a national pardon becomes a possibility, I wonder who it's really for? Those pardoned are long gone, and a pardon, by its nature, suggests guilt. Those unjustly accused by the Church and state would again be put on trial, while those who did the killing remain unexamined. As a political gesture, a pardon might change the way we talk about the victims, or, as in the case of the Prestoungrange pardons, it might be a moment soon forgotten, bringing no real change at all.

*

In the autumn of 1679, the day in Prestonpans began with the firing of the saltpans, great coal-powered vats of seawater, boiled to make salt. Many tonnes of coal were needed to produce a tonne of salt or 'white gold'. Black coal smoke roiled into the sky, obscuring the horizon. By the end of the day, it blotted out the emergent stars. Night came with the tap and hiss of a drum. The village drummer played through the streets to mark the day's margins, as well as midden time, when waste would be thrown from windows. *Right right left left,* the bouncing stick sounded the buzz and roll on the drum, and it was a sound everyone knew as well as the rhythm of the waves.

In Prestonpans, the drummer was also the witch 'pricker', a man named David Cowan. He worked with a group of men, one of whom was the town bailie, a noted drunk. They terrorised women like Elspeth Chousley, whom they abducted twice, vandalising her house and threatening her with swords and pistols. She paid the extortion they demanded for her release.

The witch-hunts in Scotland lasted longer than in any other European country. Towards the end, it became harder to gain approval from the Privy Council in Edinburgh to conduct a witch-hunt, as new arguments about witchcraft came to light. In some places, if permission for a trial could not be secured, local men took matters into their own hands. In 1678, the bailie, drummer and other men in Prestonpans violently seized the widow Kathrine or Keddie Liddell from her home and imprisoned her, claiming she was a witch. The drum sounded off at the beginning and end of each day, played by the hands of a torturer. What might it have been like for women to stand at their windows, clutching their midden pots, listening to that sound?

Keddie was tortured, and she petitioned for her release from the tolbooth – tolbooths were originally where taxes were paid, and served as meeting places for local magistrates, but they also doubled as prisons. She must have had allies in the town and the means to hire an advocate, as well as a degree of literacy, to have been able to challenge her captors in this way. Her petition pleaded her good name – she was a person of 'known integrity and untuched fame'. In a rare moment of critical reflection, the Privy Council records document her maltreatment, describing it as 'cruel and unchristian'. Keddie was imprisoned for six weeks, 'keeping her from sleep several nights and days to . . . have extorted any confession from her they pleased'. The 'pricker' inflicted life-threatening wounds, described in the record: 'The great effusion of her blood and whereby her skin is raised and her body highly swelled.' The injuries had become so infected that she thought she was dying.

The bailie and salter got off with a warning. Their crime was not that they imprisoned and tortured a woman, but that they had done so without assent from the Privy Council. David Cowan was imprisoned in the Edinburgh tolbooth and released in 1679, with the notice that he would be fined if he practised witch-finding again without permission from the Council. Despite this, he continued as a witch 'pricker', interrogating at least four other women.

When Keddie was released and returned to her ransacked home, what might she have found? No one survives alone. Perhaps a friend had restored order to what was left, folding a clean petticoat neatly in her chest beneath her one good plaid and the old, bad one. Her linen apron might have been found, mended, atop a pair of stays and a stomacher, but her good shoes – barely worn – would be gone. Keddie's Bible might have been tucked in with her kerchiefs. I imagine Keddie was a rare kin: a woman who read.

By the end of the seventeenth century, most of the male population could sign their names, but female literacy remained significantly lower, around twenty-five per cent. Keddie was perhaps one of the few who knew how to practise this magical art of deciphering the written word. In the late seventeenth century, readers learned poems, ballads and stories by heart. Oral and written history created a living, changing web of folk memory. Oral history relied on deep memory, physical and sensory, whereas reading was a linear way of thinking and processing information. To read and to recall are two different modes of understanding the world. Perhaps Keddie could do both. One could be done in the darkness of a tolbooth cell, but for the other, you must have light. What kind of reader might she have been? Imprisoned and tortured, did she recall the words of the Witch of Endor, the Old Testament sorceress who fed and aided Saul when God refused him, even after he deceived her?

*

I learned to read quite late as a child. It didn't come easily to me; the words refused to march in a line, instead dancing up and down the page in their own wilful formations. I saw letters in colours as well as shapes, and they seemed, to me, to be living things. I still use my hands to read, as if my fingers could herd the words into a linear order. It took many years for me to come into my own as a reader. In school, we were made to read stories about boys, their sporting exploits and adventures. None of these things interested me. I asked my grade-school teacher why there were no stories about girls in our reading assignments. 'Boys won't read stories about girls,' she said simply, as if it were a universal truth. What girls might want or need to read wasn't even a consideration at the time. I learned to read boys' stories inventively, to see myself in their alien world of masculine triumphs, and to imagine the space as female.

As a teenager, I embraced the intimate activity of communing with words on the page, the magic summoning of a private world. Once I discovered reading that wasn't tested and graded, I was free. I searched for books in the library's bargain box and struck gold. The box was seemingly bottomless and filled with forbidden, esoteric cast-offs from someone else's 1970s mass-market library, all twenty-five cents each. I had quarters in my pocket – the books were mine for the taking. Reading became my superpower, and I read things I didn't understand, letting them wash over me like dreams. I was voracious, devouring everything from Jean Genet's *Our Lady of the Flowers* to Philip K. Dick's *Ubik*, fished out of the bargain bin for their psychedelic covers.

Once, I found a mouldy white paperback in the bin: *The Story of O*. Of all the titles I found, none haunted me like the literary negation porn of that novel. It took on power and immediacy in my teenage brain, shaping me. O, the owl-masked woman in chains, endured branding and rape before relinquishing any claim to her own body, mind and agency. She did not survive her ordeals. In the end, she is 'of stone or wax'. Her ecstatic objectification is complete, yet her end is also the dissociative trance of one who endures violence. It was my first vision of sex and womanly desire, and I held it in my mind, a powerful curse I had to undo. Perhaps all girls have this moment of erotic knowing coupled with fear? Self-obliteration as seduction: we learn to undo ourselves in countless ways, both small and profound, in order to please others. I learned early that sexual power, for a woman, could mean death. The women embodying these states were surrounded by men, yet they were utterly alone.

We are living in a moment of witch vogue – witches are sexy. Beyond the kitsch image of a pin-up witch winking from her broom in flight, a darker fetishisation of women's suffering during the witch-hunts continues. The sexualised torture carried out in the seventeenth century has survived as a male fantasy into the present day. Not long after I began my research, I found disturbing photos online of men who collected torture devices used in witchcraft interrogations. In these digital images, they showed off their thumbscrews, shackles and scold's bridles. They posed with their trophies, some in gurning selfies wearing the face-cages and iron masks once used to silence women. Other photos posted on the Internet reveal women and men role-playing a kind of BDSM re-enactment of the trials, the woman gagged in iron and led in chains. Perhaps this was consensual, but I could not forget the original torture these objects were designed to inflict. The real history of atrocity and femicide is distorted and enjoyed as a prurient act of male desire.

The suffering of the witch-hunts is eroticised, as is the power the witch embodies. The fantasy of the sexualised witch is nothing new. While women were hunted for the crime of witchcraft, the idea of the witch was seductive and fascinating, rendered in drama and art. Across Europe, sensational details from the confessions found their way into a new genre of art depicting the witches' sabbat. These paintings were a burlesque of women of all ages, often naked. They flew on spindles and broomsticks, animated strange beasts and worked through the night, stirring potions with phallic bones. A popular theme was the witches' kitchen: a mundane, domestic space, crowded with women coating themselves in flying ointment, tracing arcane circles on the floor, flying up chimneys and – perhaps most sinisterly – reading. Deciphering words meant power, and the written word, manifested as the 'word of God' in the Bible, had equal potency within necromantic texts for summoning demons and altering the godly order of things. The paintings of sabbats are some of the earliest images depicting women's literacy, and they portray women readers as demonic.

In my search for witches and women, I glimpsed power and meaning in these paintings created as the witch-hunts raged across Europe. Most striking were the paintings of Flemish artist Frans

Francken II. He was the originator of a genre of painting called the 'monkeys' kitchen', depicting women or monkeys in kitchens as an allegory for vice. Fantastical and earthy creatures attend these chaotic folk gatherings. Working in seventeenth-century Antwerp, Francken specialised in genre painting and was greatly influenced by Hieronymus Bosch. The paintings satirise the women they depict, yet the scenes are imbued with an erotic charge. Beyond the misogynist ridicule implicit in these works, is there not, peeking out of the corners, lurking in the foreground, an illicit power? Francken renders the temporary autonomous space of the sabbat: naked witches fly up the chimney while others stir a cauldron. A table is piled with weird ingredients destined for the pot. Creatures writhe on the kitchen floor, and in the background of one painting, a church is burning: the spell is working.

In Francken's *The Witches' Kitchen*, a woman is beginning to undress. She is next in line to be rubbed down with flying ointment. She looks over her shoulder at the old woman administering the dose to another. The central figure is another young woman in elegant clothes. She wears a lace ruff, fine silk stomacher and bright yellow skirts. In the visual language of the time, the yellow may code her as a prostitute. She glances at the viewer while removing her sock, as if to say, *I see you looking*. Like the girl reading stories that were not written for me, I devour these paintings, pirate them from their original historical context. I conspire with the bare-footed woman in her bright dress. I look back. It's exhilarating: fun, even. The mundane space of a kitchen becomes a demonic workshop, where women, the young and finely dressed beside the rough and old, are engrossed in cryptic magical tomes. I imagine them reading something difficult and delicious, and they become a studious sisterhood. We work together, casting a spell, inventing new spaces in history right inside the old story told to demean, vilify and destroy us.

*

Witnesses in the Prestonpans trial records spoke of terrifying night visits, something modern historians attribute to the phenomenon of sleep paralysis. While in REM sleep, the body becomes 'paralysed' to prevent the sleeper from acting out their dreams. During an episode of sleep paralysis, the dreamer will be partially conscious, aware of themselves and the room they are in. Through this half-dream, they see a kind of umbra. Though the dreamer can't move, they feel as if they are levitating or flying, with an animal or human intruder sometimes sitting or riding upon them. This is called the 'incubus' phase, after the mythological demon that inseminates dreaming women. Suffering a nightmare, or a 'night mare', was once thought of as being 'hag-ridden.' A witch captures the sleeper and rides them like a horse through the night.

The story of Issobel Griersoune is full of nightmare. She was accused in Prestonpans in 1607, at a time when the village was overcome by feral cats. Many from the village came forward with sinister claims about Issobel. One accuser, a woman named Margaret Donaldson, experienced a kind of sleep paralysis. She said Issobel came into her house around Halloween, entering in an 'unknown way', and that Issobel pulled her from her bed by her shoulder blade and pressed her to the floor. Margaret was ill for a week afterward.

Issobel Griersoune's story confirms all the received notions of witch trials. Here was a healer with a pet cat, estranged from her neighbours, done in by hearsay and scapegoated for unexplained events. Issobel's cat was wilful – sneaking into the smith's house in the middle of the night with a glaring of local cats, one of which the man believed was Issobel herself. The summer before her interrogations, Issobel's cat went missing again, and, as she called for it through the streets, she found her neighbours gathered around a communal brew vat, drinking the 'good new ale'. When she appeared, villagers claimed the beer spoiled, turning black and thick 'like gutter dirt'. It stank; the party was over.

Uncanny accusations accumulated around Issobel, and though she tried to make peace with her neighbours over a drink, the malice persisted.

Issobel was found guilty of sorcery and witchcraft as well as 'the lying and taking off of sickness and disease' and the use of charms. She was sentenced to be taken to Castle Hill in Edinburgh, 'thair to be wirret [strangled] at the stake until dead', and her body burned. All her 'moveable goods' now belonged to the Crown. Her tomcat – I imagine him a black-and-white moggie, with a little bandit mask and bright green eyes – had to make do without her. What other possessions might this woman have had? A salt-caked willow creel and grave clothes sewn from her best dress – the one she was married in, a trimmed white shroud that was never used, as her body was 'burnt to ashes'? I can imagine these things, but there is no record of what the state took from her, beyond her life.

*

I've experienced sleep paralysis only once, just after I'd started writing about witches. I had a dream where I woke but couldn't move. Something perched on me, its tiny hands gathered over my heart. It peered into my face with enormous, feather-ringed eyes – an owl-woman, thrumming with malevolent power. In the rigid terror of my dream, this being had formed me, not the other way around. I was also aware that she was very like the protagonist in *The Story of O*. O appears naked at the end of the novel, wearing only an owl mask and chains. In this owl guise, she has sacrificed her identity and agency for her lover. Though these experiences of sleep paralysis are vague and ominous, it is only upon waking that the dreamer will make sense of them, labelling their cause an owl-woman, an alien abduction or, in the case of Margaret Donaldson and others in the seventeenth century, witchcraft.

Once I had shaken off sleep, I wondered what or who she was, this *Cailleach Oidhche* – a Gaelic term for owl or 'old woman of the night'. I remembered a painting by the surrealist Remedios Varo called *Creation de los aves*, meaning 'the creation of the birds'. In the painting, an owl-woman sits at her laboratory desk, channelling lunar rays on to paper. Where she traces them, birds come to life and take flight. It's an allegory of painting, of writing and also of reading. Owls, women, words and power are so deeply wedded in me, they ride me in my sleep. The owl-woman of my dream multiplies. She's the cryptozoology of La Lechuza, the Mexican legend of an executed witch who, at night, takes the form of a woman with an owl's face. She's Bleuddwedd, the Welsh owl goddess, and her many manifestations. She's Nyctimene, the girl raped by her father and turned into an owl by Athena. She's also the spirit of surrealist Leonor Fini, a painter of witches and female monsters, an artist of extraordinary power, now almost forgotten. Fini's owl mask inspired the denouement of *The Story of O*.

Though I'm now awake and understand my terrible dream as a trick of the brain and my sleeping body, I also believe the *Cailleach Oidhche* was there in her multitudes, staring at me, insisting I be worthy of her.

*

It's a damp summer morning in a housing development in Prestonpans. I've come to a cul-de-sac called Dolphingstone Way to visit another memorial to the women killed in Prestonpans during the witch-hunts. This statue, by renowned sculptor Andy Scott, depicts a reading witch. I can find no official title, but she is sometimes referred to as the 'Athena Statue'. She stands in a shallow pool of gravel, beside swings and a slide, part of a constellation of playground equipment, ringed by low shrubbery and tract housing.

Andy Scott's two monumental horse heads, *Kelpies*, located off the motorway in Falkirk, are better known – they're the largest equine sculptures in the world. Scott was commissioned by

Stewart Milne Housing Company to add to the public art in Prestonpans. Erected in 2011, the Athena Statue presides over a suburban enclave of the Athena Grange Housing Estate. Though figurative, she is other than human – over three metres high. Scott intended the Athena Statue as a memorial of sorts, saying he wanted to present the accused as dignified rather than victimised. But the statue is also intended as an embodiment of the name of the housing development where it resides. In an article in the *Scotsman*, the sales director of the housing company said the statue 'provides a beautiful spectacle at the heart of the development'. Can a memorial be a decorative object, something that will increase property value and sell houses, while also functioning as a witness to atrocity?

The Athena Statue wears a fine seventeenth-century style gown made entirely of filigree leaves. A lacy steel ruff frames her face, and a mask made of vines covers it. Her hair is in a tidy bun, and pale light shines through her hollow metal body. On the day I visit her, raindrops trace the leaves of her gown and drip from her nose. A large cross hangs at her throat. This Athena is a good Christian.

Scott's figurative work depicts animals and mystical beings as embodied spirits of place. This sculpture in the Athena Grange Development is undeniably beautiful. On this sunless morning, she is an elegant fairy godmother, presiding over the empty playground and its absent children. She holds out a large book ceremoniously, her head bowed as if reading aloud. With her rich dress and large tome, it is as if she has stepped directly from the foreground of Francken's witches' kitchen to stand here, dripping and forlorn, doing penance. The children who play under her perforated shadow know more than I can guess. They will have invented stories for her. Might they say that she has made them braver, a little larger? What tales does she read to them? Does the steel book in her hands tell of a woman killed by rumour? Or does it tell of others seized from their homes in the dead of night by gangs of local men? None could have happy endings, though some would be tales of women who got away, who escaped certain death.

I linger on Dolphingstone Way, taking photos of the statue with my phone. Despite the stated purpose behind the monument, there's no plaque nor panel to attribute her presence as a memorial to those who died during the trials. The monument plays at absolution from collective guilt without acknowledging the crime. The gesture is its own kind of apotropaic charm, a protection meant to banish the spectres of the past and pretend that all has been made right.

The goddess Athena's avatar is a little owl, symbolising wisdom. I like Hegel's take on Athena's owl: she only takes flight when 'the shades of night are gathering'. The metaphor means that history can only be understood in hindsight, among ghosts, after the historical moment has died. Athena's owl – Nyctimene – was a survivor of incest, a night-flier and knower of secrets, a Hegelian symbol of sense amidst a senseless history. If Scott's Athena had an owl perched on her shoulder, I would like her better.

6

Edge of the North Sea

Ellen Gray, Aberdeen, 1597

'Is thair na mair following me?'
         – Ellen Gray, looking over her shoulder as she
         was transported across the River Ythan to Aberdeen.

I had only just moved to Scotland when I found Carrie Reichardt's bright tile mural in the centre of Aberdeen, tucked away beside the malls and high-street shops in a narrow cobbled street named Correction Wynd. The mural is a monument to Aberdeen suffragists and other notable women. It's called *Gallus Quines*, or 'brave women' in the Doric dialect, and includes a panel dedicated to those executed for witchcraft in Aberdeen, with 'Hex the Patriarchy' emblazoned front and centre. 'Deeds Not Words', a suffragist slogan, appears on the second panel. Stumbling upon Reichardt's collage- and zine-inspired mural was like finding an old friend. It also honours modern, self-identified witches who have radicalised the epithet, imbuing it with an anarchic sensibility. The mural proclaims: 'We are the Granddaughters – All of the Witches You Were Never Able to Burn.'

Reichardt chose Correction Wynd for the mural's location because it's the site of the seventeenth-century workhouse, or correction house. The kirk sessions issued fines for adultery, gossip, prostitution and theft, and if someone were unable to pay the fine, they did time in the correction house. Men could more easily pay these fines, and the overwhelming majority imprisoned in the correction house were women – around eighty-seven per cent. Women who were pregnant outside of wedlock were sentenced to a month here if they were unable to pay the ten-pound fine for fornication. Other punishments, like spending a Saturday in the stocks at the market cross with a shaved head, might also be meted out. Inmates of the workhouse created textiles, their labour unpaid.

The *Gallus Quines* mural sits below the Mither Kirk, the central church in Aberdeen; stairs ascend from Correction Wynd into the kirkyard above street level. The mural watches the Mither Kirk, once a prison for those accused of witchcraft. A tile printed with a flying eyeball proclaims: 'I never sleep.' *Gallus Quines* turns the tables and looks back at the Mither Kirk. The accused were held inside the kirk's old steeple and the subterranean St Mary's Chapel. They would have been 'watched' or kept awake as part of their ordeal – they could never sleep. In the mural, feminist vigilance and witness are paired with the *droch shùil* or evil eye, a particularly malevolent witches' curse.

Whenever I come to Aberdeen, I visit the mural. Sometimes, there's another person taking it in, and there's a companionable sense of sharing a secret between us. On one occasion, I see a mother and her child together, talking about the images. It's easy to view the mural, but getting into the kirk is harder. The Mither Kirk is closed, its congregation formally disbanded. I have been trying to gain entrance to this place for over two years when I am finally granted access one day in early spring.

A long-tailed tit follows me along the cobbles to the kirk, whisking his elegant tail. The bird's small, black eyes look up through its white mask. Is he waiting for seeds, or perhaps urging me on, knowing something I don't yet realise – that inside the kirk, I will find a great piece of a forgotten puzzle? Arthur Ninfield, the kirk's organist and a volunteer with the Open Space Trust, unlocks the doors for me. The Open Space Trust is overseeing a project to transform the kirk into an accessible place for the people of Aberdeen.

Arthur and I walk around the kirk, which has seemingly been abandoned by the faith that built it. We peek at the site of the largest ecclesiastical dig in Europe. The findings span 1,000 years, and the foundation's strata lie open, a Lovecraftian void in this sacred space. The missing walls and floor disorientate me. A large wooden panel covers a deep pit that has been dug to retrieve hundreds of remains: 897 burials; three and a half tonnes of bones. When the bodies were excavated, some still wore their medieval sackcloth made of cattle hair, or jaunty silk hats trimmed with silver thread. Now, these bodies lie in boxes atop stones, beneath the stained glass windows, waiting to be reinterred. The witches' ring, used to chain the accused to the wall, hangs from the edge of the excavation site – incidental, unremarkable.

The building sighs and sings around us, and the wind off the North Sea makes a home in this empty place. The bells ring three o'clock, shaking the stone walls. This church is only the latest building to stand on this thousand-year-old sacred site. I feel like I am attending the death of Christianity as we have known it. The kirk, which held graves for the wealthy lairds, nooks for kings, and even a modern 'Oil and Gas Chapel' intended for use by the North Sea Oil industry, is gathering dust. The Church that once favoured the wealthy and powerful, and oversaw a history of persecution and atrocity, is dying, or perhaps transforming. This was a meeting place for a vast congregation of the living and the dead. I stand beside one of the last of this flock, this organist and historian: the building's champion, and an unlikely ally.

I ask Arthur to show me the church's tapestries, which I have read hang near the west door. They are the real reason for my visit. I saw the needlework listed in the Kirk's Statement of Significance, cataloguing the art and sculpture housed within. The four tapestries were created during the second wave of witch-hunts in Aberdeen, in the reign of Charles I, perhaps around 1630. The tapestries were created for a royal visit and they adorned the King's loft, his private space in the kirk.

Women embroidered them, and they depict women's stories from the Old Testament and Apocrypha – a biblical precursor to *Gallus Quines*. I had wondered what women's art created during a witch-hunt might have looked like. Here were stories of women nurturing, confronting and resisting men: Moses and the pharaoh's daughter; Jephthah and his daughter; Esther and King Ahasuerus; and Susanna and the Elders. A whole team of women created the stitches, but it was Mary Jamesone who drafted and designed the panels, and her work shows a mastery not only of the human form but of expression and depth. Jamesone used compositions and conventions from Renaissance etchings and paintings in her design; silken thread was her paint and linen her canvas. The work is epic in scale, each panel over eight feet square.

In the tapestry portraying the story of Moses in the bull-rushes, the Nile is narrow, flowing under what can only be Aberdeen's Bridge of Dee, the city skyline in the distance. In the foreground, the pharaoh's daughter and her ladies are dressed as seventeenth-century noblewomen. Their hair is modishly curled, and they wear stomachers, bright petticoats and buckled court shoes with graceful heels. Renaissance art often included biblical figures in contemporary fashions and featured patrons in the scenes, and Jamesone references this tradition. The pharaoh's daughter holds the baby Moses and looks out at the viewer. Might this figure of the pharaoh's daughter be a self-portrait of Jamesone? In the traditional story, the pharaoh's daughter saves Moses, defying her father's decree that all male Hebrew babies be drowned in the Nile. Floating in the river are several red-and-white striped parcels matching the underskirts of the women. On closer examination, they have tiny heads; they are swaddled infants floating on the current, some face-down.

Arthur suggests this panel might be a memorial to Jamesone's babies that died in infancy, and this moving reading informs the other three panels. Mary Jamesone used storytelling as a form of personal presence – a way to express her identity. Could the tapestries be her proxy audience with the King? Jamesone's selection of biblical stories spoke to the contemporary grief and horror of the witch-hunts. They speak truth to power. It's a dream I project on to the work, and they answer back with affirmation.

One panel depicts Esther bowing before King Ahasuerus. In the biblical story, Esther invites the king to dinner party after dinner party, seducing him with decorum before finally asking him, 'Why are you trying to kill my people?' The dinner parties are an elaborate charm offensive meant to win the sympathy of a king, not unlike the tapestries themselves. In this needlework, the lush costumes the king and Esther wear are displayed in ombre threads and expert colour work. He touches her with his sceptre, giving her permission to speak as a crowd forms with a gallows in the background. In Aberdeen, a gallows was built on nearby Castle Hill, and at some point in their lives, every woman working on the panels would have witnessed women executed publicly for the crime of witchcraft. The gallows depicted in the panel is contemporary.

In the next panel, Jamesone referenced Ruben's *Susanna and the Elders* from 1610. In the Old Testament story, two men watch Susanna as she bathes, and then demand that she have sex with them. After she refuses, the men have her arrested for adultery. Daniel saves her from execution by exposing the elders. In Jamesone's version, the hands, feet and bodies of the subjects are masterfully drawn with dramatic expression. Susanna is naked in the foreground, the softness of her body rendered in textured silk. Her hair is loose and she covers her breasts, gazing downward while the two elders seem engaged in an abstract argument over her body. Whether Jamesone intended this or not, I see the elders as witch-finders – a pricker and an interrogator – with a naked woman before them on trial.

The final tapestry depicts the story of Jephthah and his daughter. In this story from Judges, Jephthah promises that if he is victorious in battle against the Ammonites, he will sacrifice the first living thing that greets him as he returns home. He triumphs, but on his return, his daughter, Seila, dances out to meet him. She becomes his sacrifice, his burned offering. In the tapestry, Seila is girlish, playing a drum, and she is surrounded by dense blue stitches as dark as midnight. Jephthah looks to the sky, checking in with God, flanked by soldiers in seventeenth-century armour. Some have alarmed, expressive faces, as if they understand the atrocity that is about to take place but are powerless against it. The tapestry is darkened by fire damage, adding to the pathos of its presence.

Standing before the countless stitches made by the hands of women long dead, I marvel at their work. Here is a message, meant not just for a king, but for me, for us. We will never know if Mary Jamesone intentionally designed these panels as documents of witness *to all the women and girls sacrificed to patriarchy*, but I imagine the group of embroiderers sewing, the heavy fabric over their laps as they brought the stories to life with needle and thread, and shared other yarns. The characters rendered in the panels might have looked like neighbours and sisters, imbuing these stories with a sense of immediacy. Perhaps these artisans did not speak of the executions of living memory, but they all knew of the burning of women near the Flesh Cross and on Castle Hill. Maybe they spoke instead of Seila, and how the daughters of Israel mourned her at the quarter days of the year, their cries like the *caoineadh* – the formal keening of grieving women.

*

The first wave of witch-hunting hit Aberdeen in 1597, thirty years before Mary Jamesone and her team of needlewomen created the tapestries. It was a hard year in Scotland. Famine, plague and witch trials swept the country, with 400 people interrogated. It was the year King James VI and I published his

Daemonologie, the match to the kindling of the witch-hunts in Scotland. Reading the exhaustive records of the interrogations, trials and executions for this single year in Aberdeen, I got a sense of the scope of a mass witch-hunt: what is sometimes called a *panic*. But there is nothing panicked about a mass hunt that involved the full force of the law; it was a methodical, documented process of interrogation, torture and execution.

As the first hunt raged through Aberdeen, the pyre on Castle Hill was never cold. The smoke from the perpetual bonfires, and the bodies of those burned in them, would have choked the air and darkened the skies over the North Sea. Issobell Strachan, 'alias Scudder', was a 'common marriage maker' executed on Castle Hill in 1597. There is no record of her trial, but the expenses for killing her are mentioned in the treasurer's accounts. The list 'for the execution of Scuddie' begins: 'Item, for teuntie sex leadis of peattis to burne thame, 2lib. 13s. 4d.' Twenty-six pack-loads of peat would have made a massive, long-lasting fire. Also included in the list are the cost of tar barrels, a stake, a fathom of rope, and the labour to carry it all up Castle Hill.

Castle Hill is now home to a netball court hemmed in by a high-rise block of council flats and the Salvation Army headquarters. The grass of the hilltop is yellow, as if refusing to grow. Looking east, the industrial port busies the horizon. The city lies below to the west, with its moss-covered slate roofs. All of Aberdeen would have seen any bonfire on this hill, the conflagration visible to the surrounding countryside and to ships sailing in from the North Sea.

I walk down the hill to the seventeenth-century Mercat Cross, a large, flat-topped rotunda adorned with men's portraits and a Scottish unicorn atop a tall pillar at the centre. Before the pandemic, I'd seen this square crowded with Christmas shoppers, the multicoloured lights of a funfair glimmering off the icy street. Once, on a bright summer day, a sea of blue Saltaires and EU flags filled the square, packed with people arriving at the end of an Independence march. A ring of marchers sang as pipers played 'Flower of Scotland'.

The grey flagstones stretch out in a fractal order before me. Bus brakes hum and hiss; stray conversations and laughter drift past as I stand in the silence of the paving stones. The Fish Cross once stood nearby with a wooden bench displaying fish for the daily market. Witches were said to dance here. There is no trace left of the Fish Cross in the wide, empty square. I try to imagine dancing in this stern place, but the vision doesn't come easily. The dittay against Thomas Leydis, executed on 23 February 1597, says he led the ring dance here at midnight on Halloween. Such a dance would have been fast, perhaps dizzying. Katherine Mitchell testified that Thomas beat her because she couldn't keep up. The accused transformed into other likenesses: some into hares, some into cats, 'sum in other similitudes'.

I imagine the bustling fish market, so large it had to be marked by an iron ring in the cobblestones. Fishwives came with their creels full, laying out the catch. Feral cats wound between them, begging and stealing from the *quines*. Perhaps the fishwives threw down their offcuts to a favourite of the wee beasties, one that cried just like a child and whose eyes shone green in the dark.

*

I live an hour outside of Aberdeen, in the 'shire. During the late-sixteenth-century witch-hunts, the accused often lived in this wide radius around the city. Aberdeenshire today is a region of cold-hearted industry and Protestant thrift. Class disparity casts a long shadow over its austere beauty. Now home to the Trump International Golf Course and the oil industry, it was once the power centre of Pictish life. Before that, a vast network of Neolithic stone circles graced the land. This is a secret held fast in the heart of this hard place: it was once sacred ground.

I know well this landscape of standing stones with the

majestic hill of Bennachie in the distance; it has the uncanny feeling of return for me. Before I moved here, I'd seen it in a nineteenth-century painting called *The Weird Wife o' Lang Stane Lea* by Aberdonian James Giles. The atmospheric image of a stone circle in twilight, lit by a crescent moon, transports the viewer. A small hare in the foreground watches the central figure, the Weird Wife. The hare's little ears echo the shape of the flanking standing stones. The Weird Wife has her back to us. She carries a long staff, her plain brown plaid pulled around her against the coming night. The sun sets floridly at her back. Bennachie, with its peak called the Mither Tap, or mother breast, hails her.

The stone circle in the painting is a real place. James Giles painted the forlorn, haunted Neolithic site at Castle Fraser as the circle in *The Weird Wife o' Lang Stane Lea*. But who was the weird wife? I imagine her to be a woman named Ellen Gray, executed in Aberdeen on 27 April 1597. The trial records reveal a network of cunning women and men across the Garioch, or rural Aberdeenshire, who knew each other, shared knowledge, and often worked and schemed together. During his interrogation in 1598, cunning man Andro Man named four others, one of whom was 'ane waraye gryt weiche' [a very great witch] named Ellen Gray. Her trial records state she would change shape with her consort, Mergie. Ellen took the form of a dog and Mergie a cat, and they would wander together. Mergie was 'fugitive' – she got away.

The hunts in Aberdeen were troubled by fantasies of mariticide and castration, a common thread throughout many of the interconnected confessions. Such fantasies were also central to the continental witch-hunts. The German witch-hunting manual *Malleus Maleficarum*, or *The Hammer of Witches*, describes women collecting male organs, storing them in bird's nests, and feeding them oats and corn like pets. In the confessions, women scheme and plot revenge on men who had wronged them, and on violent husbands. In sixteenth-century Scotland, men were responsible for their wives' behaviour, and beating was permitted as a form of domestic discipline. To defend themselves against this cruelty, women of the time could employ the aid of a cunning woman, or someone who knew charms to heal as well as harm. In Aberdeen, groups of women were imprisoned in a conspiracy to cause impotence and poison their husbands.

The charges against Ellen Gray are absurd, but reveal male paranoia and misogyny: she caused Thomas Reddell of Slains such grief 'that his want lay never down until he diett' – he suffered a prolonged and fatal erection. She was also accused of discussing remedies with other 'wyse wemen'. A spirit, called 'Sathan' in the interrogation records, appeared to her like a nattily dressed Old Testament God: an elderly, bearded man in a white gown and fringed hat. 'Sathan' gave her Christian advice: 'You are a deeply troubled woman. Forgive all creatures, and take yourself to God and good judgement.'

Ellen was initially imprisoned and interrogated in the stables of Old Slains Castle. Today, only a crumbling wall remains. Ellen would have known the green, undulating hills, now turned to grazing land. Driving over the highest point in the rough road, it feels as if I will plunge straight into the sea. My peril would go unnoticed by the yawning black stone of the castle and the colony of gulls nesting there. Bulls raise their heads to me as I approach the ruins along the rough gravel road, hemmed in by hedgerow. Despite its looming presence, the castle grounds are essentially someone's driveway: a 1950s house sits incongruously on the cliff alongside an abandoned cottage with a rusted swing set wheezing in the wind out front. A Border Collie barks incessantly as I walk up, reminding me that I'm an interloper here.

It's summer. I stand along the cliff where perhaps Ellen stood, on this ground thick with new thistle and long grass. She would have known the natural harbour in the bay below and the brown kelp slouching in its crevice, glinting bronze in the summer sun. She would have *ken* this coast in all weathers: in the summer, when it was as gentle as a lake, and in the winter, with the high winds and stinging salt spray.

A wild swimmer wades out into the shallows, her red bathing costume and pale legs sinking into the tropical blue waters. She shivers and looks down into the thick clouds of *duileasg* – red dulse, moving like hair – as she prepares to submerge herself. I would like to wade into that sea along with her – let it change me, even for a moment, into something hardier. I envy the lone bather her latitude. Perhaps this longing is at the heart of my endless pilgrimages, the futile search for the footsteps of these lost ancestors. I want to find the world they knew – their extinct freedoms.

7

Just People

Helen Guthrie and Joanet Huit, Forfar, 1661

'. . . for the murther [of my stepsister] my mother did give always her mailson [curse] to me, yea and upon her death bed continued to give her mailson notwithstanding my earnest request and beseikings in the contrair . . . [entreaties otherwise].'

– Helen Guthrie's confession

The confessions from the 1661 witch-hunts at Forfar are full of wild parties and strange visions. The accused recount feasts of ale, beef and bread, and tell stories of song and dance, with the devil whistling in accompaniment as they made *gorroch* – a right mess. Isobell Shyrie, one of the accused, was nicknamed the 'devil's horse' and some said she carried them to midnight meetings, shod like a mare. The next day, her neighbour Agnes allegedly went to see Isobell and found her lying in bed, exhausted. Isobell's hands were blistered, as if she had been walking on them. She pulled off the loose the skin, moaning that it was no wonder her hands were raw, 'seeing she was so sore tossed up and down'.

In the confessions, women appear at nightmarish sabbats as demonic horses. The imaginative devices interrogators used to restrain and humiliate the accused are the fetters of the stable and barnyard. The scold's bridle, sometimes called the Forfar bridle, was used to chain the accused to a cell wall between confessions and to 'wake the witch', or maintain sleep deprivation. The Forfar bridle is based on a horse's bridle – a dehumanising method of control deemed particularly appropriate for women who were thought to be the devil's mount. This device is

93

also sometimes called a *branks*, after *brank* or bridle in Scots, which also means to prance or dress up extravagantly. An iron cage was fitted over the head of the accused with a spiked protrusion inserted into the mouth to prevent the wearer from speaking. Some examples of these face-cages are grotesque, with long noses and big ears adorned with earrings. The name 'branks' implies that a woman wearing the mask is decorated, and this misogynist satire of women's vanity adds to the cruelty of the object. The enforced silence of the Forfar bridle goes beyond voice to women's very presence. It punishes visibility, implying that a good Christian woman will keep her head down, won't make a show of herself. The branks were used as a public spectacle in the seventeenth century. The *Statistical Account for the Parish of Forfar*, *1793*, claims the accused wore the 'witches bridle' as they were led to execution.

During pre-trial incarceration, interrogators collected women's words as evidence to be used against them when seeking permission to execute them. The bridle played a role in the length and breadth of the confessions at Forfar: when the device was removed, the accused had sufferance to speak. Perhaps the women interrogated felt an urgency to say what was expected of them, hoping they would not be put in the branks again as long as what they said pleased their captors.

While the torture itself often went undocumented, the devices remain as evidence. A Forfar bridle was found 'preserved in the old steeple' of the kirk at Forfar. The date '1661' is punched into the ring beside a signature or the location of the smith, 'Angus S'. This suggests it was forged for use in the hunt beginning that year, conducted by Rev. Alexander Robertson. The note about its preservation, from the nineteenth-century archaeological record *The Archaeology and Prehistoric Annals of Scotland*, mystifies me. Was the bridle secreted away like a cursed object that could not be destroyed? Or was it found in situ, like the 'witches' ring' in the Mither Kirk in Aberdeen? Was the steeple a prison where the accused were chained between interrogations? At some point, the jailor of Forfar sold the bridle to a private collector.

When people learn that I am writing a book about the Scottish witch-hunts, they often ask me what made the victims suspect. What made them appear guilty in the eyes of the Church and landed men who sat in judgement? No one has ever asked me, what was it about the landowners and churchmen that made them so obsessed with hunting women? During the Church's terror campaign, being older and poor made a woman vulnerable, but the rest was down to luck. While healers and spaewives often gave the most elaborate confessions, the overwhelming majority were simply guilty of being a woman. If you lived in the parish of a witch-hunting pastor, you were at risk.

Reverend Robertson of Forfar was determined to find women guilty of witchcraft. His hunt was systematic, and involved processing people in batches, often on the same day, ratified by himself, Church elders and other witnesses. He presented suspects with a boilerplate confession of wickedness, along with the added sin of being 'a very drunkensome woman'. He interrogated the accused and asked for examples of general wrong-doing. He ended each confession with the statement, 'She confesses herself guilty of witchcraft and that she is willing to suffer death for it.' Beyond the similarities in the answers the accused provided, there's another a pattern – their words seem to search for the *best* guilt, the *right* contrition, no matter how bizarre.

Documents from the Forfar hunt contain a pair of confessions – the interlaced stories of a mother and daughter, Helen Guthrie and Joanet Huit. Helen Guthrie confessed to the standard admission that she had been 'a very drunkensome woman, a terrible banner [one who curses] and curser and of a very wicked life and conversatione'. Her confession was loud, conniving and blustery. Helen volunteered to act as a witch-finder, assisting

Reverend Robertson in his search. She claimed, 'If I see any witch in Scotland, I can tell whether they be witches or no after I have advised 24 hours.' She had bloody papers that she claimed could divine witches. She added, 'I will never part with them until I go to the fire. And that then I shall burn them with myself.' She cautioned that if the papers should be taken from her, harm would come to the minister and his parish.

When Reverend Robertson asked for further confessions of wickedness, Helen offered up an event from her childhood. 'About the tyme that St. Johnstoune's bridge was carried away I murdered my mother's daughter called Marget Hutchen, being my half sister about six or seven years of age.' A note in the margins of the confession states she 'killed her sister . . . by a stroak [strike] she gave hir, to the effusion of her blood, and of the which she died within a few dayes'. Her mother never forgave her. Helen felt great remorse for this act of violence, but it was not witchcraft.

Helen's tall tales include petty malefice, or harmful magic. She saw the devil in the shape of an 'iron hued man' while she was with many others she listed by name. They danced to pipe music in the churchyard at midnight, and the ground beneath them was 'all fireflaughts', or flashes of lightning. An old blind man named Andrew Watsone 'had his usuale staff in his hand . . . yet he daunced as nimblie as any of the company and made . . . great merriment by singing his old ballads'. She claimed they snuck into a brewer's house 'like bees' through a little hole, taking the 'substance of the ale'. Helen said her coven was thirteen in number, and gathered at the quarter days. They dug up unbaptised babies and made them into pies. Eating these ensured a vow of silence, though this was clearly a failed spell given the length at which she spoke during her confessions. Coscinomancy, or 'turning the riddle' with a sieve and shears in a pendulum-like motion, was used to raise the devil. Once up, he was hard to put back.

Stories of levitation and deathly curses fuel Helen's confessions. Her coven drank stolen whisky and tried to pull down a bridge by thrusting their shoulders against it and raising a wind. She met with Isobell Shyrie and others, got drunk on ale and then tried to sink a ship. She held the hawser cable while the others scampered on the rope over the sea. At Halloween, she partied so late that she could 'get no lodging and was forced to lie at ane dykesyde all nyght'. There is no mention of her daughter Joanet, imprisoned with her. Helen's confessions are rambling and fantastic, and suggest she invented stories and named others in order to please her interrogators. Perhaps her offer of using her magical witch-detecting abilities to aid the hunt was an attempt to buy time for her daughter, who was imprisoned for the same crime. Local history sites and local papers tell a version of her story, often at Halloween, with the Angus Archives describing her in an email to me as saying she was 'in her own words, a very wicked and drunken woman'. The official story claims she essentially kept the witch-hunt going by providing names, and that she was responsible for the deaths of at least nine people executed for witchcraft. Centuries later, women like Helen are still being scapegoated for the crimes of others.

The names of the men who were actually responsible for carrying out the sentencing and the murders of the accused are not central to the official story, even though they are well recorded – the judges, ministers, and *doomsters* or executioners. Forfar is the site of one of the largest witch-hunts in Scottish history. Between 1661 and 1663, forty-three accused witches were tried. Reverend Robertson conducted the interrogations with the conviction of a zealot, but it was not a single, witch-obsessed man who was responsible for the hunt. Bailies imprisoned the witches, burgesses and other townsmen sat in judgement, and notars wrote down the confessions. In Forfar, each of the eight districts was expected to furnish six men to guard the witches day and night. Surely it was not Helen but the men who had the power of life and death over her who were responsible for her murder and the deaths of others?

Were Helen's wild stories a way of stalling, a Scheherazade-like impulse to tell a good-enough yarn to survive another day? In her confessions, time is not mentioned in days or years, but by 'oat seed' or 'bere seed' time, saint's days, memorable historical events like the King's coronation or widely known disasters. Before her trial and execution, she was held for a year and probably tortured. She must have been sure she would burn, and afraid her daughter Joanet would meet the same fate.

Joanet was thirteen years old at the time of her interrogation, the youngest victim of the witch-hunts I found in my research. There is no record of the questions Reverend Robertson asked her, but we can guess it was something about her mother and the devil. The words 'carnal copulation' appear in this child's confessions; perhaps Robertson suggested them to his young parishioner. Joanet told the story of a demonic primal scene:

> One time I was with my own mother at a place called Newmanhill hard by Forfar at midnight . . . I saw the devil have carnal copulation with my mother, and that the devil having done, rode away on a black horse . . . I followed him a little way until he directed me to return to my mother . . . when I returned to my mother, she forbade me to tell my father of what I had seen that night.

Joanet said she was carried to an island within the loch at Forfar, where Isobell Shyrie presented her to the devil. He was unimpressed with little Joanet, saying, 'What shall I do with such a little bairn [child] . . .?' In the middle of the loch, she joined in the dance and the devil called her 'Pretty Dancer'. Joanet's confession continued: Isobell carried her to another meeting, where she feasted and drank but her belly was 'not filled'. Her job at the party was to top up everyone's ale. The devil kissed her and marked her, nipping her shoulder. Six weeks later, the devil came to her all in green and called her 'his bonny bird and did kiss her', stroking her where he had bitten her. She claimed, 'The devil spoke to me, saying that if I would do his biding, I should never want ... he bade me renounce my God and I answered, "Mary shall I?"'

We cannot know if 'Mary' refers to a neighbour, friend or the mother of Christ. Joanet's question strikes me as something a child would ask, a prayer for guidance in a world of dangerous adults. Joanet did as she was told, dutiful to those around her. It's a cliché that women fear becoming their mothers, but if one's mother was an accused witch during the height of the hunts, this worry would have carried serious weight. Though Joanet was interrogated at the same time as her mother, she was held in the tolbooth for at least five years after her mother's execution, and her ultimate fate is unknown.

*

Some of the most cherished folk-horror fictions were born of the fraught imaginings of doomed women. The witch trope is at the centre of the genre. She is ambiguous, connected to the land, history and the old gods. The confessions of the accused in Scotland are central to folk-horror world-building, and the Forfar witch-hunt of 1661–3 is a prime source. The modern folk-horror revival looks back to originators of the genre, writers like Algernon Blackwood and Arthur Machen. Perhaps lesser known are the contributions of Robert Louis Stevenson, who explored the witch trope in poetry, fables, and his short story 'Thrawn Janet'. In her confessions, Helen comes across like Stevenson's 'Thrawn Janet', an argumentative woman who you 'couldnae say ae thing but she could say twa [two] to it'.

Published in 1887, 'Thrawn Janet' was one of two stories by Stevenson written in Scots. Scots is one of the three languages spoken in Scotland, and it gives the narrative voice of 'Thrawn

Janet' an authenticity, as if one of the elders of the *clachan* is telling the story of a minister's attempts to save an ostracised old woman. Stevenson came of age in urban Victorian Edinburgh, but the folk ways of rural Scotland were not unknown to him. In Chapter 1, I speculated that he may have heard about the revenant grave of Lillias Adie from his Torryburn-born nanny Alice Cunningham, who no doubt knew a great deal of Scottish folklore and was a storyteller herself. The oral tradition of storytelling in pre-modern Scotland was characterised by intense dramatic pacing and uncanny details. Stevenson wrote this story of an accused witch while staying in a summer cottage in Pitlochry, Perthshire, fifty miles east of Forfar. He used elements of the Forfar confessions, published in 1848 in *Reliquiae Antiquae Scoticae: Illustrative of Civil and Ecclesiastical Affairs*, to structure his story.

In the tale, the newly appointed Reverend Soulis hires old Janet McClour to be his maid, despite the warnings from the villagers that she is kin to the devil. The village had ostracised her because she had a child by a soldier but wasn't married, and had avoided Communion for thirty years. A *collieshangie* or altercation occurs between a group of village women and Janet, and they drag the old woman to the River Dule and dunk her to see if she is a witch. Reverend Soulis stops the lynching, but already Janet has had a stroke from the ordeal. He asks her to renounce the devil and she hesitates, grimacing and teeth chattering, perhaps because of the stroke, or perhaps not. Janet next appears walking into the village, her head bent, as if she had been strangled or hung, and the villagers believe her to be a ghost. Janet becomes 'thrawn' or twisted, perhaps returned from the dead. Stevenson leaves this ambiguity to ripple out through the story, adding to its uncanny quality. The character of Janet is a liminal being, walking between worlds and possibilities.

Soulis continues to protect and defend Janet, preaching mercy in his sermons. Then, as is typical before witch-hunts, there's a stint of bad weather. It's 'het an' heartless', too hot for human or beast. Soulis goes to the old 'Papist' graveyard beyond the Hanging Wood in the shelter of Black Hill, where he likes to sit and think. He meets a stranger there, 'of a great stature, an' black as hell', sitting on a grave, heralded by seven carrion crows.

In witch-trial confessions, the devil is often referred to as a 'black man', like Helen Guthrie's 'iron-hued' devil. Though this is not exactly a demarcation of race in this context, it is still 'othering', and Scotland was very much involved in the slave trade of the eighteenth century. Stevenson suggests black as a marker of race in the mind of Soulis. He has 'heard of black men', presumably darker-skinned people, but the entity he meets in the kirkyard is *'unco'* or unrecognisable as human.

While in his study, Soulis tries many distractions, but the stranger runs 'in his heid like the ower-come of a sang [the chorus of a song]'. He looks out the window, and sees Janet washing clothes in the river. As she turns to look at him, he realises she is 'a bogle [ghost] in her clay-cauld flesh'. The idea that a dead witch could be reanimated by her satanic overlord was a real fear during the eighteenth century. Janet is a figure of terror, like the fantasies surrounding Lillias Adie in Torryburn. Soulis retires to bed, and as dawn comes, he realises Janet and the dark stranger are connected and 'that either or baith o' them were bogles'. At that moment, he hears a stamping and scuffling of feet and a wind rushing through Janet's room. Her room is empty and dark, but he persists in looking, and discovers her hanging by a single thread from a nail in the wall.

John Gregorson Campbell, a great compiler of Highland folklore in the eighteenth century, mentions a particular use of thread for divination. A ball of thread is wound around a rafter, and as the thread is pulled, the diviner asks who is at the end of 'my little rope'. In reply, something pulls on the thread and calls out its name. This strange rite echoes the uncanny rafter gallows in which Soulis finds a spectral Janet. In the end, Soulis curses

Janet, and she falls to ash amid thunder and storm. The next day, the villagers claim to have seen the black man here and there, fleeing their village of Balweary.

The fateful climax of 'Thrawn Janet' is given a date: 17 August 1712. Stevenson would have known the widely reported story of the lynching of a woman in Pittenweem, a seaside village south-east of his holiday cabin in Pitlochry. In 1705, Janet Cornfoot was violently killed by a group of men after being accused of witchcraft. This act of mob violence was well documented. Stevenson sets 'Thrawn Janet' at a time when the official, government-sanctioned witch-hunts were ending, but vigilante killings still threatened women.

*

A child of the 1970s, I grew up with folk horror and pop culture's fascination with the occult. I had access to myriad sources of dark mystery, and they became part of my formative imaginings. A latch-key kid, I was parked in front of Leonard Nimoy hosting *In Search of . . .*, its eerie synth soundtrack suggesting an ominous universe beyond anything adults could explain away. Before I could read, I pored over a book called *The Supernatural*, filled with photographic documentation of men becoming werewolves and contemporary portraits of women who called themselves witches. I made up stories for the photographs of seances and reconstructed 'spells' involving naked ladies and skulls. Even if I couldn't articulate the absolute darkness that engulfed me, my inventions localised it. I checked out a library vinyl of Vincent Price reading Edgar Allen Poe stories. In my imagination, he was the grandfather I never had (my own were long gone: one died before I was born, the other disappeared when my mother was a girl). This handsome actor with his soft, unhinged voice understood darkness, and I imagined he understood me.

I was frequently hospitalised, in and out of intensive care throughout my childhood, alone in hospital beds, mood-altering drugs coursing through my body, slowly suffocating from life-threatening asthma. The treatment at the time consisted of doses of adrenaline and steroids, medications that induce intense emotional states. Looking back, I was a depressed child, a survivor of trauma from the very beginnings of my life, dealing with undiagnosed and untreated self-harm and morbid thoughts. I sought out a darkness that could contain my fear of death. I see now that my early obsession with horror was a way to contain this fear. I believed Vincent Price, this imagined grandfather, would listen to my terrors. He wouldn't tell me my fears were simply my overactive imagination or ask me to pray them away. He portrayed campy, monstrous roles with an undercurrent of glee. His monsters suggested a safety amidst the terrors of my childhood. When I grew older, I saw Vincent Price in the Hammer Horror witchsploitation film, *Witchfinder General*, where he portrayed the 'pricker' Matthew Hopkins. It was my introduction to both this history and the exploitation of this particular suffering for entertainment. This was Price's most memorable role, and also his most frightening. The film cut me to the quick. The imagined conspirator from my childhood was no ally, after all.

This is a moment many horror fans, especially women, experience. The genre betrays us and goes too far. Women have been perpetually excluded from and left out of a genre that exploits our terrors. Our personal lives and shared history are filled with very real monsters, yet our lived experience is perhaps too horrific, too real to be included with agency and subjectivity. As I write, *Witchfinder General* is about to be remade, part of the folk-horror revival – a cinematic and literary movement that pays homage to the aesthetics of films like *The Wicker Man*, depicting rural populations as the nexus of dark secrets. The witch-hunts are Scotland's darkest secret, the human cost of which is yet to be fully understood. The Matthew Hopkins character in *Witchfinder General* was based on the English witch-hunter of the same name, but the Scottish witch-hunts also employed 'prickers'. The Scottish witch-finders no doubt used the instruction manual Hopkins penned, called *The Discovery of Witches*, now eclipsed by the contemporary romance novels and television series of the same name. In the burgh of Forfar, the witch-finder John Kinkaid tested the accused by using a long brass pin to puncture 'insensible' places on their bodies. As a sensational spectacle in film and fiction, the true horror of this history is glossed over, the humanity of the victims erased yet again.

*

A year has passed since I began visiting monuments and land-scapes related to the witch-hunts. Another winter weathered, and I've drawn up a map of sorts, hugging the east coast, wind-ing down and eventually veering west at the central belt, before zigzagging east again. I mark the map to Forfar, an hour south of Aberdeen. It's a bright, fresh day in February as I walk around the Forfar Loch, following the wide, paved circular path. Dog-walkers stumble along, pulled by their charges, and joggers speed past, warm in bright fleeces. A few families stroll together, shoulder to shoulder, and I wonder at their harmony – as exotic in my own life as seeing a unicorn. There's no atmosphere of mystery or menace here, no sign that this was the legendary place of the witches sabbat, nor that this burgh saw some of the most baneful witch-hunts in Scottish history.

I have come to find the recent memorial at the Forfar Loch – a 'cauldron' garden and carved stone. I've almost made a complete circumnavigation of the path around the loch, and I worry perhaps I've missed it. I'm ready to retrace my steps when I see the headstone, secreted away in a grotto beneath a hawthorn. The monument is sometimes referred to as the grave of the Forfar witches, but this isn't the case. The people executed in Forfar were 'burnt to ashes' and received no burial. Still, it's easy to see why that story has become part of this place. Mark and

Marie Cashley, chiropractors based in Forfar, erected the stone on their small strip of land, situated adjacent to the public footpath around the loch. The sculptor Tom Church created the memorial stone in the 'witches' circle' – a low, stone ring. The memorial, with twenty-two indentations to mark the dead, is in keeping with the Neolithic custom of tapping cup marks into stones to mark events or supplications. Uphill, a tall wych elm shrouds a squat megalith with hatch marks up the side resembling Ogham script. Perhaps this primeval stone was inspiration for the monument. Offerings are secreted here: three Brigid's crosses made of rushes.

The garden is a bowl of earth, filled with snowdrops. The delicate heralds of spring sear their way through the frozen ground, demure white wimples nodding in the cold sun. Their sisterhood crowds the space in regiments of hot, white hope. The stone is carved with simple words: 'The Forfar Witches: Just people.' It stands like a small menhir. In the glimmering February sunlight, the grove invites me to linger. Over 350 years ago, a girl named Joanet said she had been offered up to the devil here. Two teenagers pass by, a few years older than Joanet. They pause briefly before the stone. The boy explains to the girl, 'This is where they burned the witches.' She nods, her hands knotted awkwardly together. He wants to impress her, and continues: 'They burned them alive, right here.' In her silence, they move on.

Despite the clarity of the memorial's message – people, not witches – these myths loom larger than the truth. In my research, I have wondered if the men in power hundreds of years ago wanted to make sure that remembering the accused would be near impossible, and that, centuries later, we would still ape the annihilating fictions they designed. Bodies were burned to ashes, bones thrown on to midden heaps with lives unrecorded, destroyed so utterly that even the Christian God could not find them. What makes me think I can? In front of this beautifully sensitive memorial, the accused are still no more than the villains of a dark anecdote.

Marie Cashley, the woman who envisioned and funded the monument with her husband Mark, passed away in 2017. Her memorial announcement in the local paper asked mourners to 'wear some bright coloured clothes and bring no flowers'. This is good advice for those visiting the memorial at Forfar Loch. The Forfar monument is a proper cenotaph, one of the most intimate and powerful of all the memorials I have visited. This space of rest and beauty is a seed of compassion inspiring other monuments, the most recent in Orkney – a place I have been many times and one dear to me. I will visit it in the spring.

I kneel before the Forfar monument, laying out a star in a circle made of twigs and stones. A little girl and her mother stop and watch me.

'What's she doing, Mummy?' the girl's tiny voice enquires behind me.

'She's remembering people who have died, and paying her respects.'

I look back at the mother and daughter holding hands, an unspoken understanding between us.

8

Spaewife

Grissell Jaffray, Dundee, 1669

'For meikle kens she o' book-lore,
  And e'en o' grammarye, There's nae auld wife in braid
    Scotland
  Mair wyse nor learned than she.'*

– 'The Witch-wife's Son', 1860

A week after the spring blizzards began in the north of Scotland, my father died. It was the last day of March, a year into the pandemic. I'll never know the full story; I found out via email. Such is the nature of exile, of my estrangement. This silence is the latest in a long tradition; talk of death was taboo in my family. We were a long-lived people, and grief, like illness, was a sign of weakness. *Never ugly-cry and never die*. Was it a California thing? That bright place without a real winter births many fictions, and money flows like wildfire over roots and history.

When I first moved with my father to California from Chicago, he took me to Forest Lawn Cemetery, where the rich and famous bury each other. Grand follies and gauche displays, including a reproduction of Michelangelo's *David* and *The Last Supper* rendered in stained glass, mark the graves of actresses, directors and real estate moguls. Themed corners, such as the patriotic Hall of Freedom, look like something from Disneyland. The

* 'She has much knowledge and book lore,
  And even of grammar, there's not an old woman in wide Scotland
  More wise nor learned than she.'

bucolic Wee Kirk o' the Heather is said to be a reproduction of a sixteenth-century Scottish chapel. The tacky grandiosity amused my father, but he also believed it to be beautiful, a measure of transcendence. Perhaps it was the attar of his California dream, to live forever in sunlight, away from the Midwest with its personal pasts and divergent weathers. He brought me to these glitzy graves as if to say, *Look, girl: we've made it*.

But we hadn't. Poverty, hardships and ill-considered decisions – what my father called 'bad luck' – subsumed us. I'd failed to live up to my end of the feminine bargain of helpmate and mother to grandchildren. A writer and wanderer, I suspect I made no sense to him, and now it's too late for him to confirm or deny it.

On a morning in April, I walk on the coastal path at Banff Links, beside the rock formation known as the Elf Kirk. Caravans and car-campers crowded this length of coastline during the first summer of the pandemic, but now they've vanished. The bad weather of a harsh spring descends, a fitting Fimbulwinter. I'm alone at the Elf Kirk, my adopted church. The surf rolls through the pebbles on the shore, surging over my grief.

At what point did the cairns of stacked stones appear? At the high-tide mark, beside the craggy outcropping of the Elf Kirk, they stand like fey sentinels among the sea-worn stones, multiplying on the rocks further out, hovering briefly over the incoming waves. The anonymous sculptors are perhaps bored teens or parents and children finding something to do in the endless days of lockdown. Are the ephemeral stone towers actually improvised memorials to the people dying during the pandemic? Perhaps they represent all the collective mourning that should be happening, but isn't.

The sun splits the cloud cover, burning through it. The sea shifts from black to blue, and I see a man who looks just like my father walking between the balanced columns. He has the same slump-shouldered, stumbling gait, the same round head of wispy white hair and aviator glasses. He wears baggy khakis like my father's, hitched up by an old belt, and the same motley nineties windbreaker. He hobbles over the rocks, staring out to the horizon behind me, the sea at his back. Every step is unsteady, and he rights himself only to stumble again. I watch him, this ghost, for too long. The old man keeps coming. His gaze unseeing, he's intent on the hillside beside the path. Some rational part of me, the part that refuses stories and signs, turns for home.

The seventeenth-century 'fairy minister' Reverend Robert Kirk might have advised me that I'd seen a 'co-walker', an otherworldly twin that will appear to the living a few days after the 'original', their human counterpart, has died. Kirk recorded the nature of such uncanny portents in his anthropological record of the fairy world, *The Secret Commonwealth of Elves, Fauns and Fairies*. The co-walker is not made of earthly stuff, and he can't converse with the living. Kirk comforts me, claiming the 'living picture goes at last to its own herd'.

I've never visited the grave of someone I've loved. There's nothing to mark the lives of those people. Perhaps this lack drives my love of cemeteries. I'm a taphophile, a tombstone tourist. Graveyards represent spaces for grief that have been denied me, that have been denied to many in our modern lives. In my rebellious rejection of my family's values, I took to grieving, embracing this forbidden emotion with the verve of a professional mourner. Cemeteries represent something exotic and precious: space to mourn, to make peace with loss.

Older kirkyards in Scotland are fit for purpose: grim, menacing and enchanted, moss-marked and ivy-bitten. They wear decay like an honour, with a preponderance of memento mori: skulls with crossbones, skulls surrounded by hourglasses, skulls smiling at you from all corners. Carved mort bells, the winged faces of departing souls and kilted angels cavort on stone slabs, serving to remind the visitor that their life is on loan and death is part of a natural order.

Such carved headstones were expensive. These eighteenth-century stones are memorials to the wealthy, but they are also a reminder of the suffering and death that marked the lives of our ancestors. The omnipresence of death changed their cosmology, their conception of the universe and the role of fate in their lives, no matter their class. During the Reformation, Protestant faith was shaped by the fatalistic ideas of predestination. A father God, not the three Fatal Sisters of pagan legend, decided fate. Predestination was defined by a belief that the Christian God chose those who would come home to heaven. The rest were damned; it was already decided. These grave markers embody a death for which the soul was prepared. This unseen element – the dying privileged with time and resources to prepare – is perhaps their most ostentatious aspect. In past centuries, particularly the seventeenth century, ravaged as it was by war, plague and famine, a good death was a luxury few enjoyed. The carvings of skulls and angels on these older headstones are representations of ancestral fatalism, reflected in certain Gaelic proverbs: 'His hour was pursuing him,' and 'You can't give luck to a luckless man.'

My father understood these things; perhaps they ran in his blood. He was, after all, a descendant of the Scottish diaspora, his dark moods like a gathering storm over the North Sea. He loved to gamble, to test fate and rework it in his favour. Loss was a sign of doom, a dire portent – not just for him, but for me, too. I learned this at his knee, and never shook it off. Many who have died during the pandemic, including my father, did not die well. There was no way to prepare. Through this time of our own plague, perhaps we draw nearer to the realities of our ancestors.

I continue to visit the graves of strangers, noting the skull with the most winning smile, the angel with the weirdest wings, or the most beautiful carving of a pilgrim shell – the symbol of renewed faith. I am on the lookout for the next good headstone. I hear from a friend, a witchy blogger called Hag o' the Hills, that there is a beautiful graveyard at the centre of Dundee. It also houses the monument of an accused witch, so I plan a trip.

*

I visit Dundee, on the waters of the Tay in the eastern lowlands. It's morning on a late-summer day, and I'm typing field notes into my phone. It's a thrilling place – intimate and accessible in a way that larger cities like Glasgow and Edinburgh can never be. I walk the broad path along the Firth, past the grandeur of the new V&A museum, its striated silhouette reflected in the staid water. The RSS *Discovery*, a nineteenth-century ship that was once used for exploring the Antarctic, berths beside the museum. The new architecture of the V&A echoes the graceful outlines of the ship's hull. These sympathetic landmarks orientate me as I set out to find the memorials to a woman named Grissell Jaffray, an accused witch executed in Dundee in 1669.

The first memorial is part of the Dundee Women's Trail. Established in 2006 by a group of volunteers, the 'Twenty-Five Footsteps' of the trail commemorate twenty-five women, with plaques placed around in the city. Women artists, trade unionists, social reformers, suffragettes, a shipyard welder and a marine engineer are among those celebrated on the trail. I make a beeline for the memorial for Grissell, winding my way from the Tay to the city centre. I follow the pedestrianised thoroughfare of Murraygate, flanked by the same high-street shops you see all across the UK: the monoculture of Caffè Nero, New Look and Tesco Metro. I reach the narrow alleyway called Peter Street, wedged between a WHSmith and a Clarks shoe shop. Two mosaics set in the cobblestones mark the entrance to the passage. There are many modern legends surrounding Grissell, and one claims the mosaics mark the site of her execution. The mosaics resemble gramophone trumpets. One is filled with pixelated water or sky, the other with fire. They puzzle me – I don't know what they mean.

A blue plaque, the twenty-third on the Women's Trail, hangs in the dark alcove at Peter Street. It's similar to the ubiquitous blue metal plaques on historic British sites, except this one is made of resin or plastic. It is printed with the words 'Grissell Jaffray, Spaewife,?–1669.' A spaewife is not a witch; it is a Scots word meaning 'wise woman'. In Scottish folk tradition, witches performed magic with malignant intent, whereas spaewives could heal or be consulted about diseases and other mysteries. A spaewife could be relied upon to interpret dreams and strange visions – like my father's 'co-walker' at the Elf Kirk. The word suggests a tradition of healers or seers within the community – one that survived into the Reformation. But the Reformation also marked the end of miracles – Christian and otherwise. Any spiritual entities, be they ghosts, land spirits or fairies, became agents of the devil. Wise women, once seen as healers and spiritual intermediaries, were now witches in league with Satan. The witch-hunts sought to demonise the folk practices of the spaewife, like dream interpretation and herb lore, but her skills were of such value to the community that many of these practices survived.

This witch/spaewife conundrum is a version of the clichéd question, *Are you a white witch or a black witch?* Problematic race associations and moral relativism aside, this dichotomy comes from the witch-hunts and the traumatic rupture of folk tradition that accompanied them. Every memorial site and every conversation about the accused is haunted by it. Despite our celebrated modern rationality, the fear of the witch remains. Did these women somehow earn their terrible fate? This dilemma is our shared grief, a mourning that is only beginning to be formally acknowledged.

I'm in Peter Street, noting the graffiti on Grissell's plaque, which has been defaced with a permanent marker. The scrawl reads: 'Witches . . . strongmen bind.' Are the 'strongmen' bound or doing the binding? Perhaps, in the way of all toxic masculinity, oppressive male identities are bound up with the cruelties of misogyny. Myriad little crosses made with paint pens cover the plaque. The marks are reminiscent of the 'X's on Marie Laveau's grave in New Orleans. In the case of Laveau's grave, crosses are thanks for wishes come true. What does the graffiti on Grissell's plaque mean? Are they prayers, wishes or warding? Perhaps they are all three.

Though Dundee largely escaped the tragedy of the mass witch-hunts that gripped other areas, the story of Grissell, 'the last woman burned', is part of the city's history. Her accusation and death are presented as fact, but no detailed records of either exist. The only 'official' mention is in the Privy Council register's commission to try her for witchcraft, issued in 1669. She was being held in the tolbooth at the time. In my search for veracity, I found a strange ally in a Dundee librarian from the 1920s, a man named Arthur Millar. He authored an odd little tome, *Haunted Dundee*, with a cheesy cover featuring a Halloween witch flying on a broom. Despite its sensational cover and title, the chapter 'The Martyrdom of Grissell Jaffray, the Last of the Dundee Witches' neatly summarises the end of her life, and Millar's research is based on what scant records he could find. He consulted with the Presbytery records clerk, who found nothing for Grissell's sentencing nor death. He suggests the missing records might be a form of censure, noting: 'the destruction of Presbytery Records, or, at least, their silence, prevent us from knowing what accusations were brought against this grey-haired old woman'. He finds mention in the kirk session records of a commitment to rooting out witchcraft in the area. All found guilty were to be banished, but Grissell apparently faced a harsher punishment.

Millar mentions Grissell was born in Aberdeen, and his version of her story begins, like so many women's stories recorded throughout history, with her marriage. She married the brewer James Butchart. Her son was a skipper on a trading vessel and they lived in Caldendar Close, a little to the west of Long Wynd, near what is now the large mall at Overgate.

I wonder if Grissell saw the second wave of Aberdeen witch-hunts in the 1630s, or if, as a child, she'd heard stories of the massive pyres that darkened the skies in 1597. She survived the siege of Dundee in 1651, the final battle of the English Civil War fought in Scotland. Five thousand English soldiers stormed the city walls. In the initial battle, the English casualties were said to number only twenty men, but the population of Dundee was brutalised – perhaps 600 or more civilians and militia died. They were buried in mass graves. The English occupation lasted nine years, and Grissell would have survived the violence and aftermath. Perhaps she searched the bodies for friends or relatives, and helped bury strangers.

The tests for witchcraft she might have endured and the circumstances of her death remain unclear. But a record in the town council minutes does recount her last wishes before her death – that all those she had named as witches should be exonerated. This is a common thread in the narratives of execution: at the pyre, the accused often rescind their confessions, claiming their own innocence as well as the innocence of others they had named, their last words disavowing the lies they had been forced to utter by their interrogators.

The injustice took its toll on the family of the accused, who had to bear witness to the violent death of their loved one and live with their powerlessness at the injustice. A petition from Grissell's husband, dated 7 December 1669, a month after her execution, asked that he be admitted to the 'Hospital' or poorhouse. This detail gives us a glimpse of the larger societal picture of witch accusations and executions. Once a successful businessman in Dundee, James Butchart faced the end of his life in ruins. Grissell's story is embellished with the legend of her son's return from his maritime travels: he supposedly arrived at Dundee on the day of her execution. When he learned the smoke in the sky above the Tay was from her pyre, he sailed away, never to return. In leaving Scotland, he became one of the Scottish diaspora, part of the surge of immigration that continued throughout the eighteenth and nineteenth centuries.

The legend of Grissell's son is rendered in a nineteenth-century ballad, 'The Witch-Wife's Son', reprinted in *Haunted Dundee*. The ballad is sung from the son's point of view as he returns to Dundee. He is dreaming of seeing his mother's face again, and he praises her wisdom and kindness. He sees the smoke and wonders at it, and the moment of discovery is rendered with drama:

> The awesome flames had done their wark,
> Nae form was left to see:
> Naught but a grim and blackened stake,
> A ghastly vacancy.

But 'The Witch-Wife's Son' is not the only ballad about a woman being burned in Dundee. 'Bonnie Susie Cleland' is a version of the better-known ballad 'Lady Maisry'. Both ballads tell the story of a woman who was burned to death by her own family because she had shamed them by loving an Englishman. While her family makes preparations for the woman's death, she calls on a boy to take a message to her lover, an English Lord: she is to be burned, and he's to find another woman to wed. Despite the boy's valiant efforts, the message arrives too late.

In 'Bonnie Susie Cleland', her father and son make the fire.

> Her father he's caad [drove in, erected] up the stake,
> Hey my love and ho my joy,
> Her father he caad up the stake,
> Wha dearly loes me,
> Her faither he's caad up the stake,
> Her brother he the fire did make,
> And Bonnie Susie Cleland was burnt in Dundee.

Traditional musician Maureen Jelks notes that this version of the ballad may be a record of another Dundee legend: after the siege and occupation, several women were killed for consorting with the English. Perhaps encoded in these ballads are traumatic ancestral memories from a time when Christian men burned their sisters and daughters. I wonder if Grissell knew an earlier version of this song, and perhaps even sang the braided melancholy of the tune to her wee boy as she rocked him in his new linen dress, a baby death didn't take, this boy who flourished into lithe manhood.

*

On my visit to Dundee I save the cemetery at its heart, the Howff, for last. I wonder how easy it will be to find the folk monument to Grissell Jaffray, 'The Witch's Stone'. It is said to be her grave, but this is a modern invention, an urban myth. Like other 'graves' devoted to those executed for witchcraft, no remains survived Grissell's execution, and she is not interred there. The 'stone' has an altogether different, more mundane history.

The Howff is an urban burial ground dating from the mid-sixteenth century, and it's about as far from the Brigadoon-like fantasy of the Wee Kirk o' the Heather in Forest Lawn, Los Angeles, as you can get. One of its walls is the old town gate. In the seventeenth century, craft guilds met in the graveyard, gathering around a central plinth called 'the stone' – the same stone that would later become linked to Grissell in the popular imagination. The Howff, meaning 'haunt', gets its name from these gatherings. This haunt refers not to ghosts, but to a pub where the bakers of Dundee used to meet before they decided the cemetery was a better place to conduct their negotiations.

The Howff is a secret garden in the middle of the bustling city. Cascading wych elms shelter benches and ancient tombs. The monuments are carved with a lively company: a skull with checkerboard teeth, an angel with apocalyptic eyes, and a stately hourglass or two. The walls sequester the dead and their visitors. Perhaps this is the same reason the tradesmen met here, removed from the rest of the city – it feels private, protected.

I'm alone with the graves, except for a young man with a black cat on a lead. I ask him if he knows where the grave of Grissell Jaffray is. He shrugs. I clarify, 'The Witches Stone.'

'Oh, yeah, well, they're everywhere, aren't they?'

I agree. This is something people tell me when I talk of this history – most know of a Carlin stone, or Witches Stone, somewhere. They're all over Scotland, yet the stories behind them are dismissed or recollected dimly from childhood.

The cat sits down in protest as the man pulls on the lead. 'I live close by and walk here every day. You'd think I would know.'

I leave him to his stroll, and the cat watches me as I brush leaf mould from the corners of gravestones. Once I put my mind to it, Grissell's stone is not hard to find. It's a modest plinth, like a stone two-by-four stuck in the earth. I turn to tell the man and his cat, but they have gone. A two-pence piece sits in the depression at the top, and the base is ringed with offerings of shells, sea glass and stones. More coins slot into the natural crevices of the stone's sides. The little pillar has been shared and loved by nameless others who visited before me. What is this ephemeral feeling embodied here? As I sit at Grissell's stone, visitors come and go through the gates. They sit on benches to read, raise their faces to the warmth of the sun, or walk with a friend.

A group of Americans arrive, looking for the gravestone of their ancestor. This seems a luxury to me – to have such certainty of one's direct line to the past. The pull of ancestry – the fantasy of a family castle, of a bloodline, a clan – is a powerful one. I don't talk to the Americans, but I know them by their easy wealth, their new REI gear, and the innocent confidence with which they speak of the place they pass through. I might share their accent, or that way Americans have of smiling first, but the United States became a foreign country to me long ago.

I stay with Grissell's stone, relishing this temporary feeling of companionship, of home. Why would the people of Dundee invent a legend about this nub of rock? I can find no reference to its origin. For lack of a more satisfying monument, the story of the stone in the Howff takes precedence. In the nineteenth-century *History of Old Dundee*, Alexander Maxwell bemoans the state of the old graves in the Howff, and makes an argument for their preservation. He says that they represent the brave founders of the city and great men of industry. Perhaps it is fitting to adopt a stone in this esteemed place as a memorial to Grissell Jaffray, the spaewife, home at last.

Local legend claims leaving an offering at the stone will bring luck or help to those in need. Grissell's is not a vengeful spirit, and she is not feared. Like other offerings left on monuments adopted by modern visitors, those left on Grissell's suggests that these women, the accused, now look after us. It is an exchange – we remember them, bringing them the hopes and dreams of the living, and they perhaps grace us with a better turn of fate.

9

Nevin Stone

Kate McNevin, Monzie, 1563, 1615 or 1715

'Like Diana, who in one capacity was denominated Hecate, the
Fairy Queen is identified in popular tradition with the Gyre-
Carline, Gay Carline or mother witch, of the Scottish peas-
antry . . . she is sometimes termed Nicneven'.

– Sir Walter Scott

Sometimes, after a great loss all we have is a story – some invention to stand in for what's gone, a bit of folklore to tie us
together. Tales of Kate McNevin claim she was a witch and a
granter of wishes. She shares her name – the spelling as varied as
her identity – with Nicnevin, an ancient witch goddess. One tale
claims that before Kate was burned at the stake, she spat out a
jewel. If we could look inside the facets of that fable, its histories
and mythologies would multiply. Coded in that prophetic blue
gemstone, like the ones and zeros of a microchip, is the fate of
the Graeme clan, the doom of a nineteenth-century preacher, a
Scottish Goddess, and a mythic map of a village called Monzie.
As I researched the stories around Kate McNevin, they took root
and grew, inviting me to tell my own version.

*

In a time and place outside of memory, there was a daughter, one
of two siblings. She was not the favourite; that honour belonged
to the other child. Her mother didn't like children, and her father
didn't concern himself with raising bairns. On a warm day in
summer, the daughter, a girl named Kate, was out drawing water
from the old well in the shadow of the cliff known as Nicnevin's

Craig. The well has long since dried up, its source buried deep in the veins of the earth. No one even remembers its name, but some say it was once called Nicnevin's Well. In the long-ago-and-never-at-all, this well flowed with clear water known for its iron tang. The cliff was named after the well, or maybe it was the other way around; it's all been forgotten by now.

As Kate stood at the bubbling mouth of the well, filling her pail, an old woman walked up and asked her for a drink. This old woman could have been the Cailleach herself. No one really knows what she looks like; she could be anyone. This bent crone held a long walking stick in one gnarled hand, and the other trembled, reaching out towards the girl's long braid. She picked it up and sniffed it. Kate pulled away, and the two women, one old and the other relatively new to this world, stared each other down.

'Give us a drink,' the old woman asked, relinquishing the girl's braid.

Kate gave her a ladle full of well water, and the old woman drank.

'Ah, just like blood.' She smacked her lips.

'That cold?' Kate thought of the hard blood bonds of her family, and was not without a sense of irony.

'Colder!' The old woman winked.

As the crone drank, the girl loosed all the weird omens that weighed on her. 'I heard the screech of the owl in the night, and I saw the snail on a flagstone writing my name in its silver trail. I knew things would not go well with me.'

'Noisy birds and drunken snails,' the old woman said, tossing the ladle behind her, 'know little of fate, child.' The old woman made a split decision. She could have given the girl a gift – song, truth or story have their uses – but she gave her something else instead. The old woman clapped her knobby hands. The sound echoed in the girl's ears, shaking to the core of her skull. Kate coughed, sputtered, and tried to speak.

'Out with it,' the old woman prompted. She waited with her hollow smile, her three teeth gleaming in the noonday sun. This was her favourite part of any spell, that moment when it just starts to work itself out.

'You think?' the girl began, and two sapphires rolled from her tongue. She caught them and held them up to the light.

'You think!' The old woman mimicked her, giggling with delight. It was always better when the magic actually worked.

'Are they real?' Three more stones came tumbling out.

'As real as I,' the old woman declared, and then disappeared.

This is how it ends: the girl's gift is discovered by her family, and when her favoured sibling attempts to engage the woman at the well, it turns out badly. The sibling's rude utterances slither into vipers and toads. Kate, the girl with the jewelled speech, is exiled from her family home. As she wanders, she meets a royal, her happily-ever-after in human form, but they don't talk very much.

*

Some Witches Stones are not dedicated to women who suffered and died, but to legendary witches. These stones collect tales and myths as well as debates on the Internet. The eldritch goddess Nicnevin is associated with the Scottish village of Monzie, yet legend also claims a woman named Kate McNevin was executed here in 1715. Was Nicnevin a Celtic goddess, a witch or a woman named Kate? Her story is both true and false; she is real and myth. This is the holographic nature of folklore. Other women accused of witchcraft in nearby places have similar names. Catherine McNevin from nearby Crieff was executed in 1615. Another woman from Monzie called Nik Neveing was accused as a witch, named by a previous victim of the hunt in 1643. Nik Neveing, executed eighty years before Kate McNevin, was part of a lineage of women who passed healing knowledge down through their families. The Survey of Scottish Witchcraft estimates Nik Neveing was 100 years old when she was executed in 1563, but beyond this little is known of her life.

Kate McNevin's death is legendary. The Graeme Clan myth claims she bestowed a magical gemstone on the Laird of Inchbrakie, and the fate of the clan is wrapped up with this relic and the story of a woman burned alive, shouting curses and granting wishes as she dies. There is another story that claims Kate McNevin was rolled in a barrel down the hill, and the Nevin Stone marks the site of her execution. As with the spiked barrel story associated with the Forres Stone, there is little documented evidence that barrels were used as part of the theatre of execution in Scotland.

Internet records concerning Kate McNevin are fraught, and pages that mention her are riddled with fictions. Witchcraft scholar Louise Yeoman doubts Kate McNevin even existed. She commented on a post on the Executed Today blog: 'I investigated the Kate Nicnevin story at an earlier point. I also catalogued the Graeme of Inchbrakie papers at [the] National Library of Scotland. She is a mythical witch character. To say that she was executed is like saying someone executed Hecate . . . there's no actual Kate Nicnevin.'

Controversy is rife on many of the Wikipedia pages for those accused of witchcraft. Little blue parentheses riddle the information on Kate's page: 'citation needed' or 'verification failed'. There is even a 'bit of an editor war going on,' according to the Wiki Talk Page, with sections being regularly deleted. Her Wikipedia page cites a modern rhyme, with no attribution:

As long as the Shaggie* runs crookit and bent
there'll be a Witch o Mon-ie
And she'll ne'er be kent.†

---

* The Shaggie is a small river or burn with a picturesque falls in Monzie.
† 'As long as the Shaggie runs crooked and bent/ there'll be a Witch of Monzie/ And she'll never be understood.'

Repairing lost history means trying to navigate a map of missing pieces, guesses and fallacies, but in the case of Wikipedia, this mystery is also down to gender bias. As of 2021, only nineteen per cent of pages were about women, and over twenty-five per cent of the biographies slated for deletion are about women, despite their pages making up a startling minority. The overwhelming majority of editors on the site identify as male, and Wikipedia's page on gender bias puts this percentage as high as nine out of ten. How is it that this great democratisation of human knowledge is still dominated by men? The access to the history of the accused, as well as all of women's history, suffers.

The Witches Stone in the village of Monzie is called the Nevin Stone. It's named after Nicnevin, the Scottish witch queen, who presides over the great sky-raids of All Hallows' Eve. The name Nicnevin comes from many places and meanings. *Nic* is a Gaelic contraction, meaning 'daughter of'. The daughter of Nevin is not far from the daughter of *Nevis*, as in Ben Nevis, the great mountain that is said to be the home of the Cailleach. Nicnevin might be a version of the Cailleach, wrapped in her long grey plaid, brandishing her distaff, turning sea to stone. Geologic time belongs to her, as do all ancient things.

Nicnevin first appears in print in two 'flyting', or word-fight, poems from the sixteenth century. Flyting was a way to take another poet down, to prove one was the better wordsmith. Flyting poems are wildly insulting and scatological. To be associated with Nicnevin was part of the insult. In 'The Flyting of Kennedy and Dunbar', Nicnevin heads a night ride at Halloween in the company of witches, fairies, and elves. In another poem, Montgomerie's 'Flytting of Polwart', the witch queen Nicnevin adopts the child Polwart. Her 'cunning consists of casting of a Clew', or casting a story or thread. In the poem, she is markedly northern – her spells are from Caithness in the Highlands and Rosemarkie on the Black Isle.

Sir Walter Scott discusses Nicnevin in his *Minstrelsy of the Scottish Border* and his *Letters on Demonology and Witchcraft*. He equates 'Nicneven' with the queen of the fairies as well as the Gyre Carlin, the same legendary being that created the North Berwick Law. The *Gyrekarling,* from the Old Norse *gygr*, or ogress, and *kerling*, meaning old woman, is a word for female giant. Scott compared her to Hecate, the triple-visaged witch-goddess of the Greek pantheon. He saw Nicnevin as the leader of the wild hunt, 'a gigantic and malignant female, the Hecate of this mythology, who rode on a storm and marshalled the rambling host of wanderers under her grim banner'.

The legendary mother-witch Nicnevin made mythic tracks all over Scotland and beyond. Contemporary witchcraft scholars, such as Lizanne Henderson and Carlo Ginzburg, have likened her to other nocturnal goddesses like Holda, the Germanic goddess of winter. Both flew with a stormy retinue of followers. Sometimes the throng would include infants who had died before being baptised.

The name Nicnevin has roots in *Neamhain*, a Gaelic war fury and one of the Celtic Fatal Sisters, also known as *Badb*, meaning crow or witch. She is the death messenger in Irish and Scottish Gaelic folklore. In this aspect, she goes by another name, perhaps the most familiar: banshee or *bean-shithe,* literally 'fairy-woman' in Gaelic.

*

After my father's death, I dug out the shoebox of old photos, looking for him. I have one good photo of my father. It's an old, white-framed Polaroid with the date printed at the bottom – 1970. In this photo of my father and me, I'm pawing at his temple with a look of bemused incredulity, and he's bowed under my weight as if rethinking carrying me at all. He wears a white collared shirt and tie with a tie clip, his long sideburns black as Elvis's. I had remembered the photo differently – we were both smiling, and he was standing up straight, a proud new father and his happy girl. I have others where we are together: he is angry, crestfallen, or looking like he would rather be somewhere else. But this one is good, carrying with it all the love-potential of my birth. Who took the photo? Was it my mother? Another relative? In the early days of my infancy, they were around – aunts, grandmothers, great grandmothers. I found the photo stacked with others. There's a sepia one of my grandmother kitted out in Edwardian finery, and another of her in a 1950s apartment with a toy tiger in her lap. There are pictures of me in my twenties outside my old pink shack, a caravan near the desert foothills of California. Another photo has no people in it at all – just the interior of the front room of the house where I was born, purposely sparse, candles burning in trays on a long sideboard beneath abstract oil paintings and teak furniture, all modern Nordic chic. My family didn't stay, and everything, seemingly, went downhill from there.

In the old shoebox, I also found a photograph my father took of me. I'm fifteen and barefoot, crouched on a rock in the warmth of the Pacific Ocean, searching the tide pools of Crystal Cove. I'm holding a starfish. My blue sweats, pushed up to my knees, are the same colour as the sea. My hair is cut in a flaxen bob – I'd never be blonde, never wear baby blue again as a point of pride. It's the moment before everything went dark. In a few months, I'd meet with a steady diet of violence and degradation at the hands of an abusive boyfriend, trapped. That girl, the straight-A student who wanted more than anything to be an archaeologist, squints back at me. She didn't survive. That bright morning, my father knew to take me to this rippling place of fascinations. I saw a tiny purple octopus that day, pulsing through the shallows. I didn't have to smile for my father, and he took the photo anyway.

A few weeks before my father died, a shrieking cry woke me at 3 a.m. It was in the sky, just outside my window. That high chitter troubled me with its rhythmic *eeeeee eeeeee eeeeee-click*. It sounded like the *bean-shithe*. I decided it was an angry blackbird, one of the many nesting in the overgrown hedge-row at the back of my garden. In my rush to find reasons for great mysteries and be free of the irrational doom of the harbinger, I dismiss otherworldly signs. This is a particular, modern urge – to be done with fatalism and uncanny portents. It is a lost art to read signs. Is there not a use for such consolations? The *bean-shithe* is also the night washerwoman, scrubbing out the bedding and clothes of the dying, her long breasts thrown over her back. In this manifestation, she is the comforter and the guide, the psychopomp. She places her cold hand on the heart of the survivors, a severance and a mercy. Networks of inherited folklore, the beliefs of my adopted ancestors, are stronger than any living connections I might have. They flow through me like blood, answering with terrible certainty that I belong to their mystery: so says that singular shriek in the middle of the night.

*

Without knowing how much ground I will be able to cover, I've charted Nicnevin's Monzie. The nineteenth-century minister of the village kirk, Reverend George Blair, left a map of words in the preamble to his long, difficult poem about Kate McNevin called 'The Holocaust, or, The Witch of Monzie: a Poem Illustrative of the Cruelties of Superstition'. Blair iterates a version of Kate McNevin's story: she was a nurse to the darkling child of the Laird Inchbrakie. The boy named her as a witch and she was condemned. At the pyre, she spat an uncut sapphire from her mouth, like the girl in Charles Perrault's fairy tale 'Diamonds and Toads'. In Blair's lengthy preamble to 'The Holocaust', he argues that the witch-hunts were the Kirk's human sacrifice. Christian myths often claim superiority over paganism, believing Christianity is a faith that needs no immolation beyond the death of Jesus, yet the history of the witch-hunts exposes this hypocrisy. Reverend George Blair was the pastor of the village parish for only a year. In 1844, he was suspended from office for undocumented reasons.

Blair's poem relates the geography of Monzie to Kate McNevin's journey to the stake. In making my map, I wondered if there might be something else in this landscape, another kind of ceremony at its heart. I head for Monzie, travelling west from Dundee. When I arrive, I'm shattered, but the sun is out and I start walking anyway. Before drones, airplanes and cars, the landscape was understood on foot. The height of a hill or the length of a path was mapped with footsteps, and the glance of the sun pointed the way. If walking is hard, as it often is for me, these personal maps change. A short distance becomes vast. Such is the nature of disability. Before my early-onset osteoarthritis and the attendant fibromyalgia, I understood the world by walking. I walked all over European cities, through redwood forests, across vast moorland. I traced the infinite palimpsest of London over and over on foot. Walking the land is reading it. One day, I could no longer read the world fluently. Some doctors insist that depression or 'negative thought patterns' cause my pain. They have refused to believe me when I say it's the other way around – pain is hard on the soul. My sense of place in the world erodes, and this is my lived reality.

A ghostly tree, well, cliff and cave bear the name Nicnevin. I've plotted Kate McNevin's Yett, a fairy bridge over the Shaggie Burn. The hill overlooking the village of Crieff is wooded with Nicnevin's Craig, or the steep drop of the rocky hillside, looming over part of the Monzie estate. A singular standing stone, the Nevin Stone, faces the cliff on private land, past the old gate-house, now a holiday cottage.

I walk up the gated road bisecting two fields: one of grazing sheep, the other ripening barley. To the right, yellow grass subsumes a stubby stone circle decorated in cup-and-ring marks and 'dumbbell' carvings – two circles connected by a line, like two worlds linked by the thread of story. Another stone slab is covered in more mysterious cup-and-ring marks. This Neolithic rock art suggests the cyclical passage of time, of moons and offerings. The markings on these stones are some of the clearest petroglyphs I've ever seen. Excavation of this site in 1938 uncovered ceremonial urns and the burial of an adult and child, the entire site wreathed with a shattering of quartz. Heartbreakingly, someone has more recently vandalised the stones with a series of runes painted in red.

My steps are uncertain in the mud. The squat menhir of the Nevin Stone is close, silvery in the bright sun. The farmer comes by on his spattered utility vehicle with two smiling, panting sheep dogs by his side. I tell him I've just glimpsed the stone. 'Ah, you've come to see the witch,' he says, as if the stone is a woman. He smiles and wishes me well. The sun is brilliant, glinting off the craig, carving out its negative space with light and shadow. A hawk wings over all with dark certainty. I accept that it will take me a very long time to cover this short distance. I lean on my stick, each step like walking on tacks, the tension travelling up my legs to my back and neck as I brace against it. I mount the gate, and my body puzzles it out as I slip down to the earth, all ungainly. Only the sheep see me pull myself up, dust myself off. I keep walking through the field, until eventually I find her.

The Nevin Stone faces the hill. I rest against her shadowed mass and the farmer sings his cows back to the byre, his lone voice shifting on the low wind. She leans back as if yearning to see the sun or to finally lie down. The surface of the stone is abraded with millennia of rain, rivulets forming the web of wyrd. She is cracked, lichen-crusted with corners worn smooth and lanolin-waxed by the backs of generations of sheep scratching themselves on her bulk.

I follow Nicnevin's ceremonial procession through the landscape: back to the Shaggie Burn and down beside the manse to the green, past the *yett* or gate, the little fairy bridge over the tumbling Shaggie. I rest here and wonder at its beauty. It is an enchanted thing: the narrow stone arch over the stream is still 'mantled with venerable ivy,' as it was in Blair's day. Wild flowers cover the fairy crossing in a verdant crescent. I imagine a tiny company making their way over the leaping stream, their sombre din tuned to the song of the burn. According to Blair, the well bearing Kate's name is not far from here, but I can't find it in the archaeological record or on any Ordnance Survey map. I accept that I won't be able to walk to it, even if it still exists. It's a long way back to the car, and I'm already exhausted.

Scotland is full of footpaths, coffin roads and lyke wake trails. These ways once marked a public right of way, a mourning route for those taking a body to burial. They formed a walking memorial through the land. Resting at the yett, I spin another myth: what if this ceremonial route was not traversed by a singular woman to her death at the pyre, but by generations of mourners? Might it be a lost coffin road, a liminal track where the living cared for the dead?

Before ending my explorations, I find Reverend George Blair's tiny chapel, its door locked. Blair was only pastor in this particular church for a year, but the village made its mark on him. He wrote 'The Holocaust' after he was suspended from his clerical post. A flyer in a glass case beside the door lists Sunday services. The Shaggie shushes in the quiet. All is idyllic, until I see the *jougs*, an iron collar on a chain hanging from the exterior of the chapel. It dangles over a newer bench, a surreal invitation. The iron collar would have been used as a punishment for those who had transgressed the edicts of the Kirk: sinners were shackled to the building. Reverend Blair would have passed the jougs and chain every day, hanging like blackened bones picked clean by a fire. The dark ring shines with a fresh coat of black paint. Whose job is it to maintain the jougs? I stand before it, cold to the core.

Since beginning this research, I have become obsessed with jougs. I see them everywhere – hanging from the sides of churches, drilled into standing stones, dangling amidst Pictish carvings. The jougs were generally used as a public humiliation, and they were also sometimes used to bind women accused of witchcraft. In a culture that denies and obscures the role of the Church in the atrocities of the witch-hunts, the iron collars in situ are a certainty. This happened.

On my way back to the M90 at Perth, I stop at Fowlis Wester to sit and recover from the walk. I like Fowlis Wester, a tiny settlement of stone houses arranged around a central square. The kirkyard is gated and the old red phone booth is filled with books and DVDs, a community borrowing scheme. St Bean's Chapel is a lovely fourteenth-century building, restored in the 1920s to its original medieval simplicity. I stopped here before to see the kirk and the Pictish stone inside with the iron ring attached to it. The stone was moved inside the shelter of the church to protect it. It's carved with a procession of beasts and riders on horseback, one looking suspiciously like Odin on the eight-legged Sleipnir. A Celtic cross of knots and visual puzzles adorns the other side. A ring for a jougs hangs from the base of the cross, drilled into the stone in the seventeenth century. This puzzle – the inviting kirk, the ancient stone and the torture device – won't be solved on this visit. We are still in the lockdowns of the pandemic, and I can't go inside the church. A laminated sign tacked to the door is a plague-year declaration: 'Thank you for trying the door. It is locked and we are not meeting here. Pray and feel God's love for you, and know that some day we will all meet again somewhere.'

I imagine what it might mean to accept such sentiment, to set foot in a church not as an outsider, but as one of the faithful. I think of Reverend Blair and his hard words following his dismissal. I imagine Kates in all their manifestations walking the path through Monzie, maybe even down the M90 and beyond.

All of us walk together – towards what? A place in the land-scape, or, perhaps, a point in time? A moment in the turning year, a day of remembrance where forgiveness is possible. Not a pardon for the women violently killed by the Church, but an apology from the Church itself. On this day, all kirks, big and small, will echo with sermons of contrition. Only then might I go in to pray, and all the jougs would shudder in their rings.

IO

Police Tape and Ritual Litter

'Maggie Wall', Dunning, 1657

'The Tinker folk know her as their own.'

– Jess Smith

My first encounter with a cop was over thirty years ago. Nights in California were cool, expansive, and you could sit outside barefoot all year long. The lights of strip malls vied with the strings of headlights snaking over endless freeways. They pooled on the horizon, dimming the stars. The moonlight singed through the smog, and I was tangled with a boy in the back seat of his Chevy Nova, parked beside an orange grove. The logistics of losing my virginity weighed heavily on me. Like Caddy in Faulkner's *The Sound and the Fury*, it meant no more to me than a hangnail, and I wanted rid of it. The headlights of the police car found us, me and this broken boy who knew things he shouldn't have at sixteen. The policemen ordered me out and searched my dishevelled clothing, rolling a torch up and down my body. They shone it in my eyes, blinding me. It was a game.

'What colour are your eyes?' the one with the torch asked. The second stood behind him, a taller shadow in the night.

'Green,' I said. What was the right answer? I'd never thought about it in any official capacity before. I'd been told by another boyfriend, a gentler one, that my eyes were always a different colour. He'd sing me New Order's 'Temptation', with its green-eyes-blue-eyes-grey-eyes chorus, like an old-time crooner. In an updated music video for the song released in 2006, a girl is in a record store and she steals the vinyl and then some lilacs. She goes home to put the needle on the record, dancing her victory in the safe space of the song. She was like the girl I once was. Casting the circle from my record player was perhaps my first ritual.

At that moment, in the beam of the cop's torch, I remembered an article in a woman's magazine about what colour eyeshadow suited different eye colours, pink for green eyes and golden brown for blue. I was ill-equipped for this confrontation. No magazine article, no sex-ed class nor *Your Changing Body* pamphlet had prepared me for being outnumbered by powerful men.

'They're blue.' The one in front laughed, as if catching me in a lie.

'Say your eyes are blue,' the second one echoed.

I said it, and we were released. The boy, fuming and emasculated, drove me home in silence. Later, he made me pay for it, over and over again.

*

The Maggie Wall Monument might be the best-known monument to a woman in Scotland. Like the mythic Kate McNevin, it's likely Maggie Wall wasn't a single person but an accumulation of stories. There is no documentation of a Maggie Wall in the Dunning parish records. If she did exist, her life is now dwarfed by the monument bearing her name. The Maggie Wall Monument is famous on the Internet, probably because of the drama of its presence. It has become the ubiquitous image for news articles about memorials to the accused in Scotland. Despite its celebrity, little is known about the memorial: who built it and why remain a mystery. The eighteenth-century plans of nearby Duncrub Castle show an enclosed field called Maggie's Wall. 'Maggie's Wall' could also be Maggie's *Walls* or *Waas*, which is Scots for building or house. Etymologically, it's not a great leap to 'Maggie's house'. Is Maggie Wall a genius loci, an actual person or both?

The monument consists of iron supports holding a pile of stones together, topped with a cross of unknown origin. It first appears on an Ordnance Survey map in 1866, and some historians have claimed it's a folly. I found a photo postcard of the monument dating from 1910; the cross is sun-dappled, dwarfed by a dense wood of tall trees, now gone. Bright white paint spells out 'Maggie Wall Burnt Here 1657 as a Witch'. Local residents care for the memorial, regularly renewing the paint, as others have done for generations. There are those who would remember the stories of the people who died in the parish, accused of witchcraft. Exactly who built the Maggie Wall cairn, and why they did it, may not be as important as its current purpose of memorialising women murdered as witches.

An image search for the Maggie Wall Monument in Dunning will turn up recent pictures of the cross-topped cairn surrounded by a ring of policemen, their arms akimbo in their black uniforms, like a circle of wizards. In other photos, it's covered in yellow crime scene tape, the site of a murder investigation. In 2019, a twenty-two-year-old woman named Annalise Johnstone was violently killed, her throat slit and her other injuries described in the local press as 'unsurvivable'. News reports contradicted each other, with some saying she was killed at the monument, and others only that her body was found there. In the court records, her brother confessed to carrying her body for two miles and depositing her beside a path in a nearby village. Afterwards, he and his girlfriend called the police to report Annalise missing and then cleaned their car of any evidence. Two hillwalkers later found her body, claiming there had been no attempt to conceal it. Annalise was a Traveller and lesbian, estranged from her family after coming out. Police identified her using her brother's descriptions of her tattoos and piercings. She had a labret and a tongue piercing, and the words 'Lady' and 'Papa' tattooed on her chest, with tributes to four women – 'Nadia', 'Gran', 'Mum' and 'Alicia' – on her arm. Her brother was cleared; the jury found the murder charges against him 'unproven'. The investigation is closed.

Tabloids covering the murder featured photos of the monument as if the site itself were an accomplice. Macabre fantasies fuel the tabloid fascination with the witch, wedded to witches' sites in the landscape like the Maggie Wall Monument. News reports linked the monument to serial killers Ian Brady and Myra Hindley, who had visited the site on holiday in 1965. They posed in front of it, taking photos of each other. In the photo of Hindley at the monument, she perches on the cairn, one foot on the stone, the other on the wooden fence surrounding it. Her bleached blonde fright-wig obscures her face. This image surfaced at Hindley's trial and was used to indict her not only as an accomplice to murder but as a witch. True crime writers continue to look for evidence of witchcraft in the Moors Murders. Their sensationalised studies paint the murders as rituals, with Brady as the alchemist and Hindley as his witch. When Ian Brady died at a high-security hospital in 2017, a judge denied his request to have the fifth movement of *Symphonie fantastique*, 'Dream of a Witches' Sabbath', by composer Hector Berlioz played at his cremation. This piece of music is hallucinatory and grandiose. The ditty of a witches' dance is layered over church bells, a scuttering of insect-like strings and 'Dies irae', a medieval poem used as a requiem Mass that begins:

Day of wrath and doom impending
David's word with Sibyl's blending
Heaven and earth in ashes ending.

The witch is the dark matter of Britain's dreaming. The sensationalised exploitation of this history is part of thanatourism or morbid tourism; it's a version of the story that sells ghost tours, books, films and newspapers. In the case of the Maggie Wall Monument, I wondered if there might be an antidote, something beyond this grotesque fascination. I looked to the living oral tradition of Scottish Travellers in which Maggie Wall appears as real person, an ancestor.

Like people accused as witches, Gypsies and Travellers were targeted by the Reformation. Though Gypsies and Scottish Travellers are two distinct ethnic groups, they share a heritage of nomadism. The Scottish Act Concerning Egyptians of 1609 targeted Romany people, mistakenly calling them 'Egyptians'. The act accused nomadic people of fortune-telling and criminality, and gave them sixteen days to leave the realm or they would be executed. This act was in place throughout the years of witch-hunting, and was another kind of cleansing operation. Travellers were linked to witches in the cultural imagination. In Shakespeare's *The Tempest*, Caliban is the offspring of the witch Sycorax. '*Caliban*' is the Romany word for dark. Shakespeare's character of Caliban conflates the darkness of race, witches and the unknown – a fantasy that persists to this day. Until 1856, it was illegal to be a Gypsy or a Traveller in Britain.

I heard a ghost story from Jess Smith, a Traveller and renowned storyteller who heard it from Jimmy Somebody. When Jimmy Somebody was a child, Travellers would camp in places around Perth in exchange for doing work. One of his jobs as a boy was clearing a field of stones and piling them into cairns. I imagine a child, perhaps like Somebody, piling up the stones that went into Maggie's Cairn. The story goes that Jimmy's family made camp near the monument, and the children went into the wood. There, they saw a woman crouched low with a hot look in her eye, like quarry cornered by hounds. In Somebody's version, her hair was tangled, but as Jess Smith tells it, the woman's hair was a mess of twisting flames. Her clothing was torn and old: antique, even. The children called to her, but she ran past them. A black cat followed, fast at her heels. She disappeared straight into a tree, but the cat remained, brushing up against the children, circling their legs and meowing. It followed them back to the camp, and when their grandmother saw it, she got serious. The cat was a warning. They broke camp and made their way further into the wood. That night, the wood around the monument burned. Everyone from the village spent the night putting out the fire. It was Maggie Wall in the shape of a black cat that saved them. Jess Smith said the events of this story happened in around 1920. Despite historians' claims that Maggie Wall never existed, Jess believes she was a person. She said Maggie was a Traveller, an ancestor who was good with herbs.

*

I sleep in a budget hotel in Perth. These places are usually identical, with the same decor no matter where you are in the UK. It's disorientating, institutional, but this room is different. I've been given what seems like a suite – darkly panelled, the soft furnishings accented with Black Watch plaid. A print of a ubiquitous Scottish stag hangs on the wall. I toss and turn all night, pursued by the kind of dreams that were once called hag-ridden. In the nightmare, I crawl into a narrow cairn, the stones clammy and dripping. Something inside knows me, and challenges from the dark recesses with ominous clarity: 'Little witch, do you even know what you are up against?'

I plan to travel to the Maggie Wall Monument in the morning, something I have been putting off for some time, worried I would be intruding on a crime scene, or worse, that I would have to deal with police. It's early, still dark outside. I stand at the bright vanity mirror. One of the few things I like about these places is the unflinchingly clear illumination of the mirror outside the bathroom. I can get a really good look at myself. Here I am, naked and ruddy with what is probably a hot flush – a *personal summer* or *power surge* – or maybe it's just the awkward heating in the room, on and off again through the night. Vague sadness darkens my not-green eyes, and my freckled face sets in a frown. Everything's getting soft and delicate, more complex, despite all my attempts at hardening up. The tempering hasn't taken.

I rifle through my overnight bag, now a nest of crumpled black things. My travelling clothes are a long black dress, boots and a big black scarf. Is this what I should be wearing to visit witches' monuments? I let the self-conscious dilemma sit with me as I put up my hair, and adorn myself with silver hoops and rings I've forged. I brush in arched brows over my pale, sparse ones, and put on dark plum lippy straight from the tube. I'm naked without these things.

What once coded me as trad goth later became *eldergoth*, and now I've evolved into something else. Random people ask me if I'm a witch. I always answer, 'Depends on who's asking.' It's a more interesting start to a conversation than the other nosy opener I sometimes get: 'You don't sound like you are from around here.'

I know the land is alive, and our ancestors speak to us. Perhaps thinking these things makes me a witch. When someone asks me if I'm a witch, they might be one themselves. We know our own, don't we? The voice in the dream-cairn called me a witch, and a basic one at that.

The online Ordnance Survey map shows five B-roads converging like a wobbly brittle star on the village of Dunning in central Scotland, once the site of an Iron Age fort, a Roman camp, and home to a dragon-slaying saint from the eighth century. Where there are dragons, living or slain, there are sure to be mysteries, and this spot on the map is no exception. North-west of the village, hedged in by Duncrub Burn, a blank field is marked simply 'Maggie'. Zooming in expands the title to 'Maggie Wall Wood'. A small triangle, unmarked, just beside the B8062 road before the well-manicured golf course, is the monument cairn itself.

I arrive at nearby Kincladie Wood, where six women are said to have been executed in 1662. This small enclave of trees is known to locals as My Lady's Wood, marking it as a place that was once sacred, dedicated to Mary and perhaps an older goddess. It's a well-loved place, edged by a vast expanse of white polytunnels on one side, and the ramparts of the Roman fort on the other. Sunlight glosses the holly trees, the tallest I've ever seen, shining beside the bare branches of oak, beech and birch. Little elf-dens made of twigs dot the wood, and a late scattering of snowdrops blooms at the trailhead. Bat boxes, numbered like suburban bungalows, hang from trees. A map of the forest path marks the site of the witch-burnings. The archaeological record claims an old oak marks the execution site, but I suspect this is outdated, anecdotal information. I pace in the leaf mould, looking for a barren place, an uncanny glimmer. Above me, a magpie lets out a throaty bark, sounding a bit like Captain Beefheart doing a bird call. One for sorrow – the same bird who refused to weep at the crucifixion. *I had my reasons*, it seems to say as its grumpy caws grow louder.

If women died violently here, we have their names and nothing more. Isobell McKendley, Elspeth Reid and Jonet Airth were tried together. Agnes Hutstone, Isobel Goold and Anna Law were tried separately, and did not confess. There is no record of their death dates, and the last three may have been released. I make a circle with twigs and stones in a clearing, a makeshift offering, before heading to the monument.

It's just past lambing season, a sunny, late spring day, with a big sky full of clouds shifting light over the rolling countryside. A forlorn stretch of grazing land appears on the approach from the north. The stone cross is at once bucolic and foreboding, sitting atop the hillock. I walk up the three stone steps to stand before it. A shift in weather heralds my arrival, and clouds shut out the sun. It turns cold, in the way it does in Scotland: all seasons in one day, as the joke goes. In this moment of winter, I hold an audience with the imposing memorial, a rough-hewn version of the plinths seen in every village and town across

Scotland dedicated to the war dead. The police tape is gone. Six metres high, it towers over me. The white-painted lettering is as fresh and white as it was one hundred years ago.

The pile of stones form a cairn, a traditional burial marker. The Clava Cairns outside Inverness are a Neolithic example of these stone memorials on a grand scale. There is an old Scottish Gaelic saying, '*Clach air do chàrn,*' or 'A stone on your cairn,' meaning, 'I will remember you.' This is perhaps a remnant from burial customs that involved funeral parties carrying coffins for long distances. Cairns were erected at resting points, with stones being added by mourners.

I linger at the Maggie Wall Monument, where the lost trees of the phantom wood might have gentled the place, the shadows of their branches just coming into bud and dancing over this folly. But there's nothing to shelter us, the monument and me, as rain spits down. Molehills surround the cairn, fresh earth in neat piles, and I picture the little blind beings moving industriously beneath us like chthonic numina wrestling for the soul of these stones. In between tabloid headlines and police tape, something kinder waits.

The Maggie Wall Monument crowns the surrounding fields with its grim enigma. It is a lodestone of grief and despair, its cross a dark finger pointing to the mute heavens. Some sites seem to be blessed with prayer and joy; others are places of irredeemable pain. They become a challenge for the people that must care for them, and for each who visit. Tending a grave with care is not convenient nor easy. Writing in the 1980s, Perthshire historian Archie McKerracher said a wreath had been laid at the cairn each year, with a card saying, 'In memory of Maggie Wall, Burnt by the Church in the Name of Christianity.'

I consider offerings secreted in the crevices of the cairn: countless candles, an animal vertebrae, a small pot of jam. Some are things a young woman might leave for a friend: a teddy bear, lip balm, a purse charm with bells. Are they offerings for Annalise or Maggie? Locals call this 'ritual litter'. Someone regularly cleans the monument of these offerings. I circle the stones, coming to a bottle of nail polish in a raspberry-pink colour, tucked away in a crack. Its bright femininity strikes me to the heart and I think, *Annalise had grey eyes.*

II

Hedge Maze

Isabel Rutherford, Crook of Devon, 1662

'. . . I think that ye are not well, and ye are not weil [right].'
— Isabel Rutherford's confession

Witch-hunting raged across Scotland in the years 1661–2, and in Crook of Devon in central Scotland, confessions were extracted from twelve women and one man. The accused were interrogated in Tullibole Castle and processed in batches. Only one woman, Agnes Pittendreich, was spared execution, because she was pregnant at the time. Another accused, Margaret Hoggin, was seventy-nine years old. There is no note of her conviction nor execution, but she is referred to as 'deceased' in a record dated two months after the initial trials. It's possible she did not survive her imprisonment. The seventeenth-century Laird of Tullibole oversaw the interrogations. He was assisted by his bailie, the local ministers and eighteen other residents of the village, volunteers employed in 'waking the witch' or sleep deprivation. While there is no record of this torture, I guess at a pattern. The accused were held for months before their trials, and there is an ominous statement in the court record. When Agnes Murie was asked why she wouldn't repeat her confession to the judge and jury, she replied only that she had wounds, presumably from beatings, on her body, and she would have the bailie prove it to the men who sat in judgement — judge Alexander Coville and the jury of fifteen landowners from the district. She asked the bailie to lay his hand on her breast and back where 'lumps' troubled her. Her tortured body was her statement — her injuries should also be to be taken into account, along with her previous confessions. It was as if she were saying, *Whatever I confessed came with these wounds, and I will not repeat the admission.*

The judge and landowners declared the accused guilty. Only one woman, Christian Grieve, was found not guilty at the trial on 21 July 1662. This verdict would not save her; in October, she was arrested again under the same charges, found guilty by the same judge and jury, and executed five days later.

The standard demonic pact was confirmed by all the women who confessed: they had renounced their baptisms and taken exotic new demonic names like 'Rossina'. The devil marked them, and he 'made use' of their bodies. Documenting these particular obsessions was not only integral to group interrogations, it was necessary to obtain permission for a legal trial from the government. Near-identical statements of guilt appear across the Crook of Devon dittays, or trial records. Yet, when the accused described their devils, each offered their interrogators a different demonic man. To one, he appeared surrounded by a retinue of black-haired women; others said he wore a blue bonnet or a black hood. Another saw him as a 'halflong fellow with an dusti-coloured coat'. Robert Wilson, the only male member of the supposed coven, confessed to seeing the devil on a horse, wearing fine clothes and a 'Spanish cape'.

Perhaps these devils, each in different attire, were simply men. I found the trial records in a nineteenth-century source, compiled by an antiquary named R. Begg who copied them from the handwritten, deteriorating originals, translating them into print. Begg reasons in the footnotes that villages like Crook of Devon were 'swarming with discharged soldiers' in the chaotic years of English occupation and the Restoration. These aimless men may have been 'unscrupulous and designing knaves who personated Satan for their own guilty purposes'. The mythic devil multiplied, embodied in human men as well as in the imaginations of the accused – and their interrogators. He was ubiquitous, ever present. He might appear as an animal or even a haystack or other object, but most often he took human form.

Though he appeared in many guises in Crook of Devon, all the accused women seemed to agree that the temperature of Satan's 'seed' – his semen – was cold. When the accused offered this detail, it was probably not from their own imaginations, but embedded within the interrogators' salacious questioning. While the women confessed to sexual dealings with the devil, the confessions of Robert Wilson were free of such details. This is typical for men accused of witchcraft in Scotland; they were spared the line of coital questioning the women endured. The interrogators' devil was unequivocally straight.

As I transcribe them, the stories of the accused bleed into one another. Try as I may to hear them as individuals, they are a formless chorus of woe – until I hear one voice, one story call out from the rest. Isabel Rutherford's confession of 3 April 1662 echoes the others. She renounced her baptism, confessed to sex with the devil in someone else's yard, and received a new name: 'Viceroy'. The devil asked Isabel to call him 'Samuel'. Bearded and clothed in grey, he stood before her door, reminding her she had a meeting to attend in three weeks' time. She painted him as an officious and frightening taskmaster. Yet the details in her confessions, and the evidence presented against her by her neighbours, reveal a woman with a charismatic power.

The bulk of evidence against Isabel came from her neighbour. Janet Hutton met Isabel at the Tullibole kirkyard, where she asked her for a cure for her husband James, paying Isabel with a handful of meal. Isabel's ministrations didn't work; his 'disease' supposedly got worse wherever Isabel touched him. James refused further treatment and expressed remorse at ever meeting her: 'God gif [if only] he had never seen her.' He believed Isabel had stolen his health like a 'common thief', and he threatened to take his mare and ride to the Cruik, or the bend in the river Devon, to demand his health back from her. After this exchange,

Janet believed her husband had been charmed. He wouldn't let her make his bed, and although in their previous sixteen years of marriage 'there was never an evil word between them', after Isabel's ministrations, he would not 'suffer [his wife] . . . to come near him.' I project a narrative over the scant details: James is a lovesick man.

Janet also watched Isabel with another man in a neighbour's yard. She asked him to 'loose his breast' [open his shirt]. 'He did, and ye straked [stroked] his side . . . with your luif [palm of your hand].' Janet heard Isabel mumble words, but she couldn't make them out. Like Janet's husband, this ailing man was also not made well. Is it anachronistic to see sexual frisson in Janet's version of events, her portrait of Isabel's erotic power? No husband is mentioned in Isabel's formal list of charges, and she was perhaps a single woman with a tactile method of healing. The official version of events puts the guilt of these mass killings on petty squabbles, such as the jealousy apparent between Janet and Isabel. No doubt sickness and marital strife were dire threats in the seventeenth century, but so was a witch-hunt.

Neighbours like Janet called as witnesses may not have wanted the accused to die, but felt they had no choice other than to offer truth as they knew it. Once those in power demanded a version of events, testifying neighbours were already caught up in the machine of the trial.

I see Isabel as a woman with a powerful touch, one that was perhaps charged with warmth and power. Pain relief and healing can be augmented by compassionate touch. Charismatic touch – by a faith healer or another thought to be gifted with such powers – can have a curative effect. It is possible Isabel was such a healer, but the claims of her jealous neighbour and the pained fury of her patient James suggests something with an erotic charge. At a time when adultery was violently punished, might the touch of another woman carry all the power and danger of a repressed sexuality? The modern impulse to redeem the victims of the hunts often paints them as perfect, 'innocent' victims with no unique self. So little is left of an authentic life, and nothing is untainted by the eye of the interrogator. I read the scant words of Isabel's confession, and the portrait of her painted by a malicious neighbour, and wonder at James's incurable sickness – something like love. Isabel is under my skin – side *straked*, heart loosed, not made well.

*

In 2009, the current Lord Moncrieff built a monument – a 'shrine to rational thought' – dedicated to the thirteen people interrogated in his family's castle. It's an elaborate, ornamental shrubbery and sculpture built on his private grounds. Inside a massive hedge maze, a plinth is inscribed with the names of the victims. Moncrieff told the *Scotsman* that he doesn't want his monument to be 'taken over and adopted by people who believe in the supernatural'. While the maze is open to all, Moncrieff wanted to make certain that the topiary is a triumph of logic over superstition.

In his spare time, Moncrieff 'exposes bogus psychics'. Psychic nights have long been a form of popular entertainment in the UK, hosted in pubs and working men's clubs, the survivor of an older tradition of mediumship. The 'new' Witchcraft Act of 1735 made it illegal both to hunt witches and also to claim occult powers. Before it was repealed in 1951, the act was used to convict mediums and psychics. In 1944, Perthshire-born Helen Duncan was the last woman arrested for witchcraft in Scotland. Her channeling was a mixture of insight and showmanship, involving ectoplasm made of cheesecloth, egg whites and loo roll, with a spirit guide named 'Peggy' – a papier-mâché doll. She served nine months in prison. When her sentence was read, she said, 'I have done nothing; is there a God?' Being psychic is no longer a crime in the UK, but Moncrieff continues to root out modern clairvoyants.

At Halloween, the maze is used as an amusement for children. The maze itself has little relationship to the sombre message of the plinth at its centre. It has become a fun day out, the emotional message of memorial forgotten. Drone videos of the maze uploaded to the Internet show children racing each other, doing a victory dance around the plinth devoted to the dead, the memorial buried at the middle of the maze's test of endurance. Those interrogated on this land are erased again in the maze's 'test' of rationality. One memorial won't speak to all mourners; but who tells the stories, teaches the lessons? The belief in goddesses or gods, land spirits or even a Christian God is belief in the 'supernatural'. In the compos mentis world of this maze, are you required to check your faith at the door before you enter? Who is welcome to mourn? Healing will take more than right thinking and rationality; it's emotional and spiritual work. The Tullibole maze is a personal memorial, one man's response to this dark history.

There are others in Crook of Devon who have devised their own remembrance rituals for the dead. Storyteller and spirit worker Rowan Morrison recently performed a ritual she called 'Singing Their Souls Home'. Those who died at the stake were denied funeral rites and their bodies were not buried. Rowan and thirteen other women gathered together, sang a lament for the dead, and laid a small cairn of remembrance at the border of private land near the execution site. Each woman lit a candle, spoke the name of an accused person and rang a death bell 'to announce their passing'. They blessed the site of the cairn with water from a local healing well, leaving bread and water for the dead on their journey. She told me that she hopes her simple ritual will inspire people across Scotland to remember the accused in their own villages, towns or cities in a similar way. The elegance and simple power of this folk ritual has roots in Scottish funeral traditions accessible to us all. It's possible that similar quiet rituals are happening across Scotland as I write, and that they will multiply after my own work on the page has finished.

*

Backpacking across Europe in my twenties, I visited Chartres to see the thirteenth-century labyrinth laid into the cathedral floor. I'd read some medieval pilgrims traversed it on their knees, out of devotional humility or masochism. Twenty-two years ago, I scribbled my notes in a little tablet I bought in the Louvre gift shop: *The cathedral is a place of shifting emotions, a temporal temple where the circle is sacred; a pagan space amidst the Catholic finery.* I remember a feeling of déjà vu, of life coming around again beneath the surface. Initially, I was alone in the nave of the cathedral, except for a few scholars with binoculars looking at the stained glass windows, and a small crew with a TV camera.

God is not here, I noted. *This is merely a daedal shell.* A reliquary behind a large iron gate displayed a grimy length of fabric draped on a golden clotheshorse, the veil supposedly worn by Mary when she gave birth to Jesus. I lit a long white candle, wedging it into a wire rack with the other burning prayers. What did I pray for, all those years ago? Whatever it was, I didn't make a note of it. Maybe I prayed for my newly finished novel, a speculative biography of Saint Catherine of Siena. Those prayers, like so many others, went unanswered. Beside me, an old woman in a grey tailored suit bowed her head to the Madonna. I envied her faith.

As I walked the Chartres labyrinth, a woman with long dark hair in a cream twinset traversed it on crutches beside me. One circuit at a time, she hobbled out as I made my way in. We followed thousands of souls who'd wound this clockwork of faith, smoothing the stone mosaic over the last 800 years. Tour buses had pulled up before we reached the end, and we were subsumed by a loud group with cameras. The dark-haired woman was so slow. She'd been walking when I arrived and was still walking when I finished. It was beyond my imagination that walking could become so hard you might have to pray it back. I scrawled ecstatic certainty in my little travel notebook – *the way to heaven* is *heaven* – eliciting a snort of disbelief from my fifty-two-year-old self. The paradox of the labyrinth is true of faith as well as the healing journey: the further you go from the centre, the closer you are. There are no wrong turns in a labyrinth; the way in is the way out. I often think of her, that stranger on crutches. Now, I understand her resilience, and I wonder if she healed.

*

My arrival at Tullibole Castle is unremarkable. No one is here, and there are no signs to direct me. I am certainly trespassing. Peacocks, flamboyant landlords, are everywhere. Their desperate calls follow me as I find the maze beside a wood. I enter the wrong way, through the castle grounds instead of the old graveyard. It's less like Chartres and more like the hedge maze of the Overlook Hotel in Kubrick's *The Shining*. But I don't know that yet. Thinking back on everything fairy tales taught me, I should have come prepared. I check my pockets for string or crumbs, and come up empty-handed. I have brought nothing for my future self to find, so she can escape easily. Leave a trail – this is good advice if you find yourself entering a neglected hedge maze dedicated to executed people. I decide I live in a rational world, after all, and cautionary tales are metaphors, not practical advice. This is also called ignoring your gut.

A laminated wheelchair access sign marks an entrance in the wall of beech hedge. I quickly discover this is an old sign, a ruse worthy of a malicious fairy. Anyone in a wheelchair would be quickly stuck in mud and tangled in nettles. It's high summer but dark and humid. A squall waits in the heavy air. I vainly search for a shortcut to the plinth at the centre of the maze. This conundrum is 100 feet in diameter, twice the size of the labyrinth at Chartres, and the walls are untrimmed, over six feet high. I want to see the sculpture at the heart without traversing the whole thing, but I quickly become lost. Each dead end houses a stone labelled with a word on laminated paper, like a forgotten school project: 'Envy', 'Greed', 'Ignorance'. *So much for dignity or fellow feeling*, I think.

I turn and turn again in the clag of the maze. The branches of 2,000 beech trees reach wantonly from the hedge wall as if they are grasping at something or someone, obscuring all edges and corners. Their verdant dominion swallows the human artifice. Even if I'm not in the middle of a fibromyalgia flare, I like to know what I'm in for – how long I'll be standing or walking. Chronic pain is my body's way of telling me I don't live in a rational world, and some things are without reason entirely. I know this, literally, in my bones. I breath out my panic – *Brightside it*, I remind myself, *and you'll get through anything*. I try on borrowed optimism and curse my preternatural determination, its deeply emotional foundations. I sink in mud, in the trenches of this embattled history.

The maze feels haunted, every corner of it. There are fresh tracks going in, but none coming out. I hear something like scraping metal. It might be a high tree branch creaking from the tall pines above, but it sounds as if it's coming from inside the maze. This is how every horror movie begins: the innocent trusts a person, a house or a hedge-maze memorial, only to be betrayed. The final girl – the one left to tell the story – notes all warnings, and still she advances. She runs. I'm breathless, choosing a dead end at each turn. Here, disuse has created a vacancy where something else has moved in, or perhaps refused to leave. I trudge through standing water, reflecting a darkening sky, before finally reaching the centre, shattered and winded.

Here, the one-and-a-half-tonne sandstone pillar greets me. A twisting branch crowns the plinth of the memorial, infused with great sensitivity by sculptor Gillian Forbes. Wildlife embellishes the stone: a hare, frog, bees, dragonflies and a bird, lifelike among the leaves. The names of the victims are etched down the sides of the pillar: Isabel Rutherford, Bessie Henderson, Janet Brough, Christian Grieve, Robert Wilson, Agnes Murie, Bessie Neil, Margaret Lister, Agnes Brugh, and not one but two women named Janet Paton. I run my hand over the carved branches of the plinth, linger in the cool stone of each veined leaf. The small frog perched there, lifelike, is wet to the touch. I hold on to this beauty, my reward for reaching the centre. Who was the last to see the tender elegance of its detail? But it's not enough to soothe my mounting dread.

Wooden notice boards, the kind found in rural villages displaying flyers for the next Kirk Soup and Sweet or dog-walker services, surround the plinth. Warped pages tacked to the wood, rain-streaked and sun-faded, exhibit phantom missives, the vanished screed of a Lord Summerisle. One remains legible, printed with a few paragraphs about the seventeenth-century 'anti-Egyptian' laws in Scotland, which allowed the ethnic cleansing of the Romany people.

I stand at the monument, weary and frightened. I tap notes into my phone: *Writing is a descent into a past hell, and I'm disappeared into it.* I'm on the inside, now, utterly surrounded. I've traversed this weedy history only to arrive at the authoritative documents at its core, neglected and unintelligible. Here is the heart of this book, though I realise this only later. Having begun my penance for gate-crashing, for feeling my way, I now have to finish this circuit and find a passage out. I steel myself for the task. I'm no stranger to untwisting the corners of reality, threading a path through the needle of my will. I lean against the stone pillar, the names at my back, and allow myself a shuddering breath. I'm shaking.

Midge-bitten and nettle-stung, I'll pay for this exertion, perhaps for days. There will be time to process this experience while flat on my back. I tear around the muddy corners, and meet again those pedantic words beneath the laminate at each dead end. My fear hurls me forward. The allies I've chosen are long dead. They leave few threads, scraps only. They can't tell me if I've got it wrong. I follow the screams of the peacocks to a break in the hedge. It's a different opening than the one I'd entered, a ragged crack in the green wall. Something watches me from between the branches, a single eye following me out.

12

Wall's End

Annaple Thomsone and Elizabeth
Scotland, Bo'ness 1679, 1680

'The devill told yow . . . that yow wis ane poore puddled Bodie,
and hand an evill lyiff, and difficultie to win throw the world;
and promesed, iff ye walk followed him, and go alongst with
him, yow should never want, but have ane better lyiff.'*
                          – The trial dittay of Annaple Thomsone, 1679

Bo'ness is a seaside town set on the south bank of the Firth of
Forth between Glasgow and Edinburgh in the central lowlands. It's
a good three hours from Banff, where I live, and a long way to go
just to see a rock in the ground at the dead end of a private road.
I'd discovered the Bo'ness Witches Stone via a Google image search.
In some recent photographs, it's moss-covered; in others, it has
been cleaned off. It has the look of an uncanny thing, set in an
indistinct wood and carved with the words 'The Witches Stone'. I
have little documentation to help me, and I'm not even sure I will
be able to find it if I set out. There are no older photographs available online – no sepia wet plates or daguerreotypes, no black-and-
white postcard souvenirs, not even a Polaroid uploaded for poster-
ity. I wonder who scrapes the moss from the letters? And why is
there no mention of the stone on Canmore, the extensive archaeological record maintained by Historic Scotland? The stone's witch
attribution might be a recent development.

---

* 'The devil told you that you was a poor muddled body, and had a miserable
life, and difficulty to win through the world; and promised if you would follow
him and go along with him you should never want, but have a better life.'

Bo'ness is an ancient place. The Roman Antonine Wall spanning the central belt of Scotland ends at Carriden in Bo'ness. As I map the route, I realise the mudflats of Torryburn and the grave of Lillias Adie are directly across the Firth. The Venerable Bede claimed Bo'ness was named Pennfahel or 'Wall's end' in Pictish. In the seventeenth century, it was a place of industry: coal-mining, clay-mining, potteries, salt-making, and witch-hunting.

Legend claims the Witches Stone marks the execution site of five women and one man, victims of the witch-hunts in Bo'ness in 1679. These executions took place at the customary gallows site at the 'west end of Borrowstownes' or Bo'ness. Perhaps this stone marked the western boundary of the village at one time. The Witches Stone lies on the extensive grounds of Carriden House, a seventeenth-century mansion. The stone's inscription probably dates from the late Victorian era. At that time, according to the Falkirk Local History Society, the house was 'full of typical Victorian clutter. Mementoes of foreign visits abounded, such as a fur headdress, a pair of fine elephant tusks, a chair built of reindeer horns.'

The stone is one of two *muirstanes*, or moor stones – markers for the Carriden Moor, now gone. They demarcated the boundary between cultivated grounds and moorland. Annaple Thomsone mentioned one of the muirstanes in her confession. She said she met the devil at the 'Croce of Murestane', west of Bo'ness. The missing stone was a Neolithic menhir inscribed with a crude cross. It was dynamited in the early nineteenth century.

Local custom remembers the surviving stone as a fairy place. Children walk around it for luck, writing their wishes on scraps of rice paper and burying them at its base. This is part of a long tradition of fairy lore: the paper wishes are fairy meat, akin to milk or grain traditionally left for the fey to win their favour. One need only look at images of the moss-covered stone, a green beast curled in sleep, to see its potential as a fairy-thing. Before I met the stone on my travels, I wondered if it was merely Victorian tat, a bewildering garden ornament now left to re-wild itself with the mulch of children's wishes.

Like Grissell's stone in Dundee, the Witches Stone in Bo'ness marks a place in the imagination where accused witches become intercessors, the bringers of luck and granters of wishes. In the pre-Reformation Kirk, Mary, the mother of Jesus, assumed this role as an accessible intermediary with a compassionate ear. The Reformation Kirk removed Mary as a divine presence, yet this listening spirit is so necessary she persists in other guises. When God refuses to listen, there are others to ask – Mary, Brigid, fairies, ancestors and accused witches.

These diverse spiritual entities overlap in folklore and tradition. Diane Purkiss writes of fairies in folk belief: 'In some ways they *are* the dead, or the dead are with them.' Scottish witchcraft scholar Lizanne Henderson argues that 'beneath the thin diabolical crust that covers the tortured voices of the accused witches is confirmation of the tenacity and endurance of fairy belief'. In some respects, the confessions are terrible fairy stories. One could argue that these three things – fairy belief, the confessions and the myth of the witch – are inseparable in Scotland, especially where they manifest together in the landscape.

When I set out to find the Witches Stone, I use directions from a YouTube video uploaded by a drone photographer. I go up by Carriden Brae and make a left, then, when I pass the walled garden, there's a narrow path to my right, overgrown and wooded. *I've arrived*. So says my inner navigator, which is not always reliable.

It's a misting day in late summer. Boys ride by on bikes, half-standing on the pedals, skidding to a stop to watch me with narrowed eyes as I walk from my car to the wooded lot. When they see where I'm going, they take off, whizzing past faster than they'd come. Shrouded in a fringe of wood, beyond the first few trees, I see it – an old green bump. The moss has grown back since the last picture I'd found. The inscription 'THE WITCHES STONE' in caps-lock Helvetica is once more buried beneath the verdant fur. Like the countless other Carlin stones dotted across Scotland, these lonely menhirs might have been part of older Neolithic stone circles or portal tombs – they are the last stones standing. A local legend claims the devil threw the Bo'ness stone at a witch as she rode through the clouds. Less fantastically, it's possible an Ice Age glacier deposited the stone here.

As I walk around it, I notice two holes at the base – not shallow, like cup-and-ring petroglyphs on a standing stone, but deep and even. They have been made with a metal tool, like a hammer and bit. I've seen similar holes drilled into Pictish stones for the insertion of a ring, a chain to which a jougs or a scold's bridle could be affixed. The holes on this stone are empty. It's possible the holes at the base of the stone were meant for dynamite. If a large rock is considered an obstruction to ploughing, blowing it up is one way to clear it; in emails with local historian Geoff Bailey, I learn that this was the fate of its sister muirstane. The Witches Stone, like so many other Carlin stones, is a survivor.

I am standing before the boulder, the air dense in the scrap of wood, lush with summer growth, when I hear it. The stone hums. Like the whirring of a frame drum or the white noise of a mistuned radio, that wide sound is fair warning. Tiny yellow bodies surface from the earth, hovering like sparks from a need-fire – a ritual fire kindled in distress after all other flames have been extinguished. Wasps swarm up from their hive, a hole in the ground at my feet. So these witch-places are dangerous after all. I make it out, unstung, counting myself lucky.

*

Witch trials were carried out in the seaside town of Bo'ness for eighty years, the first in 1624 and the last arrest as late as 1704. In the years 1679–80, approximately twenty-eight people were arrested and at least nine killed. The accused didn't consult with the fey or land spirits, and they worked no malefice. Some drank with the devil, flirting, dancing or fucking him, but there is no evidence of evil intent in their confessions. During their interrogations, they offered stories of drunkenness, sex and spousal intimacy. The demonic pact was confirmed by marks found on the bodies of the accused, and like other trials in Scotland, interrogators saw this pact as a sexual one. Allegations of torture in Bo'ness reached the High Court in Edinburgh, and representatives from the central government were sent to investigate. They documented evidence of several kinds of torture and ordered all the suspects released. Silvia Federici argues the sexualised nature of the witch-hunts were an attempt to control women, 'by means of torture . . . as well as meticulous interrogations to which witches were subjected, which were a mixture of sexual exorcism and psychological rape'. All of the women accused, those executed as well as those set free, would have endured this.

In the late seventeenth century, there were new arguments and impediments to the local trials that had notoriously claimed so many lives. The 1679 hunt in Bo'ness was one of the last group trials conducted in Scotland, and the majority of the accused escaped execution. These debates changed and evolved over the next several hundred years, and are still being fought on the Internet today. Commissioners, judges and clergymen wondered how witchcraft could be scientifically proven in trial proceedings, and if its existence disproved or confirmed the existence of God.

As I searched for further information on the Bo'ness hunt, I met a velvet rope: the National Records Office had the pre-trial documents, but they had been re-indexed. To find them, I would have to look through boxes of three-hundred-year-old papers, searching for individual names. Reading the original texts, handwritten in Scots without any standard spelling, is exceedingly difficult and time-consuming. I was up for the challenge, but was told that only academics were allowed access to these files.

I had no institution to vouch for me, to legitimise my fascinations. Love only goes so far, and then you need credentials. I went back to the texts I did have, ones I'd found in my local library in Banff. The strange little compendium of Scottish witch lore, *Rowan Tree and Red Thread*, published in 1949, proved invaluable. I found a clue in a footnote in the chapter titled 'Witch Organisation: Dances'. A Bo'ness woman named Annaple Thomsone was accused of dancing with the devil as he played the pipes, and the trial documents were printed in an issue of *Scots Magazine* from 1772.

I found this issue digitised online; the seventeenth-century documents reprinted in their original weirdness a hundred years after the trials. Someone going by the initial 'P' submitted their findings to the publication. The Bo'ness trial record of 1679 was published by the magazine as a historical artefact, a witchcraft curio. P wanted readers of the magazine to be reminded of 'the barbarous infatuation and ignorance of former times'. They also wished 'to make some expiation to the injured names of these unhappy sufferers'. There is no further information about where or how P obtained the documents, or why they felt it necessary to use only an initial, but I'm grateful for their work.

Originally, I was frustrated by using only secondary sources, but then I embraced this glimpse into the past conversations around such fraught history. I was immersed in voices from earlier centuries, and my own work became part of a lively ancestral debate. I was listening in to others who had tried to make sense of these same events, and laying down my own responses.

The editor of *Scots Magazine* added a note to the published trial records. He had received many reactions to the trial matter from the Bo'ness witch-hunts. Some readers wanted proof that this was authentic, but others expressed 'disapprobation' that the law that allowed the hunting of people as witches, the Witchcraft Act of 1563, had been repealed in 1735. The editor reminded readers that as recently as 1743, the Associate Presbytery had considered the repealing of the Witchcraft Act a national sin. The Kirk still saw witches as a threat, even into the middle of the eighteenth century. This unexpected controversy stunned me. Were the educated readers of *Scots Magazine* really writing to the editor in favour of more witch-hunting a century after the state-sanctioned murder of Annaple and the others? I had assumed that the repealing of the Witchcraft Act and the end of witch-hunting would have been roundly embraced by the 'learned' populace that made up the readership of *Scots Magazine*. Often, this history is described as the evils done by a superstitious and unenlightened populace. Some today would like to put the witch-hunts squarely behind us, a product of 'unenlightened times', yet the issue was hotly debated by well-read, supposedly enlightened people, well into modernity.

The dittay published in *Scots Magazine* focuses on Annaple Thompson. The 'evidence' is presented in an accusatory second person: 'You . . . declared yowrself content to follow him, and becowm his servant; whereupon the devil threw yow to the grownd and had carnal copwlatiown with yow.' In these accusations, the victim of sexual violence becomes the guilty party – *you asked for it*. Modern readers, especially those who have endured such violence themselves, will find an uneasy familiarity with this evidence presented against Annaple.

Annaple confessed to first meeting with the devil at 'the tyme of your widowhood, before you was married to your last husband'. Between husbands and newly grieving, she met the devil while travelling over moorland. Her confession tells of meeting the devil on the coal hill, on the beach, and at the 'Croce of Muirstane', the sister stone to the Witches Stone. She danced at the stone to the devil's pipe music, and there was lots of ale – seven gallons at one gathering. After this heady, violent time with the devil, she settled down, married again, and was widowed once more. The bizarre stories of her confessions were perhaps a defiant offering in the face of what she perceived as ridiculous, trivial charges. Five people were tried and executed alongside Annaple – Margaret Pringle, William Craw, Bessie Wicker, and two women named Margaret Hamilton. They were all widows, with the exception of William Craw, who was an 'indweller', or incomer, to Bo'ness. The day and time of their execution is recorded exactly as Tuesday 23 December 1679, 'betwixt two and four o'clock'.

In the wake of the executions of 1679, a woman named Agnes Stewart was arrested and held in the tolbooth. When asked for accomplices, she named those who were already dead, executed in December of that year. When that wasn't enough, Agnes named others as well, including Elizabeth Scotland, Elizabeth Hutchenson and Bessie Gibb. It's impossible to know why Agnes chose to name these women as accomplices. The hackneyed story of accusation is often written off as neighbourly squabbles or jealousy. In the case of Agnes, though, I wondered if she might have named these three women, one of whom was wealthy and connected, in the hope that they could perhaps help free her.

Bessie Gibb was the spouse of a wealthy skipper, and after she was arrested, she hired an advocate who petitioned the central government in Edinburgh on her behalf. She protested the ruin of her good name and the disgrace of her husband and children. She argued that given the difficulty of proving witchcraft, there was no local judge competent to try her. She knew of none who could name her as an accomplice. If any had named her, the accusation was 'extracted from imprisoned and tortured witches who for their libertie or promise of favour would dare to delate persons of the greatest integritie and qualitie in the Kingdom their persecutors could suggest'. If anyone had named her as a witch, they had been tortured and would have named anyone their tormentors might have suggested in exchange for their freedom. Given the persuasiveness and logic of Bessie's argument, one wonders at the fate of the six executed in Bo'ness four months before, found guilty using the same methods and with similar 'evidence'. There is no way to appeal a death sentence already carried out.

The women being interrogated sometimes told stories of the devil as a husband. The two Elizabeths saw him as a kind of beloved. Though both were married or engaged at the time of their interrogations, the devil features in their confessions as another beau. Elizabeth Hutchenson worked in a shop where the devil would visit her like a trysting teenager. He appeared as a gallant young man, hanging about, and disappearing whenever someone would come into the shop. He gave her pearls and jewels, and promised to be a good husband to her. She offered him a vow: 'I am thyne and thow art mine.'

Elizabeth Scotland was a merchant's widow, and had been due to be remarried before her interrogations began. The devil promised her he would be a good husband to her, and we are left to wonder if her other husbands – the one she buried or the man she pledged to wed – also promised the same. As she sat before her interrogators, she might have wondered about broken promises. On which side, exactly, was her most intimate ally?

Men of Bo'ness – the minister, skippers, and maltmen, or brewers – conducted the trials. They knew the accused. The Elizabeths were wives and fiancées of other skippers and merchants. Their jury was made up of their husband's peers. Perhaps in these portrayals of the devil as a suitor, the accused wanted to convey a message of wifely irony: the devil was no supernatural embodiment of all evil. He resembled a human man, much like the ones sitting in judgement before them.

Of the twenty-eight suspects rounded up in the hunt of 1679–1680, all those interrogated in the latter half of the proceedings, including Agnes, the two Elizabeths and Bessie Gibb, were acquitted. After being imprisoned and tortured, the accused were returned to the communities that had orchestrated their ordeals. The surviving women, traumatised from their experiences, would have frequently seen the men who had condemned and brutalised them. The reality of survival, not only of torture but ostracism in an insular seaside community, is often glossed over in discussions of this history. Though freed, they remained prisoners of war in a battle that raged long after their official exoneration.

All over Scotland, there are stones and markers to those burned at the stake, but what marks the lives of the survivors, like these women in Bo'ness, Keddie Liddell in Prestonpans, and many others? In our commemoration of the lives of the accused, we often fixate on their violent deaths at the pyre. The reality is that the accusation, interrogation and trial could be traumatising and, in many cases, as fatal as an execution. The terrible journey from accusation to interrogation offered few escape routes. Some women managed to flee, while others were banished. Many died of their wounds or privations while in prison. A very small minority won their freedom through appeal and acquittal. Once accused, the likelihood of survival was grim, yet some did survive.

Of all the confessions in the Bo'ness hunt of 1679–80, the words of Elizabeth Scotland struck me most vividly. She called the devil by a fairy name, 'Robin,' and met him at a dam where a woman had died by suicide. She remembered in detail what Bessie Gibb wore: a red coat; a black hood with a veil of 'pearling', or silk lace, over her face; and a plaid about her shoulders. In this glimpse of Bessie, we see an affluent, fashionable woman who made an impression on the merchant's widow imprisoned beside her. The confessions are a wealth of such tantalising details. They hint at how these adopted ancestors saw themselves and each other. Elizabeth perhaps admired the delicate silk lace of Bessie's veil or her red coat; the dark, saturated colour was the cutting edge of fashion at the time. Were they things Elizabeth wished she had?

I look for the damned place where Elizabeth Scotland met the devil, the 'suicide falls' mentioned in her confessions. Such a place appears in the ballad 'Gil Morice'. The song tells the tale of a woman who dies by suicide after being betrayed by the suspicions and violence of her husband. It's the stuff of Greek tragedy or modern soap opera. In the nineteenth century, Francis James Child included a version of 'Gil Morice' in *The English and Scottish Popular Ballads*, noting it was printed in 1755. The ballad is no doubt much older. It's not too much of a stretch to imagine Elizabeth Scotland might have known a version of the tune, and perhaps the falls at the River Carron, where the wife in the ballad kills herself. The dams and waterfalls of the River Carron, ten miles west of Bo'ness, are legendary. One waterfall was once known as 'Lady's Loup', or lady's leap, and legend has it a woman drowned herself there.

I leave the Witches Stone of Bo'ness and travel west to Carron Falls, arriving with time to spare in the long late-summer evening. The River Carron has been dammed for centuries, initially to power mills and later for iron works during the Industrial Revolution. I walk the path to the dam; it's a good day, pain-wise, and I'm milking it. I want to make tracks, to soak up the negative ions at the falls, and find a shared landscape with Elizabeth. All the rosebay willowherb has gone to fluff, looking like hundreds of little distaffs losing their roving. The sound of power tools and the smell of burned hair cut through any pastoral fantasy I could summon. I pass warning signs for asbestos-contaminated ground surrounded by defiant baby oak trees. Another sign warns of 'deep excavation'. Ripe elderberries nod, looking like clusters of black pearls, the kind of jewels the devil might give to a merchant's wife.

Power lines hum above and I pass an abandoned brick hut before I decide to double back. Giant butterfly bushes hold out their last blooms. Painted ladies and bees gather in the petals. I've interrupted their seance; they scatter. A massive boulder marks the steep way to the falls. I know enough not to scramble down such descents, lest I become the next doomed lady, yet the distance down wouldn't be enough to kill you. It's not that high up. Maybe the lady leaping is not a suicide at all, but something else. The falls are dwarfed by the roaring weir, and I am baptised in its mist. Beyond, a secluded pool glimmers with coins of light. Out of the corner of my eye, I see her leap: a dark brown arc of trout, swimming upstream to spawn.

13

In the Margins

Bessie Dunlop, Lynn Glen, 1576

'Sche was gangand betuix hir awin hous and the yard of monk-castell, dryvand her ky to pasture and makand hevye fair dule with her self, gretand verrie fast for hir kow that was deid, her husband and chyld, that wer lyand seik in the land ill, and sche new rissine out of gissane.'*

> – Bessie Dunlop's confession of her first meeting with the spirit Thom Reid.

Records of the witchcraft trials in Scotland are bundled into the Witchcraft Papers, housed in the National Records Office in Edinburgh. These records span 137 years of witch-hunts and are only some of the interrogation notes and trial records for cases of witchcraft accusation. They contain confessions and occasionally the fate of the accused. Other records, such as 'pre-trial material', or confessions collected under torture, are yet to be fully indexed.

While researching Bessie Dunlop, I enquire again at the National Records Office. The pandemic and layers of bureaucracy foil my attempts to access these scraps of documentation. I'm not an academic; I can't have access. I persist, and I'm referred back through arcane information architecture to webpages that I have already seen. I'm missing essential folio

---

* She was going betwixt her own house and the yard of Monkcastle, driving her cow to pasture and making great sorrow with herself, crying very vexed for her cow that was dead, her husband and child, that were lying sick and the land ill, and she just recovering from childbirth.

record numbers, and some of the documents I'm searching for have been repaginated. I am trapped in the infinite, elliptical galleries of Borges' 'The Library of Babel', and I haven't even left my house.

I return again to secondary sources, nineteenth-century transcriptions of the original trial records. Historical societies and antiquarians diligently copied these records verbatim for their peers, and they are an invaluable resource, but I want to study the originals – the Witchcraft Papers themselves. Perhaps because it's denied me, I want it even more. As the pandemic lockdown eases, and others are going to pubs and getting haircuts, I'm holed up, writing and researching. The Witchcraft Papers take on fantastical proportions. Are the secrets that elude me tucked inside? From the outset, I've been an interloper in this historical discussion. There are few leads and even fewer conversations. Information is guarded jealously by those who keep it, and the fragments I snatch away feel illicit. In the lonely years of the pandemic, my longing takes on strange forms, bound up with reading books. The intimacy of the page replaces the physical immediacy of friendship. I know the Witchcraft Papers are no friend, but I want to hold their pages with gloved hands and sit with their physicality.

In my quest to view the Witchcraft Papers, I also begin to imagine the National Archives as a bureaucracy befitting Terry Pratchett's Ankh-Morpork. My email queries wake the sleeping golem of the Archives, and scans of some of the documents appear in my inbox. I consider the images of the 400-year-old handwritten pages, the official record of ghosts. How might this book smell? How are these pages bound, and how much space do they occupy? Are they large and unwieldy, or tiny, like an illuminated book of days?

Cunning woman Bessie Dunlop and her *bodach*, a ghostly old man by the name of Thom Reid, are grains of sand among thousands in the records of the National Archives. I study the scanned documents of her trial. An ominous mildew stain crawls up one page. On another, a drop of ink takes the shape of a duck. Beneath, the words of the ghost named Thom Reid appear: 'Gude day Bessie.'

The notar at Bessie's trial added a series of decorative dashes, as if to say, *There is more*. He scored a dark slash over an error or two, a quick scarring of the otherwise beautiful hand. Smudges of dirt and smeared ink mar the fluid script, the flourishes of a remote language, like something from a grimoire. To read it will take incredible patience. The final few words on the page are hidden, folded in shadow against the scanner. Light shines through the pages, illuminating the script on the reverse like the lamps in Borges' library, their light insufficient but incessant.

What do I think I will find here, on these pages from 8 November 1576? Am I hoping for some shred of Bessie secreted in the scans? Will I find a scrawled note that other scholars have missed? The electronic medium heightens the forensic nature of the document – it's a specimen under glass, a slide for a giantess's microscope. At a glance, the writing appears like bacterial cells dividing in orderly lines. The scan makes the page look like skin. The paper would have been made of linen rags, washed, fermented, beaten and pressed into sheets. The ink was made of oak gall, the larval casing of the oak apple gall wasp. The hollow fruits were crushed, soaked, their tannins strained and blackened with iron sulphate. The script was originally a bluish black. Now, it's the colour of dried blood. The fate of Bessie Dunlop is written in the margins: 'Convict, and byrnt.'

Historian Sir Walter Scott transcribed Bessie's confession in *Letters on Demonology and Witchcraft*. He imagined the queen of the fairies as an earthy Titania sharing a small beer on a 'clumsy bench' with the 'peasant's wife' Bessie Dunlop. Bessie believed she knew and understood otherworldly beings, particularly her dead relative, a ghost called Thom Reid. This has been termed 'fairy belief' by scholars. Fairies are the dead, land spirits or other liminal beings. The Kirk demonised them and anyone who claimed knowledge of these beings as a witch. Bessie was a healer and cunning woman who believed the source of her knowledge was fairy-given. Scott dismissed these skills as 'petty arts of deception'. Initially, I thought perhaps he was right, and yet Bessie persuaded me otherwise.

I find Bessie's trial, one of the earliest recorded in Scotland, transcribed by nineteenth-century antiquarian Robert Pitcairn in his exhaustive *Ancient Criminal Trials in Scotland*. Pitcairn retained the Scots language and aberrant spellings. In the 1833 edition, the records have a Gothic font with Pitcairn's notes in contrast – simple, serifed. Reading them, I eavesdrop on a lively correspondence between Bessie, her interrogators and Pitcairn. My own notations became a fourth voice. Pitcairn believes that Bessie's fairy-ghost, Thom Reid, is either a 'phantom of a disordered brain' or an actual man, a 'heartless wag' playing a 'fatal' joke on her. Pitcairn also claims Bessie was tortured, but that any mention in most records is brief. Though ordeals such as sleep deprivation or other tortures are not mentioned in Bessie's records, these common tactics were often intentionally elided in official accounts, and her words must be read through this invisible veil of suffering.

Her interrogators believed her visions were real and threatening to the Kirk and state. The interrogator, chancellor, and other men in power sitting in judgement were fascinated by Bessie's Thom. In their war on the devil, Thom represented a link to enemy territory. They looked for satanic intel, asking Bessie what Thom thought of the 'new law', or the reformed religion of the new Kirk. Thom said it was 'not good; and that the old faith would come again but not as it was before'. This old faith is perhaps Catholicism, folk belief, or a mixture of both.

As she offered her confessions, Bessie not only spoke for Thom, she also revealed much about herself. Her tale is one of extreme hardship and ecstatic states, with a ghost story at its heart. Bessie Dunlop was a mother of several children and a wife to a man called Andro Jak. They lived in Lynn Glen in Dalry, near Paisley in the Western lowlands. When Bessie first saw the ghost of Thom Reid, she was recovering from giving birth to another child who would die. She was grieving for a dead cow, too, and surrounded by sickness. Her husband, her child, and even the land itself were ill. Still, she worked hard, driving her other ailing cow to pasture. Through this haze of pain and grief, she saw a grey-bearded man dressed in fancy, outmoded clothing: a coat with voluminous sleeves, stockings gartered above the knee and a hat with silk laces. He was the spectre of a man who had died in a field with 6,000 other Scots at the Battle of Pinkie Cleugh in September 1547, thirty years before Bessie's trial. This battle was a bloodbath: the English slaughtered Scottish soldiers even as they retreated, and it became known as Black Saturday. This was Scotland's final battle as an independent state, part of the war with England called the 'Rough Wooing'. The last formal battle before the Union of Crowns in 1603, it was a catastrophic defeat for Scotland.

The spectre of war looms large in the confessions, and perhaps Bessie remembered news about this battle from when she was a girl or young woman. Bessie, like most of our ancestors, lived in a world of trauma and shadow: grief, privation, and literal darkness. Without electric light, half of life was spent in the murk of moonlight and candlelight. Sight uncorrected by lenses produced a world of vague forms. Other senses heightened, as well as new ways of seeing in darkness. Witchcraft scholar Emma Wilby argues these and other hardships presented the physiological grounds for involuntary visionary experience. Bessie endured the pain of childbirth, year after year. She lost multiple babies and children. The land was 'ill', and she had just come from childbed; she would have been suffering from hunger, trauma and grief. This ever-present grief created a fatalism, a constellation of beliefs that are alien to us now, even in the time of Covid-19. Waking visions brought on by extremity could provide consolation or instructions, perhaps even consulted in a process beyond our modern imagining. Scholars of this history, such as Wilby, Ginzburg and Pócs, have argued for an acknowledgement of the spiritual complexities of the lived experience of those accused of witchcraft. What we might see as hallucinations or the mind playing tricks were part of their world, as real to them as physical phenomena understood with the five senses. Bessie's visions as glimpsed through her confessions are larger than any ontological debate that might explain them.

Bessie believed Thom was a real presence. Hers is not just a story created to appease her interrogators; it's a glimpse of visionary experience. When she first encountered him, Thom Reid knew Bessie and hailed her by name. She replied, 'God speed you, goodman.'

Thom asked why she was crying for 'any worldly thing'.

She answered: 'Allas! Have I not great cause to make great dule [sorrow]? For our geir is trakit [stuff is worn out]; and my husband is on the point of dead, and a baby of my own will not live; and myself at a weak point; have I not good cause then to have a fair [weak] heart?'

He told her that she has 'crabit', or angered, God and she must make amends. He warned that the child, two sheep and her sick cow would die 'before you cume hame', but her husband would mend and be well. Thom left through a hole in the wall at Monkcastle, a place near Lynn Glen. The opening was so narrow that 'no earthly man could have gone through, and I saw I was something fleit [scared]'.

Over the course of four years, Thom Reid appeared periodically, and always at noon. He asked Bessie to be an intermediary for him. She was to go to his living relatives and 'bid them . . . mend their offences that they had done'. He gave her details to include so that his kinsmen would know the message was truly from him. She was to remind them of the day before Black Saturday when they went by the kirk of Dalry, and he bought a pound of figs, wrapped them in his handkerchief and gave them to his kinsman before they went to the battlefield.

Thom met Bessie at the hawthorn at Dalmusternock, a place not far from her home. Hawthorns, or thorn trees, are fairy trees, marking liminal spaces, but they are also meeting places for lovers. Might their otherworldly shade mark not only a door to the otherworld, but also an expansive privacy where stolen moments of intimacy were possible? In the repressive society of early modern Scotland, the shelter of a hawthorn must have been a powerful place indeed. Thom 'tarried a good while with her'. His was a strange wooing; he doled out cures, information about stolen objects, and the stings of future misfortunes, yet he wanted more from her.

'Do you trust me?' he asked.

'I would trust anybody who did me good.'

He promised her a new cow, horses and other things, and all he asked was that she renounce 'the faith she took at the font'.

'If I should be revin at horse tails [dragged by horses], I would never do that,' she said, but she promised to be true to him.

It wasn't enough for Thom, and he went away angry.

Bessie's interrogators asked if she had ever been in a 'suspect place' with Thom or had 'carnal dealings' with him. She declared 'not upon her salvations and condemnation', but that he 'would have her going with him to Elfhame'.

Thom appeared at her house and pulled her away by her apron strings up to the top of a hill. He told her not to speak and not to be afraid as he showed her a party of twelve 'good wychtis' – wights or spirits – from the court of Elfhame, or fairyland. There were four men dressed as gentlemen and eight women with fine plaids wrapped around them, 'very seemly like to see'. He promised her they would 'make her far better than ever she was'. They greeted her: 'Welcome, Bessie, will thou go with us?'

'I see no profit to go that kind of gaittis [go down that road] unless I knew what for,' she answered.

Thom asked if he wasn't enough for her: 'Sees thou not me, both meit-worth, claith-worth [well-fed and finely dressed], and good enough like a person . . .?'

She answered, 'I dwell with my own husband and children and could not leave them.'

He was 'very crabit with her', and replied as a spurned lover, 'if that's what she thought, she would get little good of him'.

Though she saw the lips of the fairy company moving, they didn't speak. They disappeared in 'an hideous ugly fowche [scurry] of wind'. She laid sick until Thom came back from their company.

Any services Bessie provided – healing, premonitions and the finding of lost things – were achieved through Thom. He advised how to help a sick animal or a child that was 'taken away with an evil blast of wind, or elf-gripped'. Thom gave her herbs and told her how to use them, 'out of his own hand'. Salves were prepared in a mixture that was powdered and sifted or 'seethed' (simmered and poured through a sieve). If the body accepted the mixture or 'drank it in', the patient would mend, but if it were sweated out, they would die.

Some of Bessie Dunlop's clients were wealthy and powerful, like Lady Johnstone, who sought Bessie's help for her daughter. Bessie, through Thom, diagnosed her with 'cold blood about the heart' that caused her to lose consciousness. The cure was a tipple of ginger, cloves, aniseeds and liquorice in strong ale, mixed together. The warming spices, alcohol and sugar, taken in the morning before a walk, worked. The young woman survived, and Bessie was paid in cheese and a peck of meal. But Thom could not provide a cure for all who sought Bessie's help. Lady Kilbowie needed to mend her 'crooked leg', but Thom said it was hopeless, the marrow destroyed and her blood 'dofinit', or dull. He warned that if she pursued a cure, it would only get worse.

Bessie used Thom's insights to find lost and stolen goods. Her confessions are full of the mundane of everyday life, and they are part of a subtle argument Bessie makes in her confession. Would the devil meddle with such minutiae? With Thom's help, she found lost casks of beer, sheets, a pillowcase, woollen hose and serviettes. Lady Blair beat her servants for the theft of her white goods, only to find out from Bessie that her friend Margret Symple had stolen them. Lady Thirdpairt lost the gold tips of her purse strings and had a 'crown of the sun', a twenty-shilling piece, stolen out of her purse. It took him twenty days, but Thom found them. There were limits to Thom's powers. He told Bessie he couldn't find a lost cloak because it had already been refashioned into a kirtle. Finding lost property could be dangerous. The original complaints against Bessie were not for witchcraft, but for false accusations of theft. She claimed two smiths, John and George Black, had stolen plough irons and a bridle. The Blacks seized her, took her to the Lord of Glasgow, and her interrogations began.

Her interrogators asked if she had ever seen Thom 'going up and down the world'. She confessed she had seen him once on market day in Edinburgh. He touched loaves of bread, just like a living person, and laughed when he saw her. She said nothing to him, as that was their arrangement. She also saw him in the kirkyard at Dalry, standing among the people, but she was forbidden to speak to him unless he spoke to her first.

Thom visited her when she was in childbed with her last son – there would be no more children, living or dead. He said, 'Take a good heart . . . for nothing should ail you.' Though she refused to run away with Thom to Elfhame, she was still damned by her association with him. Their relationship was a crime worthy of execution. The last time Bessie spoke with Thom was on a morning after Imbolc, or Candlemas. He told her 'evil weather' was coming. This harbinger forecast not only her murder at the hands of the Kirk, but also the hunts to come. Bessie never renounced her baptism, nor agreed to any fairy bargains. She had every right to expect leniency from her judges, having helped a good many people who could vouch for her character. She repeatedly emphasised that she was simply the messenger. Her interrogators asked her if Thom warned her of the trouble that would come to her for being in his company. He said her neighbours would offer testament to her good character, and she told her interrogators 'that she should . . . be well treated and sent home again'.

*

Bessie's confessions are vivid, but they only render part of her world. I look elsewhere, to ballads again, in search of other maps to her universe. In the ballad 'Thomas the Rhymer', the poet Thomas is shown many things by the Queen of Elfhame during his seven years in her kingdom. Time passes differently in this otherworld. Sometimes, seven years in Elfhame is a moment in the human world, or, more often, those visiting Elfhame for a moment find when they return to the human realm that they have been gone for seven years. Such temporal slipperiness has become a metaphor for the writing of this book. Time expands and contracts with the writing and my moments in the landscape dedicated to dead women. I understand the possibility of knowing unseen things. I commune with beings from other worlds that exist beside our modern rationality. They speak with immediacy, as if we might share a small beer, pull each other by our apron strings, or strike a bargain.

In the fairy realm, there are always rules to follow: don't eat fairy food, don't tell fairy secrets. Obey and you will be rewarded. These ideas manifest again and again in the words of those accused of witchcraft. In the ballad 'Thomas the Rhymer', the Queen of Elfhame is an elegant lady dressed in green silk velvet. She rides a white steed adorned with bells. Bessie's experiences with the fairy realm are far less glamourous. Bessie's contact in

Elfhame was the ghost of a dead soldier named Thom. The fairy queen appeared to Bessie as a stout woman who sat down on a bench next to her bed as Bessie was about to give birth and asked her for a drink.

In 'Thomas the Rhymer', the fairy queen shows Thomas three roads: one goes to heaven, another to hell, but the third goes to fairyland. It is this third road of shifting perspectives that I take as I decipher the confessions and their elusive truth. Their perplexity is as uncanny and taboo as a twilight glimpse of the wild fairy hunt. I marvel at this vibrant dialogue between a woman and a ghost preserved in trial records. Bessie, like other accused before and after, knew the Good Neighbours, the fairies, well. She was witness to the fairy raid at Restalrig Loch, east of Edinburgh. It was 'a company . . . that made such a din as if heaven and earth had gone together'.

In Dalry, Elfhame is not a magical land but a very real place. A cave called Cleeves Cove near Lynn Glen is also known as Elfhame. A map drawn in 1833 shows the cave with two openings to a marvellous network of rooms and tunnels. The map notes a 'wet passage with stepping stones' leading to a 'great court' walled with 'glittering rock'. Other passages, dead ends and 'impassible outlets' lead off this large room. The map ends with a tunnel marked 'unexplored'. It is a place peopled with long-jawed orb weavers, the damask-winged cave moth and perhaps other things at home in the dark. Equipment, experience and skill are needed to traverse Elfhame. I spoke to a friend involved in Scottish Cave rescue, who told me that children regularly go missing in caves. Their ordeal would perhaps feel like seven years lost in the darkness of an ominous court.

It's a warm, sunny day in late summer when I arrive at the Lynn Glen nature reserve. A circular walk meanders through lush woods and waterfalls over a large stream called Caaf Water. At the start of the walk, there is a well-written, sympathetic plaque about Bessie. It describes her as a spaewife. The walk through the glen is a meditation on her life. A family picnics beside a group of giant wooden mushrooms – whimsical garden ornaments that adorn the path into the glen. The wood is verdant with wild flowers, and molten sunlight reflects in the movement of the Caaf Water. Pools between white water teem with tiny fish, and the river hisses over rocks draped with hemlock water dropwort, the most poisonous wild plant in the UK. I wade out into the falls, the water misting over me. On the banks, delicate purple vetch twines about the pink delirium of soapwort and the white froth of meadowsweet.

At the northern section of the circular walk, a bridge marked 'Troll Bridge' crosses over Caaf Water. Here is Bessie's simple memorial – a rough-hewn bench carved with her name. Myriad offerings are secreted away in nearby trees: ceramic fly agaric mushrooms, hearts woven with bark, resin fairy houses, and a rusting necklace of stars. Something has happened in folk memory over the intervening centuries since Bessie's execution: she has become an intermediary between the known and unknown, someone to watch over our wishes and rest our griefs. She is an unwilling martyr to our modernity, the disenchantment of the world.

In a sunny clearing, herb robert grows in profusion, named after the fairy Robin Goodfellow. The five-petalled flowers nod as if to say, *Here you are; I knew you would come*. Fairies have not always been these picturesque Victorian fantasies. Before they were tiny winged children wearing harebell flowers for hats, they were ominous, inter-dimensional beings, and the plants and places in the landscape that marked their territory were treated with fear and respect. Walking back through Lynn Glen, the return is lined with hawthorns, markers of doorways to the otherworld.

I reach the tumult of greenery before a rock formation called Peden's Pulpit, named after legendary prophet Peden, who preached at this rock a hundred years after Bessie's execution.

He was an outlaw Covenanter, part of the Protestant movement that signed a National Covenant rejecting the changes Charles I made to the Scottish Kirk. Charles I declared war on the Covenanters, and this prosecution is called the Killing Time. Ministers like Peden preached in caves and other wild, secluded spots, like this glade with its cuboid wedge of stone above the falls. The white noise of the falls rushes behind me. A profusion of dense clusters of yarrow surround the rock; they turn their heads to the sun, pale pink into white. Peden wore a mask while he was on the run, and I have seen this uncanny preacher-man's disguise in a dark case in the National Museum. Peden's mask is made of leather and human teeth, and human hair forms its long wig and beard. In the shadowy museum case, the eye-holes are ragged and hollow. When it was worn, with the light of a man's eyes behind it, *good enough like a person*, might it resemble Thom Reid?

14

Red Threads

Christian Shaw, Paisley, 1697

'Dost thou hear this now? Thou turnest thy back to me, when I am telling the truth . . .'

– Christian Shaw, in the second-hand account
*Narrative of the Sufferings and Relief of a
Young Girl in the West, with Trial of the Seven
Witches Condemned to be Executed at Paisley*

The city of Paisley borders Glasgow to the west, eighteen miles north of Bessie Dunlop's Lynn Glen. I make my way on the winding A-road, still basking in the sylvan glow of the glen. I've come to Paisley to see the monument to the dead, set in the tarmac at a four-way intersection, marking the place where the ashes of the accused witches were buried. The memorial in Paisley is a horseshoe embedded in the intersection at Maxwellton Cross – it is a striking contrast to Bessie's dedicated bench in the fairy glen. A memorial plaque surrounds the horseshoe. Sculptor Andrew Stoddart created the framework for the apotropaic object in 2012. In folk belief, horseshoes deflect ill will and can be used to guard against capricious fairies. They were put on stable doors to prevent witches riding horses at night. Hang a horseshoe upside down, though, and the luck will run out. A local legend claims the horseshoe at Maxwellton Cross seals Paisley's luck and guards against the curse of those who died, executed as witches.

The place of execution is called Gallow Green, now a patch of lawn in a housing estate with a wide well at the centre, an incongruous hellmouth of dark stone. The black water inside is depthless, covered by a grid of wire. There's evidence to suggest that it may have been the beginnings of a coal mine that never came to fruition. Three hundred years ago, there were no apartment buildings hemming in the green. It would have been expansive, able to hold a large crowd for the popular entertainment of executions. Burning provided a public spectacle; it was a degrading way to die. It's said that before the elderly Agnes Naismith was strangled and burned here, she shouted a curse: the people gathered to watch her die and all their descendants, of which perhaps I am one, would never prosper. Her cry was so powerful, it echoes through space and time.

There is witch tourism here: the 'Paisley Horseshoe Ghost Tours' operator is located a block away. Across the street from Gallow Green, there is a small New Age shop selling tumbled stones with various properties, the obligatory plastic angel and dragon figurines, and incense. When I ask the owner about the monument in the crossroads, she shifts her weight behind the counter, pulling her cardigan around her, and looks at me blankly. I had assumed, perhaps, that the shop received foot traffic from the ghost tours that regularly visited? I broaden my question to encompass all the witch-hunts across Scotland and she nods. 'Yes, many people died.'

There's nothing more to be said. I buy a brass bell and her son, a stocky ginger lad in a plaid shirt and chinos, rings me up. This is a typical reaction I have received on my travels throughout Scotland. Most people I speak to distance themselves from this history, and many refuse to speak about it at all.

I wait for the signal at the traffic lights between Maxwellton Cross and Gallow Green Road. It's a sunny day, cloudless. I run into the centre of the intersection and have three seconds to take it in: a finely engraved brass disc framed by a wreath of flagstones, set into the road with a new horseshoe at its heart. I do this over and over, pressing the button for the light, waiting and running in. Like a spell: I go round it widdershins, crossing from the north, first. From the south, I step lightly, guarding my eyes against the sun. I cross east to west and back again, leaving an offering of rowan leaves.

On one pass, I'm able to read the lettering around the bronze frame: 'Pain Inflicted. Suffering Endured. Injustice Done.' An appeal for forgiveness and luck twined together, with fear to bind them. Breathless on the busy A-road, I wonder at the passive voice of the inscription. Who inflicted the pain, endured the suffering, and did the unjust things? Was everyone and no one to blame? Is this atrocity just part of a past full of superstition and terror? Scotland is still asking itself these questions as it tries to reconcile itself with the thousands who died during the witch-hunts.

*

The seventeenth century was a time of run-out luck in Scotland, as if all the horseshoes had been hung upside down. English occupation coincided with the nightmare of the witch trials. Famine slashed the population. Dearth, as such scarcity was commonly known, came in waves. Marching armies and the diseases they carried, as well as emigration, all took their toll. The 1690s was a dark decade in a terrible century. In August 1696, *dreich* days of sunless chill and gloom stretched on into autumn; it was the worst of the seven Ill Years, a time without summers. This coldest year of the Little Ice Age brought failed harvests. Thousands were driven from their homes by starvation, reduced to wandering far from the villages of their births to beg from strangers. There are heart-breaking accounts of women pleading and furious at market. Unable to afford the price of grain, they had to return empty-handed to the hollow-eyed stares of their starving children. This decade ended with the disastrous Darien Scheme, Scotland's attempt at colonial enterprise on the Isthmus of Panama, land belonging to the Guna people. Twenty per cent of the nation's savings was invested in the doomed project. When the English and Dutch divested from the scheme, it collapsed, bringing down the Scottish economy. The state reacted to these apocalyptic years with zealotry. In 1697, accused heretic Thomas Aikenhead, an angry young seminary student, was executed for blasphemy. He voiced his atheism with a degree of impiety so threatening that the Church-state had to make an example of him. His trial took place as the witch-hunt in Paisley began.

Seven people were found guilty, but many more were accused, including children. The role of children in the Paisley trials is particularly troubling. James Hutchison, a retired minister in Paisley, preached to the Commissioners of the Justiciary before they reached their verdict on the accused. In his eyes, witchcraft was a family matter. Hutchison argued that, just as Christian parents raise Christian children, witches will inevitably raise the devil's servants. He urged the Commissioners to issue death sentences for all.

Of the large number indicted, three men and four women were tried. The seven accused shared an advocate named James Robertson. He questioned whether the evidence presented might have reasonable and natural explanations. His arguments were part of a far-reaching surge of national doubt. The executions in Paisley marked the last major witch-hunt in Western Europe. A realisation in public discourse formed: if demonic phenomena had natural and not satanic causes, how could a legal case be built around such accusations? Despite Robertson's enlightened advocacy, the seven on trial were found guilty and sentenced to be strangled and burned at Gallow Green. The Reverend David Brown preached to the doomed on the day of their execution. Concerned with their salvation, he said, 'Ministers weep over you, as if we were seeking from you some great thing for ourselves.' But even as he spoke of redemption, he seemed convinced the accused had refused 'Christ's mercy' and were damned. The Reverend declared himself 'free of their blood' because they had 'murdered their own souls'.

I return to the metaphysical dilemmas of Reverend Brown's speech to the accused before their deaths. What 'great thing' might he have longed for as he wept over the accused? And how might one murder one's own soul? Is the eradication of the accused – their bodies burned to ashes and their memories forgotten – something beyond the Christian concept of eternal damnation? There are no answers, only horror. Perhaps this is where the devil sits, in the void of departed faith where angels and God fear to tread. The devil of the confessions is often a human man taking advantage of a credulous woman. This is the easiest way to conceptualise the bagpipes-playing, ale-drinking being who demanded sex as part of a bargain on which he would renege. What is strangely missing from the satanic parties mentioned in many of the confessions and trial proceedings in the Scottish witch-hunts is any sense of fantastic menace. Though I put the devil out of my mind for most of my life, I share this traumatic fear with these tormented ancestors.

The devil lurks between the lines of consciousness, watching me. My rational mind knows the devil is an invention of the Christian church, a demonisation of the land spirits and old gods. He's a rock star, made glamorous in films like *The VVitch* and in folk-horror images on mugs and T-shirts. He's cool, the animus to the hip witch's anima, celebrated in neopagan spell books like Gemma Gary's *The Devil's Dozen*. Or he's a figure of fun, a Krampus tweet at Christmas or a Black Philip meme. Despite my rational understanding of the devil, this party monster still fills me with dread. For the most part, the devil of the confessions is merely a happy-go-lucky charlatan, a cad and a rogue. There is no modern conception of demonic power, no cosmic horror – until we get to Paisley.

The devil of the Paisley witch trials is something we recognise from horror films like *The Exorcist*: demonic possession, full-blown Regan-esque episodes of abjection. In Paisley, the devil could woo even a child. He might live inside her, slowly devouring her soul. This is a fitting metaphor for the experience of living with trauma. I project this idea on to the story of the young girl Christian Shaw, scapegoated for the hunts at Paisley.

According to the official story of the Paisley hunts, an eleven-year-old girl orchestrated an industrious deception, inciting a witch-hunt in Paisley, feeding the flames of the pyre with wild claims of demonic possession. She manipulated all around her – her family, doctors and the judge and jury in the witch-hunts in Paisley – causing the deaths of seven people. A sensational seventeenth-century pamphlet invented this fiction, and an eighteenth-century lawyer elaborated on it. The story was novelised in the 1970s, and is repeated endlessly on ghost tours. The myth is so all-encompassing, any evidence to the contrary so buried, that to doubt it feels like a stretch of the imagination. The story of Christian Shaw exemplifies the struggle we have in separating the wheat of history from the chaff of legend – the fictions that survive possess a potency that persists even down the centuries.

The pamphlet *Narrative of the Sufferings and Relief of a Young Girl in the West, with Trial of the Seven Witches Condemned to be Executed at Paisley* was published in 1698, a year after the trials. The *Narrative* is fiction based on hearsay. It describes Christian Shaw suffering delirium and violent fits. She was seen flying about the house, dancing and tearing off her clothes. Grown men couldn't restrain her. She pulled stuff from her mouth – burning coals, plaited hair and dung. She quoted scripture and mumbled a ballad of her sufferings in regular meter. The *Narrative* explains that the old woman Agnes Naismith was working with Katherine Campbell, a Highland incomer and newly hired housemaid, as part of a coven from the village. They bewitched Christian, who later named other tormentors: a midwife named Margaret Lang who lived on a smallholding with her husband and her daughter; a man named John Lindsay, and his brother James. The witches 'crew' also included a second John Lindsay, a tenant farmer, and Margaret Fulton, a 'beggar wyfe' blamed for several unexplained deaths in the area, among others.

The author of the pamphlet is unknown, but the *Narrative* may have been written by Christian's uncle, John MacGilchrist, town clerk of Glasgow, using notes from the case. Another possible author is local minister Reverend Andrew Turner, who led the Tuesday fasts intended to help Christian, and who may have transcribed the tale for the meeting of the Presbytery of Paisley held on 14 April 1697. The reverend was perhaps inspired by an account of the Salem witch trials printed in London in 1693. The Salem account is strikingly similar to the Paisley *Narrative*, even down to its title. The Salem account bears the unwieldy name *A Brief and True Narrative of some Remarkable Passages Relating to Sundry Persons Afflicted by Witchcraft, at Salem Village which happened from the Nineteenth of March, to the Fifth of April, 1692*. Both pamphlets feature the supposed demonic possession of a young girl.

In 1785, ninety-two years after the trial and publication of the *Narrative*, Hugo Arnot laid out his imposter theory in his *A Collection of Celebrated Criminal Trials in Scotland*. Describing Christian, he wrote, 'she seems to have displayed an artifice above her years', and 'this actress was abundantly pert and lively'. Arnot cites the *Narrative* as his source, claiming there was no written record of the trial, yet these records exist in the National Records of Scotland archives. The documents include evidence of her condition as given by Reverend Brisbane, but Christian herself made no statement, and her situation was not central to the official legal case against the accused witches. Arnot's portrayal of Christian has become definitive in this history – she is the infamous 'Bargarran Imposter'. This cynical myth persists to this day.

There is documentation of other children in Renfrewshire exhibiting similar behaviour in the shared hysteria of the witch-hunts in Paisley, but Christian Shaw is the most well-known. The traumatising impact of the hunts was far-reaching, and those who witnessed the executions and survived the hunting of family members, friends and neighbours were changed by it. Modern medical historians pathologise Christian's behaviour. They surmise Christian suffered from conversion disorder, a condition where acute stress manifests as seizures, paralysis and other physical symptoms. Current research affirms that many people diagnosed with this disorder have a history of childhood sexual trauma. In the *Narrative*, the devil appeared to Christian as a 'naked man . . . having much hair upon his hands and his face like swine's bristles'. He repeatedly tempted her with gifts: fine lace, good health and a 'brave man to marry'. The devil said she must renounce her baptism as part of the pact, and he asked her to become a witch. She refused with a great show of mania. Christian's sexual descriptions of the devil are concerning from a girl living in the sexually repressed culture of the 'godly society' of seventeenth-century Scotland. The bristly nakedness in her description of the devil suggests a young girl's sexual encounter with an older man.

During the witch-hunts of the seventeenth century, the church defined the demonic pact as sexual intercourse, an imagined sex crime. One wonders how much of this did the public know and understand? What forms did this information take when passed to children? It's possible that children like Christian Shaw struggled to understand the sexual nature of the pact, yet it was part of their reality. Her private hell will never be fully understood – was she the victim of molestation?

I've guessed at her life. What did children make of this devil that made grown men so fearful they would burn others to ashes? Perhaps Christian's survival manifested as a question of identity: *If this devil wants me, might I be a witch, too? What does it mean that he has chosen me?* The devil's mark is also the predator's mark. A survivor must live with the question, *Why was I marked as quarry?* This question manifests in the body in myriad ways. It changes you, perhaps on a molecular level. As a survivor, this is something my body understands, even if my mind refuses. We carry these questions with us for the rest of our lives.

Later, as an enterprising young woman, Christian Shaw was pivotal to Paisley's early prosperity. The daughter of a laird, her family had many privileges that continued into her adulthood. She married Reverend John Miller in 1718, but was widowed just three years later. She went on a European tour with her mother, where she saw fine thread spun in Holland and brought these ideas back to Paisley. She set up Bargarran Threads, which became the Coats company. She died at the age of fifty-two in 1737, and is buried in Grey Friars Kirk, Edinburgh. Bargarran House stood in ruins in the nineteenth century, visited by touring Victorians excited by the sensational story of Christian's demonic possession. The ruins would have intrigued the Victorians' gothic sensibilities. They claimed the girl's chamber remained mysteriously untouched. Her carved oak bed frame was whole among the rubble, and a fine tapestry, faded and green with moss, still hung on a crumbling wall. This room and its surrounding ruins are gone now, as is the truth of her story.

*

Many of us hope to find distant relations that root us to the past, but we may not like what we discover. Genealogical charts and DNA swabs will only go so far in providing a personal past beyond our immediate family. A cultural inheritance is larger than the confines of biology and genetics, and presents more challenges. I share a surname with Christian Shaw. While researching her, I wrestled with the nature of ancestry. I know very little about my family tree, and will never know if I share any direct descendants with Christian, yet I still claim her.

How might I explain myself, a woman from another land across the sea, one of the vast Shaw clan? I might start with paisley. In the 1980s, I was a teenager living in midwestern America. We had no geography classes in my schooling, and I didn't know Paisley was a place. The Persian teardrop motif is named after the town in Renfrewshire, which produced textiles with this design. I was into the Paisley Underground – jangle pop from the West Coast of America. I loved paisley patterns, and would doodle them in my school notebooks with a ballpoint pen, filling the swirls of ornate apostrophes with floral art marks. They were part of my threadbare inheritance: I had a paisley maternity dress in day-glo sixties wool, a hand-me-down from my mother's pregnancy with me, and a green-and-pink paisley scarf that belonged to my grandmother, Flora Gunhild. She would wear it babushka-style, tied beneath her chin to keep the rain off her curled hair. I still smell her face powder, just vaguely, in its web, though it has been a good forty years since she wore it.

I have very little from the people who came before me, but I do have some things. Before her death, my aunt sent me a copy of a photograph of an extended family standing in front of a barn in Wisconsin. My grandmother is at the centre, the only one smiling. She is young and well put together, in a crisp, white lace blouse, threading her long-fingered hands together in a gesture I recognise – I do it, too. I have a few rings she gave me. One is a large emerald, worn down to a dimpled, matte surface; she washed dishes wearing it. Where did this woman, a domestic servant and Skilsaw factory worker, get an emerald like this? She also gave me a rocking chair that belonged to her grandmother. It's narrow and creaky. I have had it re-caned, and one arm is broken. My black cat sleeps in it, and I like to think she is sitting on the lap of my great-great-grandmother.

There is another thing willed to me – my grandmother's fear of the Christian devil. She was a survivor of two World Wars and the Great Depression, the widow of a suicide, yet the thing she feared most was this supernatural being. As a child, I associated her courage and long life with her faith, which included a profound degree of superstition. She wouldn't eat devil's food cake, devilled ham, devilled eggs. Supernatural danger was mixed up with human men, and she made me promise never to kiss a man. I was just a little girl, and the promise seemed a simple one to keep at the time.

My grandmother taught me all the prayers I know. They are few, but the King James version of the Lord's Prayer remains. During the hunts, some interrogators asked accused witches to recite the Lord's Prayer as proof of their innocence. I can still mouth the words, the inevitability of their order, *for thine is the kingdom, and the power, and the glory, forever.* The repetition is more satisfying than the meaning. I feel the solid rhythm of syllables, the last of my inheritance, a list of petitions and empty promises. Before Matthew iterates the prayer, he warns that it is a heathen practice to vainly repeat words just for the sake of hearing one's own voice. He cautions against a performative Christianity devoid of actual Christian ideas. I wonder at this heathenry – how widespread it is. I am guilty of it, repeating the words just to see if I still have them. I wonder, if my life depended on it, could I say the prayer in front of an audience of hostile men in black – lairds, ministers and councillors from the capital? Would I forget the first bit and go straight to asking for mercy, a stay of execution: *give us this day . . .?* I couldn't actually say *forgive us our debts, as we forgive our debtors.* No doubt the accused prayed, but perhaps not the Lord's Prayer on demand. I imagine it as something we share – a raw call to the universe, a yelp into silence. *Deliver us from evil.*

Writing this history is like mending a tear, but as I stitch it up, the rend grows and the questions multiply. My grandmother taught me to sew. Her needles are tucked up in an envelope printed with a picture of a gilded lion, with a window cut in the paper. They're old; she had them for over half a century. We used red thread, unrolling it from a wooden spool and cutting it with sharp little scissors. She licked the end and twisted it before threading it through the needle's eye with her arthritic hands. I was fascinated with the spool, as old as her needles, decorated with links of a chain: the Coats Threads logo. We sat in a tiny apartment in a tall public housing building in the middle of America, *kingdom come*. She taught me how to patch and mend, *thy will be done*. We started with dolls' clothes because they were simple and small. Then, we mended socks with a darner shaped like a wooden knob for a door that will never open. We stretched the fine wool over the surface and joined the rend while we practised praying. I said it after her: *Hallowed be thy name*. One word, one stitch follows the next, whole again.

15

Roadside Shrine

Marion Lillie, Spott, 1698

'Of *withered beldames auld and droll, Rigwoody hags would speak a foal.*'[*]

— Robert Burns, 'Tam o' Shanter'

'Tam o' Shanter' is Robert Burns's famous witch poem, recited in Scotland at Halloween. Much of Burns's work is a record of Scottish memory, taught in schools and performed during Burns Night celebrations. What was once part of the oral tradition is codified in his verse. In Seamus Heaney's poem, 'A Birl for Burns', he says that now even the simplest Scots words must be *glossed*, or checked in a dictionary, but 'In Burns's rhymes they travel on/ And won't be lost.'

Tam's spirited tale is at the root of modern, burlesque fantasies surrounding the witch. The poem details a jolly image of the Scottish witch as a capering old woman, cackling with glee and dancing to bagpipes. The poem's 'wither'd beldams' are in stark contrast to the reality of women tortured and killed for the crime of witchcraft. Burns based his rollicking poem on an anecdote from a farmer who claimed he was once chased by witches. 'Tam o' Shanter' was published in 1790, just seventy years after the last woman was executed for witchcraft in Scotland. Though Burns would have had no personal memory of women at the pyre, surely he would have heard stories from others who did remember. These bleak, gruesome incidents were quickly folded into folklore meant to entertain.

[*] 'Of crazy, old, and withered grandmothers, these tough hags would put a foal off their milk.'

A drunken Tam witnesses a sabbat in a haunted kirk and then flees from the witches chasing him. It has Burns's characteristic saltiness, full of vernacular texture and sex. The narrator jokes about Tam getting drunk after market day, lingering too long and avoiding his wife's advice. The iambs canter along as the narrator paints the scene: Tam gallops for home through a downpour, drunkenly singing as he approaches the haunted kirk of Alloway in Ayr. The chapel is ablaze with light, music, and dancing. The narrator describes the details of the sabbat: coffins standing upright and opened like cabinets, with the dead in their burial finery, each holding a light. A makeshift altar displays a murderer's arm in gallows' shackles, unchristened babies, bags made of lawyers' tongues, and rotten priests' hearts. Before this altar, the devil pipes and old women dance, casting off their clothes, sweating and stinking. The speaker interjects a voyeuristic wink; he thinks if only the old women were teenagers, he would have given his only pair of *breeks,* or trousers, for a peek at these young girls. He wonders why the sight of the old women doesn't turn Tam's stomach.

One woman catches Tam's eye; she wears a 'cutty sark o' Paisley hairn', or short shirt made of Paisley linen. Tam is excited by how revealing her shirt is, and he roars a catcall at her, 'Weel done, Cutty-sark!' [Well done, short-shirt!]. The festivities immediately end, his cry marking him as an intruder. The witches pursue him and, just before his mare makes it over the running water of the River Doon, a witch pulls off the mare's tail. The poem ends with a moral: if you ever get distracted by drink and scantily dressed women, remember Tam's mare.

The poem sexualises young 'witches' while making a joke of older women, their redundancy painted as repugnant and evil. Darker still, the poem's whimsical tone and fantastic details are far better known than the actual stories of accused women. The same fictions dominate the public's perceptions of this history of atrocity. Is this glossing over of mass death all in good fun?

This question is larger than Burns's beldames, and is central to our understanding of how women – and witches – are represented in the present.

*

Burns died young. Like a Hollywood leading man, he will always be a boyishly handsome thirty-seven. He is Scotland's national poet, but his notoriety is far-reaching, celebrated across the Scottish diaspora. When I lived in Los Angeles, I was removed completely from Scottish history, relishing instead the kitsch of old Hollywood. I wore red lipstick and 'Betty bangs', or a straight fringe. Vintage forties dresses were cheap; the dry climate of California preserved them like treasure in a pharaoh's tomb. I mended and re-mended dead women's dresses and wore them out for cocktails. The downtown I knew looked closer to the elegant dystopia of *Blade Runner* than the gentrified loft space it is now. Those years in Los Angeles were like waiting in an anteroom of hell, wondering about my future. *Am I really damned to this place?* I haunted Hollywood's golden age: drinking dry martinis at Musso and Franks, 'blood and sand' cocktails in the Dresden Room, Scotch neat at the Tam O' Shanter Inn.

The Tam O' Shanter is the oldest restaurant in the city. What passes for tradition in Southern California is often not traditional at all, but a mimicry of the Old World. The Inn celebrates Burns Night with kilts, bagpipes, whisky and haggis. The Tam O' Shanter dates from the 1920s and was Walt Disney's favourite restaurant, the kind of simulacrum on which he built his empire. Modelled after an English country pub, its faux-Tudor facade forms part of the surreal landscape of Los Angeles, where restaurants are shaped like bowler hats or space stations.

Like most Americans, the first Burns poem I ever heard was 'Address to a Haggis'. It was an inauspicious beginning, yet to be redeemed. I still don't get Burns. His lascivious glee and poetic bonhomie is meant for another reader. The sexuality in his poetry is one-sided and off-putting – especially a poem like 'The Yellow, Yellow Yorlin', which deals so casually with rape. The voice I hear in these poems is what poet Liz Lockhead has described as 'sex pest' Burns.

Despite my distaste for Rabbie Burns, his work is full of details of a landscape I share with him, and intriguing linguistic puzzle pieces. In the Burns poem 'I'll Meet Thee on the Lea Rig', the speaker implores his lover to meet him at the *lea rig*, in the gloaming at midnight in midsummer, a transitive time belonging to the fey. Lea rigs, or ridges of unploughed fields, were left unsown for wild oats to grow. They sheltered lovers from dominant sexual norms. Here also is the *lea* of *The Weird Wife o' Lang Stane Lea*, the Aberdeenshire painting by James Giles. Before the Reformation criminalised the practice, sections of unworked land were left fallow for the *Hynde Knight* or fairy king. These 'Goodman's Crofts' or leas were offerings for a capricious land spirit. The lea was a wild place, a sanctuary not just for lovers but also fairies and old women, weird and wise *carlins*. Advisors to King James VI and I suggested all farmers be forced to till their fallow land or it would be forfeit to the King, effectively ploughing under these genius loci. In the sixteenth century, the Kirk scoured the countryside, rooting out suspected witches as well as uncultivated land. The Reformation orchestrated a complete cultural overhaul, changing people's relationship to the land and each other. Older women who could no longer have children – the crones and carlins of the witch trials – were suspect. Like land left fallow, they were perceived to be useless – no longer fruitful or sexually exciting.

Burns's romantic, pastoral lea rig is also a window into the many dimensions of the Scots word *rig*, the ridge formed when land is tilled. It also means spine, as in *rigbane*. The Scots language is poetic and suggests a living earth, where land is body. *Rig* is part of *rigwoodie*, a derogatory word in Old Scots, meaning tough and bony. It's preserved in 'Tam o' Shanter', where an old woman dancing in the kirk is a 'rigwoodie hag' – wasted, devoid of sexual appeal. Marion Lillie, a woman accused of witchcraft in the village of Spott, was known as the 'Ringwoodie Witch', and indeed 'rigwoodie' was often used in conjunction with 'witch' by witnesses in seventeenth- and eighteenth-century cases of slander and criminal proceedings. Rigwoodie can also mean 'one of durable frame, one that can bear a great deal of fatigue or hard usage', or 'stubborn or obstinate . . . wilful, perverse'. As a noun, it's also 'an antic, caper, feat of agility'. Marion Lillie was not a witch, but perhaps she *was* rigwoodie – bony, wilful and hardened. She could have been single-minded and sprightly beyond her years, different at a time when such things could cost you your life. Or perhaps she was none of these things, and the name was applied well after any memory of her was long gone.

Words are alive; they change and grow, reseeding themselves in our verges with all their wild hybridity. *Woodie* has several meanings in Scots: the binding of a broom, a willow switch, a marriage bond and a gallows. Its meanings are a brief poem of a woman's life, the life of the accused – work and flight, broken bonds, punishment and death. I hear the words shift again: 'rigwoodie' into Marion's 'ringwoodie'; rig turns to ring, like a circle dance. Witches were said to dance in rings at the sabbat, but this formation is also a folk dance, the oldest dance.

I have my own fantasies about witches and the unbridled joy they embody. Modern self-identified witches tread carefully, reclaiming 'witch' while paying witness to the terrible history of the hunts. It is a tightrope, strung treacherously between fantasy and reality. Like Walt Disney at his favourite booth in the Tam O' Shanter, are we also yearning for a past that never existed? If we turn our backs on the glib, salacious treatment of the witch, is there nothing happy left for us?

I imagine it anyway, the ring dance, knowing perhaps I turn atrocity into merriment. Do I repeat the very mistake I find so distasteful in Burns's 'Tam o' Shanter'? Surely Marion danced and sang, held hands with neighbours and friends, and laughed. I see her step it widdershins, the echo of her rigwoodie footsteps in time with the distant song of a ceilidh.

*

There is a stone dedicated to Marion in her village of Spott in East Lothian. It sits incongruously in edge land, what is known as 'soft estate' – a term used by the Highways Agency to denote verges of natural habitat lining roads. The marginal land-flanking roads are modern lea rigs, makeshift nature reserves, shelter for myriad wildlife and vast species of wildflowers. Recently, local authorities have recognised the importance of this space as a micro-ecosystem. Rather than cutting back the verge, it's left to flourish. This is a small piece of a larger re-wilding dialectic, a renewal of an ancient but long-dishonoured contract between the earth and the people living on it. The soft estate is a fringe of earth left fallow for bees, insects, the fey and the ancestors. At Marion's stone, this green verge also shelters our memory of the accused.

The companion to the verge is often the hawthorn, that ubiquitous marker of liminal space – the tree where Bessie Dunlop met Thom Reid. The hawthorn is a plant of edges and boundaries, a line between this world and the otherworld. A tree of contradictions, its lovely white flowers smell like decay. Margaretha Haughwout is an herbalist, permaculture programmer and member of the Coven Intelligence Program, a 'techno-botanical coven' or collective of artists and scientists whose mission is to 'track and encourage emerging revolutionary ecologies of work between plants and machines'. Haughwout sees the hawthorn as an ancestral plant. She describes the tree as a healer of broken hearts and explains its history as a plant used to mark the new boundaries between enclosure and common land. Hawthorns were planted as fences, their thorns a very real barrier. In her words, the common people were driven off their land and became 'a landless proletariat'. The story of the hawthorn is one of fences, removals and clearances. As people were moved off their lands, sometimes walking long distances, hawthorns could feed them. Once known as the 'bread and cheese tree' and 'wayfarer's friend', walkers could stave off hunger by folding a berry into a leaf and eating it. A common plant of the hedgerow, it's also friend of the modern hedge witch.

Many self-identified witches are at home in this wild verge. We are hedge witches – philosophers on the margins. In neopagan ideation, the hedge witch is solitary – we work without a coven or group. We might also be good at riding metaphorical hedges, jumping all sorts of boundaries. We're at home in metaphysical lea rigs, working with the spirits of plants and places in a reparative, visionary tradition. Much neopagan thought has distorted the history of the witch-hunts, mining a complex and traumatic period selectively for its own purposes. As in popular culture, some neopagans are guilty of conflating the fantasy of the witch with the reality of those real people who suffered and died. Yet, some who reclaim the name 'witch' are radical thinkers, examining intersectional feminism, ecology and spirituality through folk practice and history.

The hedge witch is a shamanistic figure or spirit worker travelling between worlds. This exploratory way of thinking is often dismissed as modern woo-woo, but the way of the hedge witch is more than a New Age fad. Historic roots of ecstatic folk practice are coming to light in modern scholarship. Academics researching the witch trials, like Carlo Ginzburg and Emma Wilby, have found parallels between the spirit helpers of seventeenth-century cunning folk and animist belief in pre-Christian shamanic visionary traditions. Recent work by scholar Julian

Goodare has examined evidence of a native shamanistic tradition recorded in Scotland called the cult of the 'Seelie Wights'. Wights are otherworldly, in-between beings or fairies able to exist in different realities simultaneously. In the cosmology of this cult, the fairy *raid*, might also be a road or a spirit journey. This is a traditional shamanistic ritual where the soul can leave the body and visit other worlds, communing with spirits of the land and ancestors. Indigenous people throughout the world accept this notion as fundamental to life, yet it remains an ontological debate that we, as a culture, are perhaps not ready to consider thoroughly. Spirituality is often suspect in our 'enlightened' society, or otherwise seen as best left to the experts of organised religion. What cannot be argued is the fact that working with the spirits of place or, more reductively, *fairyland*, was once part of Scottish folk belief.

*

Marion Lillie's stone is a roadside shrine. The 'Witches Stone' is part of a long tradition of wayside altars found in many cultures. Sacred space for the traveller is common in Shinto Japan and on Catholic pilgrimage routes. Other roadside shrines are erected to honour victims of accidents or as waymarkers. They become a witness to the journey itself, a place to pray for safe passage. Travelling has always been a dangerous undertaking. Like Grissell's stone in Dundee, the Witches Stone in Spott may represent a benevolent presence, a chance to make good with these adopted ancestors – people accused as witches.

Tracing the story of this Witches Stone led me to land dedicated to pilgrimage, hedge witches and Burns's poems. Like the stones of Bo'ness, Forres and Monzie, it's another ancient menhir, an unassuming rock in the ground. It may be the remnant of a Neolithic site, the fragment of an ancient monument. The provenance of waymarker stones in Britain is often attributed to a giantess dropping them from her apron, like the Giant Bell's stones on the North York Moors. In Scotland, they are some-times said to be rocks thrown in a battle between a witch and the devil.

The Witches Stone of Spott lacks a poetic lineage. It wasn't carried by a giantess nor thrown by the devil. In 1913, it was almost entirely covered in road scrapings. Until recently, a sign stood behind the stone claiming: 'Marion Lillie, the Ringwoody Witch was burnt here in 1698. The stone is reputed to stand on the site of the burning of the last witch in the South of Scotland.' The original sign and iron fence may date from the 1950s. The stone was not intended as a memorial, but it has since taken on this distinction. Of the people tried for witchcraft in Spott, we know very little. Marion Lillie was unmarried, named as a witch by another person, and her fate is unknown. In *The Old Statistical Account of Scotland* (1791–9) I found a request to try her, as well as a mention of 'many witches' executed atop Spott Loan in 1705, followed by the ominous statement, 'the Presbytery meet at Spott as a committee of censure'. Eight residents of Spott were accused of witchcraft in the seventeenth century, with the majority executed in the witch-hunts of 1661. There is no record of Marion's execution.

In recent years, the original, mistaken sign has been replaced. The new sign reads: 'This stone has become a place to commem-orate those local people who were once persecuted as witches. We cannot undo the hurt, but we can let their souls go free.' A group of women and children updated the monument, organ-ised by artist Allison Weightman. Weightman is a master of *raku*, a Japanese style of glazing that roughly translates to 'happy accident'. Echoes of cup-and-ring marks, lunar symbols, and Neolithic petroglyphs mark her work, and she is most noted for vessels punctuated with bullet holes. Weightman was shot in the leg as a child, and these vases and bowls are visceral objects exploring the violence of gun crime. They are a far cry from the floral tiles she helped create with local children for the Spott

Witches Stone. These ceramic tiles surrounding the dedication plaque feature the impressions from pressed local botanicals with medicinal properties. In her research, Weightman found Marion was arrested for witchcraft twice and, after her second accusation, she died while awaiting trial. Weightman told me, 'Marion Lillie has a place in my heart forever.' She included medicinal plants in the monument because she 'live[s] by the notion that the healing is out there for us all. Most people have just lost the "feeling".' The memorial reminds us that we are feeling our way toward healing this history together.

I asked another local artist, photographer Denise McNulty, about her relationship to the stone. She returns regularly, and it has become a guiding force in her creative work. 'My time with the stone has helped me deepen my spiritual practice as a hedge witch, which influences and directs my photography working with botanicals and being in nature,' she explained. The new memorial is a 'celebratory, colourful remembrance of lives lived and lost. It is pleasing to know that the memorial [has] not been forgotten, and it is alive and fresh in the minds and hearts of others.' One memorial inspires the next, as one artist's work speaks to another. All over Scotland, a movement began years ago to remember those accused. In many ways, the legal gestures and developments of recent years are just catching up.

*

The village of Spott is east of Prestonpans and North Berwick, on the nub of land jutting into Blackness Bay. As I make my way to the village, the day turns dreich as twilight gathers. The sky is close and dim, the clouds like a sheet laid over a blasted glass dome. I double back through East Lothian with the Firth of Forth and North Berwick on my left. The stone is on the narrow High Road leading into the village, and there's no clear passing place or layby. I realise too late that this roadside shrine is best visited on foot.

After I park, a pair of distant crows break the silence. I find the stone, caged by a small, iron fence, as if it were a creature that could turn into something else entirely if you were to open the cage and break the spell. Without the iron bars, the stone would be easily missed. It's unremarkable, nestled into the hawthorn hedge, the brown leaves of the wayfarer's friend shivering in the wind. A black sign mounted on the bars reads 'Witches Stone', the letters painted in white. Coin offerings fill the stone's quern-like bowl, evidence of those who came before. The tiles surround the stone, full of fascinating details. A ceramic ladybird crawls up the side; pressed images of holly, wild garlic, and other plants ring the plaque. Hawthorn has pride of place at the front.

I visit this stone with the same weight and intention as those before me. The journey of this book is a long corpse road. I repeat the ritual of pilgrimage, knowing I might be the first to brave the whole of this undertaking – visiting the shrines and monuments across Scotland devoted to the accused. I trust I will not be the last. I leave a five-pointed star made of twigs, laid atop each other. They may blow away before another sees them, but it's a sign: *I'm with you in witness.*

16

Come the Shipwreck of the World

Elspeth Reoch, Orkney

> 'Come tak me noo, an tak me a' . . .
> Tak hert, an harns, flesh, bleud an banes,
> Tak a' atween the seeven stanes,
> I' de name o' da muckle black Wallowa!"*
>
>   – Orkney Witches' Charm, recorded
>   by nineteenth-century farmer and
>   folklorist Walter Traill Dennison

As I prepared to travel to Orkney, I read Robert Louis Stevenson's spooky fairy tale 'The Song of the Morrow', and it struck me to the heart. Here was a bedtime story for the woman I am now, at the fulcrum of my life, looking forward and back. 'The Song of the Morrow' is one of his fables, the last of the twenty tales, philosophical puzzles published posthumously. It is a story of cyclical transformations: a young princess, innocent of the world, happens upon 'the loneliest beach between two seas, and strange things had been done there in the ancient ages'. She meets a crone at the tidemark, and the old woman scolds her for not considering her own power. It's as if the old woman casts a spell on her, and the princess spends nine years in contemplation until she is called by pipe song to the same eldritch shore. She finds the crone dancing widdershins, against the sun. In the old woman's ecstasy, she falls on the sand and disappears into 'stalks

---

* 'Come take me now, and take me all . . ./ Take my heart and mind, flesh, blood and bones,/ Take all between the seven stones,/ In the name of the great dark Völva!'

of the sea tangle, and dust of the sea sand, and the sand lice hopped upon the place of her'. The old woman is taken by the sea margin. After learning the 'Song of the Morrow' from the piper, the princess trades places with the old woman.

Not long after reading 'The Song of the Morrow', I found the Orkney Witches' Charm, recorded by the nineteenth-century folklorist Walter Traill Dennison, and I wondered if Stevenson knew of it when he wrote the fable, or if it were just another uncanny coincidence that the two things should overlap so profoundly. In the Orkney Witches' Charm, it is as if we hear the voice of the young woman in the fable embracing her power, and also that of the old woman, dancing on the beach, ready to be subsumed. The charm includes the imperative '*Fae de how o' da heed/ tae da tip o' da tae*' [From the top of the head/ To the tip of the toes]. Many Scottish folk charms of healing and warding involve a promise from the top of the head to the toes. During the witch-hunts, this was demonised as a deal with the devil. I guess at the 'muckle black Wallowa' – might she be a *völva*, a seer in the pre-Christian Norse tradition? Norse influence is ever-present in the culture and folklore of Orkney. The incantation is a call to one who knows and sees, and who has come before. It's a wanton call of devotion that flies in the face of Christian doctrine and the Protestant Kirk's insistence on shame and docility. What's at the heart of these words? Is it just nonsense – part of witch mythology written down by a nineteenth-century folklorist? Or might it be a seed of volition – will to power – with a heady mix of joy and love?

These questions shadowed me as I researched the witch-hunts in Orkney. The Fair Folk peeked from between the lines of the trial documents, as real as the interrogators and the accused. Uncanny men made promises of power. Ghostly visitors stalked and raped. The Fair Folk inhabited hillocks and certain stones – all conspicuous and mysterious landmarks belong to them. Orkney has a lot of those places; the islands are a metropolis of hollow hills and ruined *brochs*, or Iron Age roundhouses. Here, the sea reveals Neolithic houses and then takes them away. It's an archaeologist's polestar, the entire island covered with burial mounds, standing stones, cairns and portal tombs. People have been burying their dead here for millennia. To our seventeenth-century Christian ancestors, who wished to stamp out old folk beliefs, the landscape of Orkney was menacing, full of demonic beings.

In his *Daemonologie*, King James VI and I claimed witchcraft was 'most common in such wild partes of the worlde, as Lap-land, and Fin-land, or in our North Iles of Orknay and Schet-land'. Lapland refers to northern Norway, and the native Sami people who live there were erroneously called Laplanders. To this day, the Sami maintain a strong shamanic tradition, demonised in the seventeenth century during the witch-hunts in Norway. In many works of art and references to the Sagas, Laps or Fins are synonymous with wizards and witches. Women with second sight were called *völvas*, and *seid*, or shamanic trance-work, was 'women's work'. Orkney was under Norwegian law until the fifteenth century, not fully part of Scotland until 1472. The transition from Norse law to Scottish law was not an easy one. The Orkney court established many new laws in the early seventeenth century, including acts against sin and edicts affirming the power of King James VI and I. It was a time of anarchy and rebellion for the islands. The culture of Orkney was seen as 'other' by the Scottish mainland. It was against this fraught storm of change that the witch-hunts in Orkney began.

During the hunts of the seventeenth century, eighty-one people were accused of witchcraft in Orkney, seventy-three of whom were women. In 2020, nine more cases of witchcraft accusation were discovered by Orcadian archivists, so this number is far from static. Women confessed to meeting fairies, and these entities were turned to demons in the official records.

These fairy-demons cast a pall over everything in my life, and I put off writing because I'm afraid of falling into their world, losing my way, and being unable to crawl back up into modern life. While I felt this at every stop on my grand tour, it was researching the Orkney trials that really amplified this unease. The Orkney trials haunt me. The writing is a fairy offer, a gift with a trick. The land spirits say, *You're writing about witches in the landscape! Why not go to Orkney?* And then they see fit to drown me in women's stories so urgent, complex and disturbing that I'm stunned into silent procrastination. The voices of the accused are like a single sack of fairy coins that soon turn to mounds and mounds of gold, filling rooms and burying gardens, on my plate at dinner and crowding my bed. The more I consider them, the more I learn, and the bigger my thoughts on the accused Orcadians grow. How can I wrestle it down, this fell angel, into something contained within a finite number of words? Has the taboo of speaking *Fairy* come to silence me, too? In the end, of all the accused and their incredible stories, their tragic and cruel fates, I choose Elspeth.

*

The record of Elspeth's life ends with her sentence: to be taken to the *lockmane*, or executioner, at Gallow'ha at noon to be 'wirryet at an staik quhill she be deid. And thereafter to be burnt in assis' [strangled at the stake until she be dead. And thereafter to be burnt to ashes]. She was an unwed teenage mother, a survivor of brutal violence and perhaps incest. Most remarkably, she was a wanderer, hungry for knowledge. Elspeth's story roams over the Highlands, and her short life ends in Orkney. Found guilty of 'giiving ear and credite to the Illusions of the Devil' and 'fenyeit herself dum' [pretending to be mute], she was tried and executed for witchcraft in Kirkwall in 1616. There's evidence she may have been involved in the Kirkwall Rebellion of the previous year. Her trial came soon after a time of great unrest in Orkney. Two years before, the Earl of Orkney's twenty-two-year-old son, Robert Stewart, had led a rebellion against King James VI and I and the Earl of Caithness, Elspeth's father's old employer. Stewart amassed 700 rebels in Kirkwall before the King laid siege to the town, pitting one earl against the other. In her confessions, Elspeth mentioned Robert Stewart and his father, as well as Patrick Trail, the father of her child. She saw them all drinking together before the Earl of Caithness's arrival. She was swept up in the events, and it's possible that her trial was politically motivated. She was singled out; her punishments were a deterrent.

Elspeth was born in Caithness, an area in the Highlands encompassing the northernmost tip of mainland Scotland. Before she was orphaned, she may have travelled with her father, Donald Reoch, a piper to the Earl of Caithness. Was she a Highland Traveller, a Summer Walker? In Timothy Neat's book *The Summer Walkers*, he explores the idea that the Highland Travellers are perhaps the direct descendants of the Picts, the indigenous people of the *Gàidhealtachd*, or Gaelic-speaking area of Scotland.

After Elspeth's father died, she went to Lochaber in the central Highlands. She was twelve years old when she had her first encounter with men who she thought were fairies. They came to her as she waited beside the loch for the boat to take her to the other side. One man was 'clad in black and the other with a green tartan plaid about him'. The man with the plaid called her 'an pretty', and promised to 'learn her to ken and see any thing she would desire'. One of these fairy-men promised knowledge, like the proverbial serpent in the garden. To young Elspeth, this had value – knowledge was something she wanted badly. This meeting of two adult men and a twelve-year-old girl casts a shadow over any fairy-tale reading of Elspeth's confession. The man in black warned the other that she was not worth advising because she would not keep a secret, and the man in green said he thought she could, and that he would vouch for her. He advised her to wash her hands and eyes with the sulphurous 'sweat' from a roasted egg. After three Sundays of this ritual, she would know anything she desired.

Two years later, when Elspeth was fourteen, she had her first baby. The father was a man named James Mitchaell who lived in Balvenie on Spey, at the very eastern edge of the Highlands. She delivered the baby in her sister's house, back in Lochaber, south of Loch Ness, near Ben Nevis. She had just given birth to a child outside of marriage, in a borrowed bed, when the second fair-man from the loch paid her a visit. He was the one in black who had distrusted her. Was this a human man, stalking her for years across the Highlands? Or was he a fairy-man? In Highland folk-lore, childbirth was the classic window of opportunity for fairies who wanted to switch human babies with their own: this danger-ous time is filled with fairy lore about abductions and change-lings. Women and children frequently died in childbirth, and fairies were thought to prey on new mothers and their infants. Pain and postpartum depression summoned the uncanny just as effectively as any formal ritual.

The man in black told Elspeth he was the ghost of her kins-man John Stewart, who was slain 'by McKy at the down going of the sun. And therefor neither dead nor living but would ever go betwixt the heaven and the earth.' He stayed with her for two nights, preventing her from sleeping and 'persuading her to let him ly with her'. If she complied, he said he would teach her to *ken*, or know, anything, but that this knowledge would make her mute. He also warned her that if she spoke, 'gentlemen would trouble her . . . she might be challenged and hurt'. The fairy-man behaves like a human abuser, threatening punishment if she tells anyone what he has done. Yet, she experienced this in her sister's house after giving birth. Despite Elspeth being unmar-ried, she would have had family and other women around her. How could a man get past them, into a tiny house, to menace Elspeth? Who was this fairy intruder?

Like many who witness the uncanny in their beds, Elspeth may have experienced sleep paralysis. Might this man have been a spectral visitor in her sleep, one that seemed very real? Her visitor might have been a predatory human man aware of the fatal punishment for second sight and fairy knowledge, or equally aware of the censure and fines for 'fornication'. In Elspeth's experience, he might have been a ghost, a fairy and a man all at once. On the third of his nightly visits, she was asleep when the man in black 'laid his hand upon her breast and waked her. And thereafter semeit to ly with her [seemed to lie with her]'.

In the morning, she was mute. Elspeth had survived her pregnancy, as had her child. She was only fourteen and unmarried. Like Christian Shaw of Paisley, historians have diagnosed her with conversion disorder. Whatever the cause, her silence was real, and it was punished, first by her brother and then by execution by the state for this 'crime'. Her brother beat her with a branks 'until she bled'. When she still did not speak, he put 'an bow string about her head'. He took her to church three Sundays in a row, asking the congregation to pray for her.

She left for Orkney. The confessions give no sense of the fate of her child, nor the reasons for her relocation. The Highlands were not a happy place for her, but in Orkney she was an outsider. She earned money by using second sight to advise people, and she had another child. The father was a man named Patrick Trail, who was wrapped up with political intrigue at the time, as was made clear by her confession – the meeting she described seeing between him and the Earl of Orkney suggests treason, a plot of rebellion against the King.

The fairy-man followed her from the Highlands to Orkney. At their final meeting on Yule, he lay with her, warning her to leave Orkney, a 'Priestgone' country with too 'many Ministeris in it'. This uncanny presence warned her that 'if she tarried she would be hurt'. The notar described the fairy-men as manifestations of the devil, though this was not what Elspeth believed. This fairy-man cautioned Elspeth against the church, his warning a blasphemous detail in her confessions. She found her voice again in her confessions, and it was as if she had to tell her story, even if she knew speaking would kill her. She broke the fairy pact, told all the secrets.

Fairies embody the unsayable, and whether the fairy-man was a human or a dream figment, both would have known these taboos. Fairy bargains in ballads often come with a vow of silence. According to some folklore, even saying the name 'fairy' is forbidden. One must instead address them as 'The Fair Folk' or 'The Kind Knight' or 'Goodman'. In the confessions, *fairy* encompasses the unsayable, lived experience beyond the narrow confines of the Protestant Kirk. What was the nature of Elspeth's silence? Was it self-censure, a fairy curse, dissociative disorder or an assertion of power? Perhaps it was all of these things.

Literary witchcraft scholar Diane Purkiss writes that fairy belief in witchcraft confessions represents something that could not be said under any other circumstances, yet speaking it was essential. The fairy stories told by the accused 'are paradoxically liberating, though told under terrible duress. Duress might even serve as a kind of alibi.' Elspeth was one of several accused in Orkney who lost the power of speech at or before their interrogation. Their silence was demonised, unrecorded. At a time when the ruling men gathered up women's statements in order to kill them, might silence have been power? Mute refusal would be the ultimate in self-containment at a time when women's words were stolen between blows, through the spikes of a branks. In the darkness of a cold cell, silence was sovereignty.

Much of women's history is a long silence. Ours is the silence of erasure. We guess at lives from the mute artefacts – fragments of textiles, a spindle whorl washed up on a beach, a bone comb in a glass museum case, scattered beads and fossilised remains. The witch-trial interrogations break this long

silence in a flurry of agonised voices, singing ballads, telling
fairy stories and repeating the words of their captors. The
confessions are perhaps the richest source of the voices of early
modern folk we have, especially women's voices – and they are
a poisoned well. What can I learn from these terrible fragments? In writing these lives, my own experience surfaces.
Silence is double-edged: it might protect you, or it might damn
you. Invisibility has its uses. In speaking my experience as a
survivor, I risk being marked, a target for further threats and
violence. Emerging from a long silence, I write. Their last
words give me a voice.

*

I travel over the Highlands to the edge of mainland Scotland.
Night descends as I reach Scrabster, with its yellow-trimmed
lighthouse and ferry terminal, a squat industrial building. There
are only a few of us going to Orkney tonight. It's off-season, and
late. For those who live on the island, this ninety-minute trip is a
commute, but for me, a journey by sea, no matter how short, is
a kind of transformation. I sit on one of the wire chairs affixed
to the outer deck of the ferry, whipped with salt spray and wind,
the hood of my anorak pulled up against the cold. The black sea
is rough, the roll of the ferry coursing deep inside me, a molten
power. If I claim any ancestry, it is this: I was born with sea legs,
a descendant of seafaring people. As I stare towards the conver-
gence, the horizon heaves up and down like a black plaid tossed
over the night.

The daylight in Orkney is painterly, a filtered gold shifting to
steel grey or shroud white. The sea can play with the sun, creating *gaas*, or sundogs – rainbows behind the sun. On the night I
arrive, clouds roil and dance over a crescent moon pinned to the
sky. The moonlight is equally captivating. An almost-rainbow,
what the Doric dialect of north-east Scotland calls a *watergaw*,
shimmers in the distance, nacre on the mussel shell of the moon.

Past Kirkwall, the road beyond the headlights moves foot by foot in absolute darkness, like a velvet curtain.

Orkney, just to be on your flat expanse is magic. Like the speaker of the Orkney charm, I could give myself heart and lung, from the mound of my head to the soles of my feet, to this network of sacred islands. There are moments when I feel a power surge connecting me to the land. It's a hot flash, a heart-ache, or it's in the fierce wind of the north-east – an Orkney wind, too. These rough gales have the force to sweep through you, to scour away both your equilibrium and ego.

I arrive at the converted barn where I stay when I'm on Orkney. Quiet, tidy and modern, with a view from the kitchenette to the hills and the wide sky. I make an easy fire and sit beside its blaze, spreading my arthritic feet over the heated slate floor. Perhaps this is why I come here, year after year, to feel the warm stone, and to sit with a fire that asks nothing of me but that I be here. Tomorrow, I'll find the monument on Gallow'ha. As I lay my head down to sleep, I dream of a lonely beach at midnight under a full moon, tracing a circle in the sand with a staff of driftwood. I work at the tide's ebb, a narrow channel in time. In the dream, I'm myself and other: a rebel and a Summer Walker with dark secrets, the piper's daughter, Elspeth.

The monument on Gallow'ha, now called Clay Loan, isn't hard to find, but it still feels hidden. The slab is set into the top of a low hill surrounded by modest, modern houses. Behind it, a box hedge marks the location of the gallows. The stone is carved with a stylised sundial and the words in Orcadian dialect: 'They wur chuest folk', meaning 'They were just people.'

Buried beneath the carved slab of Orkney sandstone is a time capsule containing sound files, stories, as well as a witch bottle made by potter Andrew Appleby. It's filled with tears from Orcadians involved with the memorial, collected in cotton wool, along with a few cat hairs. The capsule beneath the memorial is a community outpouring. I want to know more about what is inside the capsule, and what kind of ceremony went into the memorial's placement, so I make my way to the Orkney library, where documents related to the memorial are kept. The white lace and ribbons that adorned the monument at its unveiling now wrap the documents in the archive. I work my way through them, reading, taking notes and listening to sound files in which diverse voices of Orcadians share their grief, outrage and wonder. Perhaps most moving are the letters addressed to the accused penned by adults and children from Orkney. My favourite element of the time capsule is a song sung in a round by Kate Fletcher and Corwen Broch, based on the traditional song 'Drive the Cold Winter Away', a tune the accused might have known. Fletcher and Broch's composition combines the traditional lyrics with words from the confessions. At a workshop day with members of the community, lines of mournful poetry contemporary with the witch trials were collaboratively reassembled into lyrics:

Mark me not to endless pain
I am condemned e'er
or come the shipwreck of the world
the heavy state of night
Happy they that in Hell
feel not the world's respite.

I imagine the lilting melody, its interwoven voices, playing in the earth of Gallow'ha beneath the carved stone slab. The sound mingles with buried tears, echoing through time and space, the last ingredient of this healing spell.

*

I need air and I need light, and Orkney has these things in abundance. The Loch of Stenness on the Mainland is an otherworldly place on this late afternoon, the sky reflecting in the unbroken surface of the loch, skimmed only by a pair of swans, gliding past. Here is another world so like ours, I could fall in and through, perhaps finding myself in a fairy place.

The Ring of Brodgar stands watch. As I draw closer, the megaliths seem to turn and face me. The thinnest slabs appear hollow-backed, like the Fair Folk in the old stories. The heather has gone brown, dry enough to feed a bonfire now, perfect kindling to light the peat at Gallow'ha. Silhouetted against the horizon, the stones mark slow time, aeons. They are hoary with lichen. I walk the circle widdershins, stick in hand. My pace is pained and sagely. Clouds hang low, already shifting imperceptibly to a lacy scatter. Fallen stones covered in sheep droppings dot the ring, while others are sheared down the centre as if lightning-struck. Flecks of pink mica glimmer. Some of the stones have random initials and serifed graffiti with now meaningless dates – 1924. Those marks erode, leaving the stone scaled, scarred with fissures like a living thing.

Booming base fills the circle from the stereo of a passing van. A baby cries somewhere in the distance. I share this landscape with the accused. Elspeth *stravaiged* – roamed. No doubt she knew this ancient ring of stones on her adopted isle. What did she make of their oracular grandeur? I slide down next to one of the stones. As the sun sets, a shadow forms beside me. Together we watch the last, clearest light before nightfall, a golden hour glancing over the hills.

17

Rough Music

Janet Cornfoot, Pittenweem

'All I have confessed, either of myself or of my neighbours, were lies . . . God forgive the minister. He beat me with his staff when I was telling the truth. Alas, alas, I behoved to say [I was a witch] to please the minister and bailies. For Christ's sake do not tell them that I have said so, else I will be murdered.'

– Janet Cornfoot, 1705, as she was
visited in prison by three noblemen

In 1705, in the seaside village of Pittenweem, on the Fife coast, a woman named Janet Cornfoot was lynched by a group of men. They beat her and dragged her by her heels through the streets. They hung her from a rope between the mast of a ship and the shore, and some swung at her while others pelted her with stones. After three hours, they laid a door over her, weighting it with stones until she was crushed to death. Afterwards, her body was repeatedly run over with a horse and sledge. None of her attackers were arrested.

*

Twenty-eight people were accused of witchcraft in the years of witch-hunting in Pittenweem. The families of the accused bore the expense of the executions; husbands and sons were served bills for the murders of their wives and mothers. Those women released after being imprisoned were expected to pay back the cost of their keep during interrogation. At the time of Janet's Cornfoot's lynching, witch-hunting was ending in most of Scotland. In the hunt of 1704–5, the minister and local

217

government received permission for a trial, and the accused were to be taken to Edinburgh, yet the trial did not go ahead. Some of the accused were bailed out by friends, while others were released after they were examined by the Lord Advocate James Stewart, the same prosecutor who condemned Agnes Naismith and others in Paisley, and also issued the death penalty for young blaspheming Thomas Aikenhead. Stewart decided there was not enough evidence to try the accused in Pittenweem. Despite the central government changing its mind about the trial, the local minister and many men in the village wanted to punish someone for the crime of witchcraft. Some historians claim the mob violence against Janet Cornfoot in Pittenweem was a singular event, but there is evidence of similar persecutions in Prestonpans and Dornoch. In 1750, several women were seized in Tain by a gang of men who dragged them from their beds and cut their foreheads with an iron tool, scoring them 'above the breath'; making this incision was thought to remove a witch's spell and Sir Walter Scott refers to the practice persisting into the nineteenth century. We will never know the extent of these late vigilante hunts. This 'rough music', or folk justice, was rare, but it became more common as it grew harder to obtain final authorisation for a formal trial from the Privy Council.

In June 1704, Minister Cowper and the local government of Pittenweem sent a petition requesting permission to try 'several witches' held in the tolbooth. The men in power claimed to have a case of demonic possession on their hands, and cited the case of Christian Shaw in Paisley in their application. After an argument over some nails, a young smith accused a woman named Beatrix Laing of bewitching him. He named others, including Janet Cornfoot and the elderly Thomas Brown, who died of 'hunger and hardship' in the tolbooth despite his daughter bringing him food.

In July, the central government in Edinburgh granted commission for a central trial, but by August, five of the surviving accused had been bailed out by friends and released. The survivors spoke of their ordeals: one of the accused was kept awake for five days by being pricked with pins until she bled profusely. Beatrix was pricked, endured sleep deprivation and was held in a 'dark dungeon' alone, for months. She petitioned the Privy Council, detailing her tortures. In October, the central government demanded the release of all the remaining prisoners. I found no mention of Janet Cornfoot. What we do know, though, is that before Janet's escape from the tolbooth and her death at the hands of an angry mob, she was imprisoned and interrogated.

The *Annals of Pittenweem* note that word of her confessions spread and some 'gentlemen' visited her in hopes of seeing a real witch, but came away disappointed when they realised she wasn't actually a sorceress but merely an imprisoned woman. While she was in the tolbooth, three 'noblemen' came to visit her, and one of them recorded Janet's plea for help in an anonymous letter. Afterwards, the Reverend Cowper threatened her and commanded she be kept in a room with a low window. The anonymous nobleman writing his account of Janet's story theorised that this would have enabled her to escape, and that the minister had a hand in organising the mob that killed her. That night, Janet climbed out of the window and ran. The minister and bailies offered £10, a large cash reward, to find her. She managed to make it to a village eight miles away; the local minister there sent her back to Pittenweem. According to the nobleman's account, she was delivered to local men in Pittenweem and Reverend Cowper told them to do as they wished with her. The family of the minister, as well as the magistrates, watched Janet's murder, coming to the scene to encourage further violence. Janet Cornfoot's daughter hid in their home as her mother was killed, afraid she might be next.

I've woven together Janet's story from multiple conflicting sources. Several witness accounts detail the violence of her death, but the events leading up to those last hours are unclear.

Cornfoot is sometimes spelled Corfitt, Corset, Corphat or Crowfoot, perhaps after the wildflower crowsfoot, which has caustic sap and is also known as 'cursed buttercup'. Her death is well recorded in the burgh records, wedged in between 'Riot at a Likewake' and 'Insult to the Town Clerk', and in the Privy Council minutes from February 1705, titled 'Murder of a Pittenweem Witch'. The bailie was meant to secure her in the tolbooth, but when he arrived, she was not there. Later, he found her 'half dead lying within the sea mark'. The bailie ordered four men to carry her to a house in town, but none of her neighbours were willing to take her in. The men left her at the door of another accused woman named Nicolas Lawson. She had named Janet as a witch while she was imprisoned six months previously. At Nicolas's door, Janet 'changed her head cloaths', presumably because they were bloodied. There, she was attacked again, 'cast into a gutter, and a door laid upon her, and stones upon the door, whereby they putt out her lyfe'. The Privy Council minutes take pains to describe the attackers as 'incomers' – 'a school boy, actors and two English men who fled afterward'.

An anonymous pamphlet entitled *A Just Reproof*, published in 1705, defended the events in Pittenweem. The writer argued that the witch problem was international in scale, mentioning trials at Paisley, Salem and 'Lapland' (Vardø in Finnmark, Norway). With an undercurrent of outrage against the inaction of the central authorities, the author goes on to detail the confessed guilt of all the accused of Pittenweem, including Beatrix Laing and Janet Cornfoot. The writer defends Minister Cowper and concludes Janet was not deserving of a Christian burial because she had renounced her baptism.

In October of the same year, Beatrix Laing was afraid she might also meet a violent end. She asked for a guarantee of protection from the Council, but was denied. Her request renewed the inquiry into 'Cornfoot's Murder'. The Privy Council ordered all those involved in Janet's murder be held in the tolbooth in Edinburgh and charged the local magistrates with failure to keep the peace.

Four years later, Beatrix Laing was arrested again, and the central government issued permission for a trial, but there is no record of the proceedings. A year after Beatrix's second arrest, an interesting development appeared in the record. The bailie William Bell apologised and compensated Beatrix Laing for her sufferings. He said his actions were 'proceeded on idle stories', and he acknowledged his 'rashness in having a hand in the foresaid wroungous imprisonment . . . I beg God and her [Laing's] pardon.' William Bell's apology and compensation is a singular event. Of the hundreds of cases I have reviewed, this is the closest to a statement of contrition or reparations I've found on record.

*

I sleep in a chain motel on the edge of Dunfermline. The room is hospital-like and utilitarian; anywhere you go, the same art hangs on the wall, with the same mauve textiles. This room could be anywhere in Britain, but I am back in Fife. Beneath the lurid purple nightlight, I dream of Pittenweem. It looks nothing like it does in pictures. It's not a picturesque fishing town with colourful cottages lined up along the shore. In my dream, it's a green, craggy place of cliffs and stones, with the tide gone out. I'm flying over it, like a bird, a drone or a witch, and I'm looking for Janet Cornfoot – *Crowsfoot* – cursed buttercup. The stark line where sky meets sea might be a Neolithic coastline, an ancient topographical map come to life. There are no humans here, no sign of modern habitation. I don't find her.

The pressure to forget unendurable truths – both personal and societal – is great. Private memories and public historical records both take on a dubious quality. Did they really happen? In our collective forgetting, much has gone missing. Traumatic memory is a shattered lens – the pieces don't fit. This erasure doesn't just excise the terrible moment. Swathes of the past darken with it. I confront my own missing time as I piece together the violence visited on Janet Cornfoot. Years dim in the distance, lost. I write at the hotel room's narrow desk, but the words are subsumed in the blurred chaos of my own past sufferings. What I survived is in no way comparable to Janet's ordeals, but my limbic system identifies with her. I'm beyond fight or flight – frozen. The hard, necessary thinking crumbles and the work shuts down.

I decide to take a shower, start the day again. Wreathed in the sour smell of mildew from the shower curtain, I turn away from the mirror and sink on to the cold floor. The white towel tucked at my heart comforts me, smelling vaguely like nag champa. A memory returns like a loan long forgotten: you are sixteen, an incense smell, the upholstery of the back of a car where he's over you, before you disappear. The vinyl is not quite black, the thick stitches gone grey with age. There will be blood. You'll tidy away that spilled self – a piece of your soul irretrievable now – mopped up and all the rags hidden. You nurse a bruise in the centre of your forehead – lurid, dark purple, astoundingly symmetrical. You don't remember how you got it, but you endured much at the hands of this abusive boyfriend. You are alone and somehow you manage it, the cleaning, the hiding; this realisation is the red thread connecting you to our past, to me.

I get up, wipe down the mirror with my fist, get myself together. I tie up my hair, put on my dress and the lipstick that smells like fairy cakes. I pack my bag. When I leave, the lights go out behind me.

I hike down the cliffside to the coastal path in Pittenweem, through the brine-blackened umbrels of hogweed and dense cloud, as the tide rolls in below. The grey waves lap at three low concrete walls built into the tidal waters, an outdoor swimming pool, empty in the October gloom. I try to imagine the hardy people of this place going for a swim on a summer day, staying in for as long as they can stand it, and perhaps warding their children's bodies against hypothermia, an inoculation against the sudden shock of the sea. Maybe there is laughter. As I stand looking out over the coastline, I recognise these cliffs from my dream, primordial and brooding. In the distance, the gaily painted fishing cottages, perhaps once the residence of some of the accused, line the shore. Further in the mist, I see the natural port, rows of dark stone where Janet Cornfoot was lynched.

I keep searching. I'm groping in the dark for something, a clue in the landscape, a marker. For lack of a locus, I go straight to the cave, a Christian shrine that was once a prison for accused witches. I wonder if it's perhaps the 'dungeon' where Beatrix Laing and others were imprisoned in solitary confinement. I haven't been able to corroborate this idea, but it feels like it could be true. Winding my way from the shore into the village, I pick up the key to the cave door from the Cocoa Tree Cafe, a pretty little chocolatier's shop in a village of lovely shops and charming streets. A part of me wishes I could ignore those who suffered and died here, and just enjoy myself. Maybe this is the point of my long, winding trek, spanning years and the length and breadth of Scotland. It will be ending soon, with one more stop in the Highlands and then Edinburgh. If I can build a monument of words – create a humanising space for this horror – I'll be home.

I walk past the tolbooth and the kirkyard. The cave entrance is on Cove Wynd below. It strikes me that the topography of the tolbooth, kirkyard and cave is at the heart of Janet's story. Pittenweem is named for the cave, now called St Fillan's. *Pett*, meaning portion, is the Pictish root of many Scottish place names, and *weem* comes from the Scots Gaelic word for cave, *uamh*. The shallow, naturally formed cave was rediscovered in 1900, when a plough horse fell into it. It is set into a craggy yellow stone cliffside, dotted with a rock garden full of pastel succulents. A naive shell-and-glass mosaic in the shape of a cross gives the cave the feeling of a Victorian seaside shrine, but this addition is modern, made by the school children of Pittenweem in the early 2000s. The doorway-shaped opening dates from the seventeenth century, though the iron door, decorated with another cross, seems as new as the mosaic.

Electric lights on a motion sensor flood the place as I enter. Before me, plastic flowers decorate a shiny new altar. The ancient, crumbling cross has clearly been brought in from some-where else. A contemporary sign tells the story of St Fillan, whose glowing arm illuminated scripture in the darkness of the cave. For much of this cave's history, it was used as a dump, until it was cleared out in 1935 and consecrated to St Fillan. It's now a place of worship, with a Christian myth attached to the cave, claiming St Fillan used it as a place to convert the Picts. This legendary figure is the patron saint of the mentally ill. Church lore says he spent most of his life as a hermit here, and that the unwell could be cured by being chained in the cave overnight. A natural spring oozes from the wall, trickling down the stone, as if the cave were weeping. Carved 'beds' and nooks for candles lie empty. Beside me, rough-cut stairs ascend into darkness. Despite the domestication of the floodlights, plastic flowers and ersatz Christianity, it retains an otherworldly austerity. At some point in the cave's history, the sea would have washed up to the entrance. A sign requests silence. For whom? Perhaps the urge to scream in this place is universal, and the Church knows it. I howl into the fluorescent brightness, and the dripping stone answers in echoes.

I leave the key with a family arriving at the cave. The children scramble into its shallow depth, shouting. I wind my way past the tolbooth where Janet was held. It's my moment of dark tourism, the first and last stop on a private ghost tour. The ghoulish curiosity I normally resist floods in as I look through the broken window into blackness. Its mouldy smell of disuse is beyond dereliction. Here is a place of suffering. I shake off the feeling and make my way to the harbour, where a few tourists watch the fishing boats bring in their catch as the autumn sun sets early, casting everything in a warm ember glow. In the seafood restaurant beside the docks, the cooks with striped aprons carefully ponder the evening's menu. Two meticulously carved pumpkin lanterns, one with a skull and the other with a little kirk, wait in the window for dusk to fall, ready to be set alight.

*

Ten years ago, a group of Pittenweem locals proposed a memorial to the accused. Half the village voted in favour, but it was rejected by the council. Seven years later, a memorial was erected in Pittenweem, but it is not for Janet Cornfoot, nor the others imprisoned with her, but for fishermen lost at sea. The Pittenweem Fishermen's Memorial Association erected a bronze statue of a woman dressed in Edwardian clothing, gazing longingly at the horizon while her son clings to her skirts, looking up at her. The life of a fisherman is fraught with danger. Those of us who live in fishing communities all know families who have lost someone to the sea. Witch-hunts were fervent in seafaring villages. Witchcraft was to blame for violent weather, shipwrecks and loss of life.

At certain points in history, war and the sea took an equal share of Pittenweem's men. Sixty years before the lynching of Janet Cornfoot, the Battle of Kilsyth ravished the male population. One hundred able-bodied seamen died, devastating the village for generations. Seventeen ships rotted in their moorings. This was ruinous for the women who survived, as it was taboo for them to go to sea. They could prepare the fish and take it to market, but they could not sail. It was considered bad luck even to have a woman on a fishing boat. Perhaps one day we will understand what it might have been like for these women. Did they defy convention and take matters into their own hands?

Was their self-sufficiency a threat in later years? Perhaps Beatrix Laing's grandmother lived through these times, and taught her granddaughter to challenge men in power. I can only assemble further fictions.

In 2012, some of the locals opposed the suggestion of a memorial to the accused with the argument that it was living in the past to dwell on the witch-hunts. Yet the memorial to the fishermen of Pittenweem is nostalgic and sentimental, the figures dressed in old fashions of the past. The bronze wife has her back to West Braes, the cliffside where the accused were strangled and burned during the hunts. The plaque at the statue's feet reads, 'This memorial is dedicated to the men and women who make their living from the sea and to those who have lost their lives in so doing.' The proposed memorial originally included a longer sentiment: 'May we and those who have cause to pass this way in the days to come look upon this woman and child and reflect on the cost of fish down the years, on those who have experienced the shocking breakability [sic] of life in pursuing their calling; a mother's son, a husband, a father, a grandfather, a sweetheart.'

As I walk back over the cliffs to West Braes, I see a possibility. One wet summer, wild crowsfoot will grow in profusion. The white-petalled flowers will bloom beside a cenotaph and seat looking out to the natural harbour. I imagine the plaque: *Look to the sea mark and reflect on the shocking vulnerability of our community and those lost during the witch trials: our neighbours, daughters, wives, mothers, grandmothers and lovers . . .*

18

A Lingering, Voracious Image

'Janet Horne,' Dornoch, 1722

'The date of the last executions is often given as 1722, and a rude stone in a cottage garden adjoining the links marking the spot bears this date.'

– George F. Black, *A Calendar of Scottish Witchcraft*, 1938

The Witches Stone in the Highland village of Dornoch marks the final execution of a woman for the crime of witchcraft in Scotland. Postcards and snapshots document its unassuming presence. The earliest image, from the late nineteenth century, is grainy and occluded, the stone a forlorn figure in the foreground, framed by an unremarkable landscape. The stone is clean of lichen and moss, as if it had just been erected, and '1722' is etched in shadow. The stone appears on an Edwardian postcard with a handwritten note scrawled across the bottom: 'This stone marks the spot where the last witch was burnt in Scotland.' In another Edwardian photograph, the stone has company: a woman and three children, nattily dressed for a tour of the Highlands, pose around the modest monument. The woman sports a fashionable curled fringe, a cap and long plaid skirt, while the children stand stiffly, frowning in their Sunday best. Someone has placed a pot of flowers in front of the stone. Another postcard from 1922 shows the lot surrounding the memorial grown over with bracken. In a black-and-white photo from the 1930s, the stela begins to look as it does today, a low picket fence surrounding a neatly trimmed lawn with the stone in the centre, framed by a ring of gravel. In the 1970s, it's subsumed by a Kodachrome efflorescence of azaleas. This cenotaph has attracted tourists and offerings for at least a hundred years.

The Witches Stone of Dornoch, also called the '"Janet Horne" Memorial Stone', has a page on *Trip Advisor* and is ranked number eleven out of twelve things to 'do' in Dornoch. Some visitors have left reviews rating their experience (average: four out of five stars). One visitor notes that the date is not right on the memorial, referring to the fact that the stone says 1722, but the execution was also said to have taken place in 1725. Other reviews register disappointment: 'Not a lot to see . . .'

The peaceful village of Dornoch is an unlikely place for a memorial to the 'last woman burned'. There were no large-scale witch-hunts in the Highlands, and scholars still debate why Gaelic-speaking areas of Scotland were spared. Witch-hunting did occur, but not with the same intensity as in the central belt and on the east coast. The reasons are complex, and probably down to cultural differences in the Highlands: vestigial Catholicism, clan social structure or the persistence of fairy belief.

The earliest account of the execution of this nameless woman killed in Dornoch appears in Edmund Burt's *Letters from the North of Scotland*, written in 1730 and published anonymously in 1754. Burt was an English rent-collector and engineer working in the Highlands after the Jacobite uprising of 1715. He mentions the arrest of a mother and daughter charged with the crime of witchcraft. He makes a distinction between the superstitions of the Scots and the rational English, claiming that the notion of witches is 'pretty well worn out' with 'people of any tolerable Sense and Education in England'. The last witch legally executed in England was Alice Mulland in 1685. Burt believed that in Scotland, witchcraft was still greatly feared, even by those in power. His summary of the arrest of the unnamed mother and daughter is cursory. They were tried by the deputy sheriff, and confessed to being witches. Burt wondered, ironically, if they had been denied water, as local folklore claimed 'witches will never acknowledge their guilt as long as they can get any thing to drink'. The daughter escaped prison, but the mother 'suffered that cruel Death in a Pitch-Barrel'. He had heard that many women had met the same fate 'within the compass of no great Number of Years', and claimed 'the matter is not worth speaking of further', except to say the law criminalising witch-craft should be abolished. He questions the endeavour of a pardon for those found guilty of the crime of witchcraft, wondering 'if any one may properly be said to be forgiven a crime they never committed'. It's a compelling assertion, still relevant to discussions around the legal gesture of a pardon today.

One hundred years after Burt's recording of the arrest of the mother and daughter in Dornoch, Sir Walter Scott tells another version in *Letters on Demonology and Witchcraft*, writing: 'In the year 1722, a Sheriff-depute [sic] of Sutherland, Captain David Ross of Littledean, took it upon him, in flagrant violation of the then established rules of jurisdiction, to pronounce the last sentence of death for witchcraft which was ever passed in Scotland.' Scott describes the victim as 'an insane old woman', and repeats the old chestnut that she warmed her hands by fire that was being made to burn her. He notes that the woman's daughter was 'lame both of hands and feet', and goes on to say that her disability was a result of her mother transforming her 'into a pony . . . shod by the devil'. According to Scott's source, the Countess of Sutherland, the disabled woman's son was marked by 'the same misfortune'. The countess claimed to have known the boy personally; he was a recipient of her charity. Scott remarks that though large-scale witch-hunting had ended, the belief in witches persisted.

The last woman killed as a witch in Scotland has become known as Jenny or Janet Horne. Her name is a 'Jane Doe' of Scottish witches. This tradition may stem from ballads like 'Tam

Lin', where brave Janet saves the poet Tam Lin by holding him fast through his torments and transformations. At the time of Janet Horne's execution, the minister of the parish church was Robert Kirk, the son of the famous 'fairy minister', also named Robert Kirk, author of the weird little anthropological treatise on unearthly beings, *The Secret Commonwealth of Elves, Fauns and Fairies*. While the short book reads like science fiction, it is a source of fairy lore and a glimpse into the ontological nature of ancestral thinking. Communion with *sìthichean*, or fairies in Gaelic, was dangerous, and doomed the elder Robert Kirk. One day, he disappeared into a fairy hill. What role did the younger Robert Kirk, a man whose father was lost to the *sìthichean*, play in the execution of the last woman burned as a witch in Scotland? The details of the case are unrecorded or lost, but it's certain that fairy curses and disability are central to the story.

In Highland folklore that survived into the nineteenth century, fairies could maim a baby when the mother wasn't vigilant, leaving it deformed. Illness, disability and the Fair Folk were linked. The elder Robert Kirk equated certain symptoms of mental illness with fairy abduction – literally being 'away with the fairies'. Changeling children were thought to be fairy children left in place of a kidnapped human child. Women who had just given birth could also be taken away, a captive nurse to fairy children. When the fairy child was weaned, its nurse might die, be brought back to the human world or stay forever with the fairies. If she returned to humankind, she might find that no time had passed since her abduction, or that many years had gone by in her absence.

Childbirth is a dangerous time for mothers and babies. For women like Janet in the eighteenth century, childbirth would have been a liminal time between life and death. The experience of fairy abduction parallels postpartum depression, and it's something we see echoed in the ghost-fairy confessions of both Bessie Dunlop in Lynn Glen and Elspeth Reoch in Orkney.

Perhaps it is anachronistic to pathologise these beliefs, but the difficulties modern women experience around pregnancy and childbirth were no doubt shared tenfold by the women of past centuries. Women died in great numbers in childbirth, and infant mortality was high.

Children like Janet Horne's daughter might have been considered changelings: they survived infancy with birth defects or chronic illnesses, and this marked them as something other than human. According to Robert Kirk, the changeling was a 'lingering voracious image' of the missing child. He remarks on a melancholy, silent woman who fasted for many years and claimed to have slept on a hillock one day while she was out herding her sheep. She was transported someplace else, and later gave birth to a child. She was 'like an unextinguished lamp, and going in a circle, not unlike to the faint life of bees and some sort of birds that sleep all the winter over and revive in the spring'. This is an apt description of someone dealing with depression or perhaps chronic pain – invisible illnesses that defy medical science. That they might be fairy-wrought is as good a reason as any for these afflictions.

A person taken by the fairies was a *sìthbheire*, a term of contempt according to the nineteenth-century compiler of Gaelic folklore, John Gregorson Campbell. In old Highland tradition, precautions could be taken against fairy abductions: an old shoe thrown in the fire, doorposts sprinkled with piss, a father's shirt wrapped around a new baby. A child suspected of being swapped out for a fairy changeling could be tested by being passed over the fire or left at the hem of the sea for the tides. Some presumably survived this test, as fairy foundlings were known to reveal themselves unwittingly by their fondness for music and dancing. Unnaturally precocious, they might let on that they were much older than their earthly years. As the changeling grew older, they were said to have been 'taken out of themselves'. They had spent time away in the domain of the Fair

Folk, in *sìthein*. This was justification for ostracisation, but also a mercy.

The prejudices that damned the woman now called Janet Horne and her unnamed daughter persist. Backward ideas still dominate conversations about illness and disability, prevalent even in the mindset of some medical practitioners, who think illness is a moral failing or a curse of wrong-thinking. Some still believe the sin of the mother is visited on her children, and physical disability is a marker of God's disfavour.

*

One of my earliest memories is of enclosure – of being alone in a box. Later in life, I pieced this together as one of the times I was in an oxygen tent as an infant. I was convinced I'd been forgotten, abandoned in this place of tubes and beeping machines. I plotted my escape, looking for a way out. Was I really too small to think these things? Yet I did. Traumatic recollection is not the same as normal memory. Incidents of trauma are vivid yet fragmented, calcified with a hoar of impossibility. They carry with them the whiff of figment, terrible and immediate, as if the bad thing happened yesterday, or is still happening. I see them as *cuimhne sìthiche* – fairy memory.

In Highland lore, fairies could be spiteful, but also merciful. Should the *sìthichean* find a child that has been left alone, even for a moment, they might look after it. It's also well known that fairies are thieves. They don't steal things or people, exactly. They steal what is known in Gaelic as *toradh*, the essence or goodness. As I've learned to live with multiple chronic illnesses, I've found this idea comforting. I've had severe asthma from infancy, and I've made my way in the world despite perpetually suffocating. I often thought I must be from somewhere else, in the wrong element entirely – I'd just not got my gills yet. As I survived, accruing years and beating my prognoses, my illnesses developed illnesses. PTSD and depression emerged from the untreated trauma of severe asthma attacks and the struggle to access medical care. The bones of my feet are growing spurs and phantoms: random sensations of other toes beneath my own, ephemeral stabbings, the burning ambush of nerve pain. I remain a mystery to doctors, a puzzle they abandon like a half-worked crossword. One doctor said if he diagnosed me with fibromyalgia, I would be stigmatised. He gave me the pamphlet anyway. A specialist told me that my crippling pain was caused by my 'bad attitude'. It would have been more comforting, and perhaps as useful, if he had said this was a fairy curse. There would at least be inherited folklore to help me cope with such malefice. Whatever my diagnosis, I am now considered a problem patient.

During the witch-hunts, vulnerable or difficult people were singled out, and some historians have argued the hunts were an attempt to get rid of 'unwanted people'. This is an uncomfortable connection I carry with me on this journey, through a pandemic that takes the old, disabled and chronically ill first. There are many now, in the time of Covid, who have endured similar experiences to my own. Surviving a life-threatening illness is like returning from a fairy abduction. Illness brings myriad emotional and spiritual states and dark ecstasies. There is missing time, and a sense that one has been elsewhere – but where exactly, no one can say.

When I was a little girl, my grandmother would hold me tightly as I wheezed and coughed, her hymns sibilant over me, our sounds rhyming with the creaking of her rocking chair. The women of the family were Christian Scientists, and their prayers should have cured me, but they didn't. They said they could see the fight in me, that I wanted to live. Where did the fight come from? As a young girl, there was a family consensus that I was far from God. I was smothered by would-be miracles, suffocated with unanswered prayers. What if I belonged to a different god entirely? A god of the creatures that nest in corners, in holes in the earth, in little webbed places? Perhaps I belonged to those capricious folk in the hollow hills?

My Highland ancestors marginalised their disabled neighbours. They were exceptional – stigmatised but powerful. They had survived against the odds. Being fairy-touched was an exchange. A disability could also come with other faculties to compensate for the loss. I claim this idea. I live in my singular body in two places at once: occupying this world and another place of pain and wonder. There are no talismans – no tossed embers, no salt in the porridge, nor iron nails beneath the bed. Yet there are stories of those who came before, luck-bringers like Janet Horne's daughter, their wilful souls between worlds, with all their gifts unaccounted.

*

I'm putting in the miles to the Highlands. Neil Young is on the car stereo. Blue sky and fluffy clouds cover the distance, keeping pace as I go west. This American's love of the road happens to be true, and my heart breaks open through Gowdie country, Isobel's places, that beautiful stretch through Moray. I'm still grieving, getting my head around the idea of never going back to California. Neil Young's 'L.A.' is next on the playlist. His is the Los Angeles I remember best: smoggy, uptight. There's no reason to go back, put the needle in the groove of that heartache. My father is dead, and I can finally put paid to homesickness. No one would be waiting for me at Arrivals. There would be no more negotiating the alien familiarity of freeways, the dead stop of traffic through the leaden blur of jet lag.

My life was different in that sunny place, and every time I returned, I looked for a comforting version of a past. Over a Zoom call, one of my California friends asked me, *Remember frivolity?* I remember margaritas at El Coyote with her, gossiping about who we'd seen, what we'd just watched, the minor obsession of lipstick. But I also remember disasters, natural and otherwise: evacuating brush fires and hiding in doorways during earthquakes. The *nevermore* of it all, my Cali.

I remember hiking in the Sierra Nevadas. Once, I saw a wolf bounding up the path ahead of me – the last of its kind. He turned in the sunlit brush and stared me down. His long-muzzled smile was unmistakable. Yet seeing him was miraculous. Wolves were wiped out in California in the 1920s. Before wolf packs returned to the area in small numbers in 2015, a lone, radio-collared male named OR-7 trekked all the way from Oregon to California, looking for a mate. He travelled back and forth between the two states so many times he earned the nickname 'Journey'. It's near impossible to see a wolf in California, yet I had seen one. Did I see Journey? When he looked at me with the storm-cloud intensity of his amber eyes, did he see a woman or a witch? Together, we lingered as voracious images – wildling koans.

It's Friday the thirteenth. Of the lives I've been granted, which one am I on? Rowan trees festooned with berries shimmy in the wind off the road's soft shoulder. Fields of ripe yellow corn ripple in the sunlight, and the Black Isle darkens the horizon. Culloden Moor is in the distance on my left. I've seen it packed with tour buses full of Americans visiting stones marking the graves of their clans. It's an emotional place for many, a pilgrimage site for the Scottish diaspora, but I've never understood the fascination of battle sites. Those lean expanses of nothing much hold no interest for me.

Skirting Inverness, I travel over the Kessock Bridge on the Moray Firth to the Black Isle. The expanse of the Highlands is the epitome of Scottishness for many. The Highlands feel wild, remote and empty, but they weren't always like this. During the clearances in the late eighteenth and nineteenth centuries, tenant farmers were forcibly removed from the land. Many were put on ships to North America, while others were relocated to the north-east of Scotland. Their ancestral lands became pasture and their crofts crumbled. The clearances made room for sheep and myths. The Brigadoon fantasy, clan identities and Highland dress are central to the American dream of Scotland. Many tourists arrive in Edinburgh and skip over most of Scotland, going straight to the Highlands or Skye.

The distant hills are dusky with heather as I hug the coast north, passing over the choppy grey water of the Cromarty Firth. The sky gets big around Balnagown, and then at Tain the land flattens out. I take the bridge over the Dornoch Firth, and the sky shifts to low cloud. Miles and miles of planted woodland spread out west. I'm almost to Dornoch. As Dorothy Wordsworth travelled through the lowlands in 1803, she remarked on the fir plantations, and her observations fit the landscape here as well, haunted then as now: 'It is a very beautiful district, yet there, as in all the other scenes of Scotland celebrated for their fertility, we found something which gave us a notion of barrenness, of what was not altogether genial.'

My arrival in Dornoch is like any other tourist coming for a day out. The village is busy, despite the pandemic putting a damper on international travel. As I wind my way to the memorial stone, families with ice creams wander down the main road, and a woman passes me with a 'Jail Dornoch' shopping bag. The nineteenth-century prison is now a boutique beside the tourist information centre. In a parcel of lawn adjacent to the stone, a Historylinks museum sign shows an illustration of a witchcraft trial. An old woman stands in front of a group of men, and a notar writes down testimony worthy of the heroine of a melodrama. The image is captioned: 'I've tried to lead a good life, but my people are strangers to me now. My girl has a twisted hand and they whisper terrible things about us. Why do they hate us so?'

The lack of any material evidence implies that Janet Horne did not have a legal trial, and if anything she said was recorded, those documents have since been destroyed. The sign also claims

she was burned alive, an assertion for which there is only anecdotal evidence written down over a hundred years after the
event. There is no mention on the sign of the deputy sheriff
Captain David Ross's rogue justice. The sign speaks of the
daughter who 'escaped punishment', yet those responsible for
this atrocity, the ones who literally got away with murder, are not
named.

Up a slight hill from the sign, the stone sits before a quaint
cottage. The grass is as green and even as the golf course across
the fence. The sound of elf-shot – the swift breath of golfers
teeing off – greets my arrival. There's a stretch of blue sky
above the course, but here it's wet and dark. Warm, fat drops
of rain blacken the stone and my jacket as I stand before the
gravel ring, where shells and pebbles circle the memorial.
Stones painted by children lay before it: a waterfall, a white
rose and a whimsical 'wild haggis'. Coins brighten the top, so
many that it resembles a coin drop machine, with more piled
up at the base. A blue AA chip marking six months sobriety is
secreted between them, with the Serenity Prayer embossed on
one side: *God grant me the serenity to accept the things I
cannot change; courage to change the things I can; and wisdom
to know the difference*. An AA chip is a worry stone on a difficult journey, a physical token of inner strength and a powerful
offering indeed. I feel kinship with all who have left a piece of
themselves at the stone, knowing also that someone must come
and clean this 'ritual litter'. Lichen forms its own language over
the monument. Phrases of black, minuscule dots of green and
ruffled pinks mark the stone like notes of an alien song. The
date 1722 is painted in, but the lichen is winning, and if left
undisturbed it will cover the marking completely, erratum and
all, with its silent music.

Over the grassy knoll beside the stone lies the Witch's Pool,
now called the Royal Dornoch Pond. It's adjacent to the seventeenth hole of the golf course, surrounded by groomed, verdant

plane trees. Lanky stems of wily cat's ear grow in profusion, defying the herbicides of the Royal Dornoch course. The pool is dark and deep, contained within the fencing and barbed wire. In some accounts, witches were 'swum' here, although there are no official records of this practice in Scotland. It might have been a 'drowning pit', where women found guilty of other crimes were executed in the Middle Ages. Men were hanged, and women were drowned. If there were no suitable body of water nearby, a hole was dug and filled with water for the purpose.

In summer, the pond stagnates. According to pitchcare.com, a trade website for the turf-care industry, golfers at the seventeenth hole found it odious, and so an aerator was installed that perpetually churns the black water. In the overcast darkness, it looks like *a hell-broth boil and bubble*. The pool's one million gallons of water irrigate the golf course. A bright orange lifesaver hangs on the fence, should anyone find themselves sinking into its depths again. This pool and its attending narratives persist in the imagination, as if collective memory is subsumed there. The nameless last witch is the genius loci, the lady of this little lake, or the Cailleach of the borehole.

As I head back to Banff, the sun filters through fog over the Dornoch Firth. At Tain, the rain comes in earnest, darkening the Firth and hills to a gunmetal world. I keep thinking about Janet Horne's daughter, the nameless one, that got away. At the time of her arrest, Horne's daughter would have been old enough to have children of her own. If we are to believe the tale Scott tells of her child, the family remained in the place of their grandmother's torment. So much of our women's history is unrecorded. Often, as in the case of Janet Horne, ill-fitting fictions exist in its place. How unsatisfying these embroidered scraps are, penned by those who indulge in base sentimentality about the suffering of others. How did Janet's daughter escape? Did she try to free her mother, or did she just run? Was it the kindness of strangers or her own ingenuity that set her free? What about revenge – did she think on it at all, and what would it have looked like? I lay new stories over the old, but none seem to fit. We will never know who exactly the last accused witch in Scotland was, or if vigilante trials persisted unrecorded after the dubious date of 1722. What is certain is the multivalent idea of the witch survived.

The last witch, so brimming with life force – voracious and guileful – got away. She survived her ordeals, and multiplied. In Lizanne Henderson's study of Scottish witch trials, she parallels the ending of the witch-hunts with the disappearance of the Scottish wolf, hunted to extinction in the seventeenth century. Many claimed to have killed the last wolf, displaying their prey as a trophy in various locations well into the eighteenth century: 'While hunters celebrated the slaughter of the last wolf they could not be certain whether another still roamed free in the mountains.' The witch-hunts were concurrent with the machine of trophy-hunting that ushered in a new era of mass extinctions. A century before Janet Horne's death, the last dodo expired in the forests of Mauritius, along with the Rodrigues owl, starling, pigeon and night hen, as well as the saddle-backed and domed giant tortoise.

The last witch has no documented confessions, stories of midnight fairy raids, or knowledge of herbalism or midwifery. Whoever was hunted to extinction during this time of mass killings was not a witch. Yet witches flourish, an endangered species reintroduced into the *spiritus mundi*. What would it mean to re-wild the witch? What does the idea of the witch look like when freed from the pyre of her extinction? As we rework the word into one of power and subversion, we travel far and long to find a safe haven.

The witch has evolved over time from the church's fantasy of a demonic woman to a fairy-tale villain, a pop culture icon and a multifaceted modern identity. She is a paradox: a New Age money-spinner, a visionary thinker and a feminist firebrand. I am a witch. When I say this, I hear Walt Whitman's 'Song of Myself' – filling and emptying the terrible past and the uncertain present, looking to imbue the future with meaning:

> Do I contradict myself?
> Very well then I contradict myself,
> (I am large, I contain multitudes.)

We are many. We are in your book group; we hot-desk at the office with you, and live next door. You, perhaps, are one of us. We are witches. Just to say it is to challenge centuries of persecution. We are witches – and we remember.

19

Homecoming

Alisoun Pierson, Edinburgh, 1588

'Scho had freindis in that court quhilk wes of hir awin blude,
quha had gude acquentance of the Quene of Elphane, quhilk
mycht haif helpit hir . . .'*

– Alisoun Pierson

At seventeen, I was homeless, sleeping on sofas and relying on
the kindness of friends. I burned through their generosity as I
shoplifted bags of carrots and day-old bread. How I survived
mystifies me. I buried the memories of that vulnerable girl nurs-
ing the psychic and physical wounds of sexual assault, rejected
by her family. That sofa-surfing, traumatised teenager inside me
is still running.

I've approached the notion of 'home' through a process of
deduction. Home has to be more than ceremony, Home Office
paperwork and fees. Finding home is bigger than making peace
with years of culture shocks and pangs of homesickness. My
homecoming is not a return to the familiar past, and it's unre-
lated to the idea of family. I reject any oath of nationalism. The
lonely search for my adopted ancestors is fraught with suffering.
I've not yet answered the burning question: how is it that this
beautiful country, with its terrible history, has claimed me? I'm
left with a singular guess – could home be a place of healing?

Decades ago, long before I lived in Scotland, I was in Edinburgh
for a night and a day. I walked the jagged contours of the Gothic

---

* 'I had friends of my own blood in the fairy court, who had good acquaintance of the Queen of Elfhame, which might have helped me.'

cityscape in a pink-purple fog. The buildings were blacked by centuries of soot and grime, dirt sunk deep in the pores of the red sandstone. The narrow closes and cobblestones had their own dank weather. I ignored the 'Thistle Do' tourist shops and imagined all the stories set here, stories I might write. I noted that the Wallace Monument at dusk looked like a giant Geiger sculpture, and techno music blared from the shops selling plaid scarves, shortbread and stag key chains. I was in my twenties and ignorant about much of Scottish history. Like most tourists to the city, I didn't know that hundreds of women tried for witchcraft were taken to Castle Hill and burned, more than anywhere else in Scotland. While the kirk sessions oversaw local trials, central trials were conducted at the highest criminal court – the Court of Justiciary in Edinburgh. The accused travelled to the city over miles of rough roads, often by cart. Their journey, and their lives, ended here.

I spent the night in a fancy hotel. In those days, before the Internet changed everything, you could show up in a city, drop by the tourist information centre, and ask if there were any rooms going cheap. Sometimes it was a dump, but on other nights you could get lucky and find a good room, glimpse the luxuries reserved for wealthy business travellers. My travel diary from that brief stay holds few details. I noted with glee that the hotel had an ice machine – a measure of civilisation to my American mind – but I found the shower tepid. The wide window framed the rooftops of the city like an intricate sky-maze glinting in the night.

Beneath the high thread-count sheets of the posh hotel, I dreamed of Los Angeles and a friend of mine who had just killed herself. Her suicide had disordered my world, and I went travelling to set it right. Wendy was a brilliant scholar who could make tax documents from the Italian Renaissance interesting. She worked as a PA in Hollywood while I was a temp at a mortgage bank. I spent my days removing staples from endless boxes of documents, and she ran errands for demanding industry people. Wendy was always honest; she thought I couldn't work a room, that I needed to think bigger, and that I was an unconvincing brunette. She once told me, in a particular moment of my own despair, that I always did what mattered most, and she liked that about me. After she died, I wondered what happened to her dog, Daisy. Why didn't she ask me for help, and how could I have not seen how bad things were for her? I wandered far from the soul-deadening indignities of Los Angeles, a city that had no place for the likes of us. She chose one way of leaving, and I was looking for mine.

*

Alisoun Pierson was one of the countless accused to be executed on Castle Hill. Next to Bessie Dunlop in Lynn Glen, Alisoun's is the oldest trial I have researched. Her ordeals predate the group trials and systematised confessions found in later hunts, and her confessions read like a nightmarish soap opera. Poets at the time took full advantage of her sensational story. Alisoun's dittay is transcribed in Pitcairn's *Criminal Trials*. It's difficult to hear Alisoun's voice, rewritten in the third person by the notar, and then transcribed again by Pitcairn in the nineteenth century before I, too, note it down. I read between the imposition of the interrogator and the infiltration of slander and rumour circulating at the time, trying to find what might authentically be her lived experience. Her wild tales of herb lore, a tithe to hell, cursed books, fairy raids and otherworldly menace at her bedside all have a common thread – the capriciousness of those in power, and their use of threats and soul-extortion to get what they wanted.

The accusations read at Alisoun's trial contained hearsay and reconnaissance. James Melville, the nephew of Alexander Melville, a leader of the Presbyterian Kirk and principal at St Mary's College in St Andrews at the time of Alisoun's investigation, gathered information on her. James Melville was no stranger to witch-hunts. He witnessed an execution of another witch in St Andrews overseen by John Knox, 'against which Mr. Knox delt from the pulpit, she being set up at an pillar before him'. Melville recorded the story of Alisoun and the Bishop of St Andrews, Patrick Adamson, without mentioning her by name. He claimed they met on 'King's Hill' or Arthur's Seat in Edinburgh. Supernatural harbingers peppered the intelligence. Melville writes in his diary that a cosmic omen marked the year Patrick Adamson took the bishop's seat: 'This year, in the winter, appeared a terrible Comet' with a long tail that was 'a flaming besom in the sky'. Like a spectral witch on her broom, the comet also heralded a new age of demonising women.

The witch-hunts began in Scotland as women's networks were criminalised. Women's connections to each other were travelling webs of information, a threat to the new world order of the Reformation. They gathered at lochs and streams, doing laundry. Together, they collected water from wells, met at bakehouses and helped one another during childbirth. Women in the late Middle Ages used collective action to resist economic policies they saw as unjust. Brewsters worked together to protest the regulation of ale prices. In many Scottish towns, including Edinburgh, women were prohibited from setting up independent households. Laws forbid landlords from renting to single women. Living alone as a single woman was a criminal act, and living with other women was scandalous. *Scaldrie*, or scolding – a woman's use of her critical voice – was also illegal. In the sixteenth century, the Edinburgh town council prohibited arguments on the High Street. This offence was punishable by six hours in the jougs. After the Reformation, the policing of women's moral behaviour became central to the Kirk's agenda.

Heated arguments in the marketplace were outlawed, as were wandering minstrels, the newscasters to the folk. In 1548, the Dumfries council outlawed all but the 'official' burgh minstrels, and in 1574, Glasgow attempted to banish pipers, fiddlers, minstrels and vagabonds. An act of parliament that same year outlawed idle folk, including minstrels, songsters and storytellers. Outlaw minstrels and poets had power. Like the feared figure of the witch, a poet could bring shame on a public figure. The satirical ballads were effective at character assassination. They were considered so dangerous that slanderous writings, including books, ballads and songs, as well as 'blasphematiounis, rymes or Tragedeis' were illegal. This prohibition spurred the rise of the *pasquil* – a satirical statement posted publicly under the cover of night.

The sixteenth-century satirist and poet Robert Sempill was no stranger to gossip or blasphemous rhymes. One of his poems, 'Maddeis Proclamatioun,' is narrated by a kale-seller, Maddei, who hears all the news circulating at the market and is able to spread it freely. In the late sixteenth century, poets had a lot in common with talkative kale-sellers. Both were a threat to King and Kirk. Sempill satirised Alisoun's friendship with the bishop in 'The Legend of the Bischop of St Androis Lyfe callit Mr Patrik Adamsone'. The poet rendered the bishop abject, impotent and in league with witches. Unlike the kale-sellers and brewsters, poets had real power.

At a time when women's speech was demonised, poets employed gossip and insults, their own kind of curse, in the form of flyting. This poetic form enjoyed its place in court. King James VI and I had a retinue of poets and considered himself one, penning *The Essayes of a Prentise, in the Divine Arte of Poesie*. Sempill's 'Legend' influenced one of the King's court poets, Alexander Montgomerie, who penned the 'Flyting of Polwart', with its famous mention of the 'Scottish Hecate' Nicnevin. Both Montgomerie's 'Flyting' and Sempill's 'Legend' employ sensational witches as objects of ridicule. The gist of the sections of Sempill's poem concerning Alisoun is that the bishop was a swindler who visited several different witches, including

Alisoun, 'a carline of the Queen of the Fairies', who arrives with the seelie wights at Halloween. The poem mentions details from her confessions, such as her acquaintance with her uncle's ghost, William Simpson. Sempill accuses the bishop of visiting her while she was imprisoned in his castle. He confesses to her, 'my tool won't grow', and she 'blesses it twice or thrice with her holy hand' and restores his 'pure potency'.

Whatever is true of this scandal, Alisoun was connected to those in power, like the bishop. She was born in 1533 and lived to the age of fifty-five, just a few years older than I am now. For part of her life, she lived in Byrehill, in Fife, near St Andrews. She may have also lived on Lothian Road in Edinburgh, a busy street now filled with cinemas, bars and restaurants. For sixteen years, she was in demand as a practised healer. She worked with the ghost of her *guidschire* – or uncle – William Simpson. He was her spirit guide. Her friendship with the Bishop of St Andrews was investigated by the kirk session in 1582. She was investigated for witchcraft twice, once in 1583 and again in 1588. He betrayed their friendship and turned her over to the kirk session the following year. She was initially held in the castle at St Andrews before she escaped. Rumour claimed the bishop let her get away. This calumny had legs – even Queen Elizabeth I's secretary knew of it. In 1588, the bishop was excommunicated and Alisoun was hunted down. Alisoun's sentence is not formally recorded, but '*Convieta et Combusta*' – convicted and burned – is noted in the margin.

During her interrogations, she confessed that her uncle William Simpson taught her healing and charms. Alisoun's uncle William was dead or between worlds, 'carried away out of middle earth'. Like Bessie Dunlop, Alisoun used her ghost as a consultant. William learned these arts from an 'Egyptian giant' who took him to 'Egypt'. Romany people and Travellers were mistakenly called Egyptians at the time, and perhaps this detail hints at a fostering arrangement. The dittay also describes

William as Alisoun's cousin and mentions William's father, a smith, died because he looked at a forbidden liturgical book. William taught Alisoun which herbs heal and how they could be used to cure different illnesses. He had once been a great scholar and doctor of medicine practising in Edinburgh, and she studied with him for seven years, perhaps in his ghost-form, beginning at age twelve. He remained her advisor and, years later, helped her diagnose the Bishop of St Andrews. The bishop had an incredible list of ailments – fever, heart palpitations, dysentery and weakness in his back. She was to rub a herbal salve into his body and prepare a quart of Claret with medicinal plants for him to drink.

During one of their meetings, William warned Alisoun that the Good Neighbours were coming for her. A whirlwind marked their arrival; they were looking for a soul to pay their tithe to hell. In fairy folklore, every seven years, these beings must pay a hell-tax, offering one of themselves. Satan will accept a human in their place. Pitcairn noted this tithe was a kind of annual 'decimation' – from the Roman word meaning 'one in ten is taken as an example'. Capricious fairies held Alisoun hostage and made demands of her soul, perhaps not unlike the Bishop of St Andrews and her interrogators. It seems the Good Neighbours spared her, but the Protestant Kirk, eager to establish the Reformation in Scotland and make an example of a cunning woman, could show no such mercy.

Between stories of fairy encounters and healing techniques, Alisoun's confessions are weighted with her chronic pain and the loss of feeling in her limbs. On one occasion, she said, her suffering was so great that she laid down sick along the Grange-mure, an area just inland from Pittenweem, ten miles south of St Andrews. *Grange-mure* suggests a stretch of barren land, perhaps a moorland. A man clothed in green came to her and offered to 'do her good' if she would be faithful to him. She answered, 'If [you] come in God's name and for the good of

[my] soul, [you] should tell.' He went away before answering, only to appear to her again – this time with a group of 'lusty men and women'. She *sained* or warded herself, making a protective gesture of the cross, and prayed as the uncanny folk danced and piped, making merry with wine casks and silver goblets.

She was an outsider to both their world and her own, without anyone to trust except her uncle's ghost. She said she journeyed to Elfhame regularly, but the first time, a fairy gave her a severe blow. It took all the power and control from her left side. The violence left her with a discoloured mark, a wound so terrible that she had to lie in bed for twenty weeks to recover. She confessed to camping in Elfhame and meeting with the Good Neighbours and the queen of the fairies over many years. She had relatives and 'friends in that court' who were in good standing with the queen. During one of her visits to Elfhame, she watched the Good Neighbours make their salves in pans over fires. They gathered herbs before sunrise, just as she did. They might have helped her, but sometimes she was too unwell to visit them.

The Good Neighbours were an uneasy company. Terrifyingly, they came from Elfhame to her home and sat beside her, promising that she should never want if she were faithful and kept her promises. If she spoke of their ways, they would *martir* her, or murder her, making her a fairy martyr. Metaphorically, this bedside fairy menace is also the experience of someone with chronic illness and pain. Convalescence is akin to dark mysticism, a place outside the ordinary world where one surfaces between dreams in an endless wait filled with heightened awareness. The immediacy of this section of Alisoun's confessions, loaded with the lost time of chronic illness, spoke directly to me. I project my own sufferings on to Alisoun. Fibromyalgia, or 'pain amplification syndrome', is as much a mystery to doctors as it is to those living with the condition. Though PTSD and other illnesses, such as osteoarthritis, can trigger it, there is no cure. I imagine it as sci-fi disease, as if someone with a tricorder-like device is switching on pain centres in my body. Some pains are as precise as elf-shot; others are symphonic performances, nerve riots. While it's impossible to pathologise Alisoun's experience, especially through the distorted lens of the confessions, I feel a kinship. The reappearance of fibromyalgia symptoms can be mysterious – a sudden, specific weakening out of nowhere, seemingly fairy-wrought. Many doctors don't believe it's real. Others guess that the nerve pathways to the brain no longer perceive of pain proportionately: the circuits have overloaded, as if they have repeated *pain* – both physical and psychological – so often it's as alien as a threat from Elfhame.

*

I return to Edinburgh, to negotiate the droves of tourists milling down the Royal Mile, the crowds wearing a tawdry groove in this city. I visit the National Museum of Scotland, where a portrait of the boy-king James VI and I holds court in a beige room filled with exhibits of branks, shackles, spiked jougs and thumb-screws. In the centre stands a guillotine called 'The Maiden', once used to behead criminals in Edinburgh. The machine, invented in Scotland, predates the French Revolution. A grey-haired tourist in khaki shorts runs his hand along the 'The Maiden', measuring the blade with his fingertips. If a place can hold prayers and loving thoughts, becoming a storehouse of blessings, surely the reverse might also be true. Hatred and pain also leave indelible energetic marks, and perhaps that is what is on display along with these objects.

In the US, museums have had to reconsider how the torture devices and restraints of slavery are curated, considering they are a repository of so much human suffering. Yet here, there is little sensitivity used in the presentation of torture devices, and scant recognition of the human bodies and the souls they were forged to break. Private collectors and ghost-tour operators use these objects as part of their Grand Guignol, their amoral horror show. Rather than the grisly sensationalism often attending these devices, or the bland curators' notes, there needs to be an understanding of all that was lost – the people and histories destroyed, and the suffering caused by these things. Generations were traumatised – and perhaps, as a culture, we still are.

The centre of Edinburgh is full of beauty, tat and the curious jetsam of thousands of years of history. I wind my way from the museum to Market Street on my way to Princes Street Gardens. I pass the Edinburgh Dungeon tourist attraction, but don't go in. The franchise's red slasher font repeats in the windows, above photos of the scares inside. In this time of mass death from the pandemic, what could its shows offer tourists? In 2021, the Dungeon introduced a Covid-19 testing scheme for those entering, called the Rapid Witch Test. Those infected with Covid-19 are 'witches'. The Dungeon makes light of this modern plague, as well as femicide, capital punishment and the sufferings of the past, including the witch-hunts.

In a city where hundreds met their deaths because of accusations of witchcraft, the Edinburgh Dungeon's 'The Witches' Judgement' experience is perhaps the most well-known representation of this history in the city. Thousands attend the show each year, with a soundtrack and spinning room. Actors playing a witch-finder and a witch about to be burned at the stake frighten the audience with jump scares and special effects. Agnes, 'the baddest hag in town', casts a spell to menace tourists. From the Edinburgh Dungeon website:

> Agnes Finnie – accused of witchcraft in 1645. She's mad, she's bad, she's not to be messed with! But are you a witch too? Protect yourself from accusations of sinister sorcery or you might be burned alive! Let's face it, nobody wants a human barbecue . . . How much more deadly is the female of the species?

The website also asks: 'Have you met Agnes? She loves a good pricking.'

Atrocity is glossed over for entertainment, feeding a myth that has twisted the reality of thousands tortured and killed during the witch-hunts in the seventeenth century.

I walk through Princes Street Gardens, a long, narrow valley of manicured green with war memorials and lawn-mowing drones. All the greenery was once submerged by Nor Loch. Legend claims it was the site of the 'swimming test' for witches. As recently as 2014, an article in the *Scotsman* asserted this myth with grim relish. Drowning was once used as a form of execution for other crimes, and its use was outlawed in 1685. As I've mentioned, in all my research, I've not found a single piece of evidence this test was ever used on suspected witches in Scotland, yet the idea persists.

I've walked this stretch of urban park in midsummer when it was filled with reddened sunbathers. On a short day in midwinter, holiday market stalls light its expanse. The sky is dark as I make my way to the Royal Mile, normally heaving with tourists. Today, it's emptied out, weirdly quiet. A busker sporting a plaid dress and mohawk claims her corner by setting up a spinning wheel, as a few groups of tourists form wide, distanced circles along the cobbles. Freed from my year-long isolation, I feel Coleridge's voluptuous, trembling joy at being out in civilisation again.

I walk with purpose toward Castle Hill and the Witches Well, knowing I follow in the footsteps of the hundreds of accused who met their ends here. My journey is different. The geography of the city suggests a story – you start here, in an unassuming jumble of random shops and cafés. You walk up and up, slowly, and there will be music and little distractions, like whisky, 'Celtic' jewellery, and the promise of a grand view. Like a good daughter returned to the land of her ancestors, I pay each piper, dropping a coin in their cases. I marvel at their dignity, standing in full regalia, which they wear in blazing summer heat, surrounded by gurning selfie-takers, and also today, piping only to the paving stones and a lone passer-by.

I search for the Witches Well between souvenir shops. Eventually, I come to the Esplanade before the Castle itself. I've seen the castle grounds filled with massive bleachers set up for the Royal Edinburgh Military Tattoo and a Proclaimers concert. One in ten accused witches were tried in Edinburgh, and this is where two-thirds of all accused tried across Scotland were sentenced to death. All accused were imprisoned and interrogated locally, after which some faced a local trial, either in an ad hoc criminal court or by a travelling circuit court, while others were transported to Edinburgh to be tried by the highest criminal court, the Court of Justiciary. Countless women like Alisoun met a state-sanctioned murder here. The Visit Scotland website claims there is a 'Witches Wall' at the Esplanade, but this is a typo. The map app on my phone knows where the Well is, and it tells me where to go, but I can't see it. I see The Witchery instead, a posh, Gothic-themed hotel, cashing in on the site of atrocity. Their website claims that the hotel 'takes its name from the hundreds of women and men burned at the stake as witches on Castlehill during the sixteenth and seventeenth centuries.'

I'm almost ready to give up when I finally find the Well, tucked into the rear facade of a biscuit shop. A large man sits on it, smoking. I stand, waiting for him to move, working up the courage to ask him to shove off. His friend, seeing me waiting, prompts him to get up. He apologises to me, totally unaware that he was sitting on a memorial. When I get a good look at it, I realise it does actually look like a big, art nouveau ashtray. The Well was originally a drinking fountain, but has sadly gone the way of all public drinking fountains, and no longer runs with water. Its cast-iron basin is filled with flowerpots. The plaque beside it says it was sculpted in 1894 by John Duncan, a 'leading Celtic Revival artist'. Another sign marks it as item ninety-one of a tourist trail that tells the history of Edinburgh in 101 objects. The frame of the Well features two heads, 'the wicked head and serene head', according to the plaque above the fountain. An older woman's grimacing profile is paired with a younger, demure one. The serene head is bowed and her eyes are cast down. A stem of foxglove and a snake wrap about the faces, the snake's head protruding toward the viewer, crowning the opening where water once flowed. The plaque above says: 'Some used their exceptional knowledge for evil purposes while others were misunderstood and wished their kind nothing but good.' It explains the snake and foxglove are symbols of duality – evil and wisdom. Foxglove is highly poisonous, but in the right dosage it is used as a heart medicine. The front of the Well's basin is decorated with swirling vegetation, each side representing further dichotomies: with 'hands of healing' holding a bowl on one side and a glaring, crows-footed 'evil' eye on the opposite. The monument suggests that while some people killed here were innocent, others were actually evil. The fountain and other so-called memorials still frame the accused as suspect.

*

My last stop is the National Library. I wander through the convalescing world like a Romantic poet, a masked flâneuse. Pain slows me down. Long gone are my days of endless walks in London, what Virginia Woolf called 'street haunting'. A journey on foot is still at a turtle's pace, but now it's often a short, sharp shock. With all the tourists gone, the rough sleepers seem to be everywhere. Are more people homeless because of the pandemic, or am I only just seeing them now? Other groups are hammered, their loud camaraderie out of place. I make my way past closed cafés and shops, to the unassuming facade of the National Library. The wide, heavy doors have thistles on the brass handles. Immediately, I'm greeted by a masked employee, my appointment double-checked.

Libraries have always been a kind of spiritual home, yet for many, they are also quite literally a shelter. When I worked in the Western Addition Library in San Francisco, people without adequate housing would come and flip through the Zip Code Directories, simply because they were stacked by the heaters. The library was a place to get warm, have a wash and sleep unmolested. The National Library in Edinburgh holds no such amenities. You need to book to get into Scotland's Fort Knox of books. After the guard finds my appointment, I go from the registry desk, where a photo is taken documenting my road-weary state, to the room of wooden lockers with brass numbers, where all belongings, except for a notebook and laptop, must be left.

In a city brimming with stories, here is the beating heart, the treasure house. My numbered desk sits in an alcove lined with tomes on Scottish history. A pile of books waits for me and my heart sings – *home*. The library is an unfussy place. There's no grand hall illuminated by a skylight, no dark oak shelves or spiral staircases. It's a utilitarian space. Long readers' desks like unused banquet tables flank the low-ceilinged corners. Histories I'd long searched for and given up on ever finding just happen to be on a shelf beside me. How did the kind librarians, my fairy godparents, know to put me in this particular book-filled nook?

On the shelf beside my desk, I find *A Source-book of Scottish Witchcraft* in its unassuming yellow library binding. Compiled by Christina Larner in 1977, it's the first study to systematically use the primary sources of the central government records. In her introductory notes, Larner says that she initially believed she could quantify the accused by going through the Privy Council records, but she quickly realised these records were part of a much larger picture of prosecutions. The confessions extracted during preliminary incarceration were often the only evidence used to condemn someone to death. This 'pre-trial material' contains the stories of people who were held, tortured and interrogated, but who never went to a formal trial. There are gaps in these records, and many are missing. Going through every box of pre-trial material all over Scotland was beyond the funding and scope of Larner's initial study, and even that could not give a complete picture.

Holding Larner's *Source-book* is an emotional experience. The list of thousands of names, going on for pages and pages, is a bleak document. Devoid of a cover or front material, it's typed up in Courier on an actual typewriter and printed from a mimeograph. Each name of the accused has a number and coded abbreviations beside it. At first glance, it looks like a phone book or census record. While searching for the few souls that have eluded my research, I face proof of a genocidal operation. Larner's work was borne out of comparative studies in persecution and extermination, specifically the echoes between the Holocaust and witch-hunting. I knew this going in, yet the weight of their names is far heavier than the volume I hold in my hands, or the one you now hold in yours.

I plough through the pile of books set aside for me, pulling others from the stacks. I only have five hours. I transcribe what I can into my laptop. There were some women's voices I thought I would never hear at all, even in a fragment, yet in these nineteenth-century sources I find them quoted with a sparse and heartbreaking immediacy. I find more evidence, missing pieces and terrible discoveries. It's a sprint and a marathon. My hands cramp up as I type my notes, and I reluctantly take breaks to stretch. My notes are a wild, troubling word-hoard and I hope they're enough.

I retrace my steps through the streets of Edinburgh, relishing its attar of Scottishness even when emptied of tourists. I have a long way to go, travelling back to the north-east. My field notes are in my laptop on my back, a collection spanning years spent combing archives, trial records and markers in the land. When I set out on this journey, I considered compiling a gazetteer, an index of memorials and Carlin stones in Scotland. I soon found this list growing, changing. The history of the witch-hunts subsumed me – it was older than the place I'd come from, the place I once called home. I'd been taken in, but what or who had received me? The voices of the accused became more than a remote historical record. It was as if they spoke directly to me – to us. Even if it would take hundreds of years, someone would hear them. Their voices braided into the roads – narrow gravel paths, motorways and tidal verges. They echoed off the haze of distant mountains, susurrated in the purple of high-summer heather and roared with gannets nesting on cliff sides. I thought perhaps when I was done travelling, the map of long-dead women would go quiet, but their voices have grown louder and more insistent. They have become part of me.

I head towards Banff, where a home waits for me. On the road north, I feel the pull of my wild garden. The apple tree heavy with little green fruits, and the old stone washtub brimming with rainwater. Club moss, *Lycopodium* or creeping 'ground pine', grows in its shadow. It was once a charm against elf-shot and fairies. The dried seed pods are flammable, an incendiary staple for special effects on the Victorian stage and an ingredient in fireworks. *I'm coming home*, I tell all the lush green things that wait for me there, and I imagine a cloud of spores alight, each a burning word of witness, a name, a scattering of fire.

Epilogue
Sifting the Ashes

'Me too, I make do, I anoint what cannot be fixed.'
— Hélène Cixous, *Hyperdream*

Years ago, I was on a ship in the Norwegian Sea when a storm hit. The tempest was a stark world, with the rippling sea crested white and black, like mountains covered in snow. I found the far north grim – heavily bombed in the war and rebuilt in a post-war, modernist expediency. The colour harmonies of Trondheim – mustards, reds, slate blues, olive greens and dove greys – gave way to the industrial coding of beige and steel, broken only by the bright fishing boats, with their fluorescent net floats dangling like eighties jewellery.

I was travelling to Vardø to see Louise Bourgeois' last sculpture, the Steilneset Memorial, entitled *The Damned, The Possessed and The Beloved*. Her collaboration with Swiss architect Peter Zumthor, the memorial is set within a larger structure on the craggy coastline far beyond the Arctic Circle. Mirrors surround a burning chair in a dark glass box. They reflect the viewer and a perpetually burning flame. The monument is a memorial for over one hundred women, girls and Sami men executed in 1621. The hunts in Vardø erupted after a sudden, violent storm ravaged Finnmark, sinking ten boats and drowning forty men, devastating the small fishing village. Three years later, the union of Denmark and Norway enacted a new law against witchcraft, a law quickly enforced by the Scottish witch-hunter John Cunningham, who oversaw the trials in Finnmark.

As my own storm raged, I clung to the bed in my tiny cabin. Everything fell about – a water bottle, my books and a toiletry bag slid down back and forth on the floor. Sometimes I was almost upside down in the small space, shifting to another plane of gravity a moment later, like a terrible fairground ride that lasted twelve hours. The waves were three metres high and the windspeed force was eleven on the hurricane scale, meaning 100 kilometres per hour. The next morning, pieces of the ship's railing were missing.

We couldn't dock in Vardø. I never saw the monument, but I witnessed the northern lights. The Norn-spun spectacle undulated on the illusory horizon. It was long past midnight, the sea was calm and the ship repaired. I had the deck to myself, wearing only a sweater and my pyjamas in the Arctic night as I watched a pale green dragon of light twist above me, breathing a blast of radiance, flitting to the horizon, sparking white into a fern-frond spiral, a Catherine Wheel. Here, gods played ball with walrus skulls and dead maidens danced, veiled in solar flares. A pale web fanned out across the stars, now a white shroud unrolling.

*

I'm finishing the final pages of the manuscript, perched in my little house in Banff. The high street, full of hairdressers and kirks, is back open for business after two years of the pandemic. A sagging vinyl sign close to my house suggests that we TRY PRAYING. When I walk by, I hear its acerbic tone, the ending to a bad joke about lost faith. This writing – the necromantic, dirty work of the psychopomp – has changed me. I have lived in the world of the dead for years, a ghost alongside greater spectres. Often, my courage failed me, yet a voice insisted that I wasn't done yet. I had work to do. I wondered what it meant to write about memorials during the pandemic and the loss of my own father. Just as there was no shared familial space for my personal mourning, there has been no cultural space created for grief during the pandemic. A broad conversation about loss is missing from the public sphere. There is overwhelming pressure to 'return to normal' – when we will no longer have to protect ourselves and each other from the killer virus.

Why talk about memorials dedicated to long-dead people when there is so much death and unrest in the present? This history is essential to this moment. One could argue that all the things we see manifesting in the broken capitalism of the white elite – the legacy of slavery, the commodification of the body and the exploitation of the earth – have origins in the social restructuring of the 'Enlightenment'. Might the privatisation of common lands concurrent with the witch trials be the original disaster capitalism? These outmoded ideas we untangle now were burned into women's bodies in Europe as colonialism and the slave trade began.

The day I sat down to write this book was not momentous. The writing was a stitch in my side that wouldn't go away, a knot I had to untangle, and that I pick at still. Before writing the first chapter, I checked for any local news and saw a community wreath-laying ceremony planned for Lillias Adie's grave in Torryburn on the 315th anniversary of her death. The synchronicity was a sign. What is magic but this kind of accord? It was the sort of sympathetic concurrence by which my adopted ancestors lived. Their charms of red thread and rowan branches, widdershins dancing and bent pins thrown in wells – what were they but calls to the universe for expedience, for life to be put right?

I travel to the places of execution; I write to them. I take measure of the archives and read between the lines of the kirk sessions' scribes. Every morning, I tap away, making words stand in for physical space, for a true memorial to the atrocity. New cases and monuments come to light as I write, and no doubt this will continue after the writing is complete. These discoveries and attempts to memorialise will be ongoing, and new voices and perspectives will emerge, deepening our understanding.

On 8 March 2022, International Women's Day, Scottish First Minister Nicola Sturgeon issued a formal apology to those accused of witchcraft during the witch-hunts. Her speech framed the history with compassion and her words were powerful, setting a precedence of clarity on this issue. The day after I read this news, I just let it sink in and wash over me. As a survivor of sexual violence, Sturgeon's words felt deeply healing to me. Witness to the atrocities of the witch-hunts remains occluded by lies and silence. It is part of the erasure of women's suffering on a global scale. Violence against women remains the 'hidden' pandemic. In Scotland, police statistics show rape, sexual assault and Internet-related sexual violence have increased dramatically over the last ten years. Their figures reflect only what has been reported. Rape crisis centres have their own statistics that reveal that half of the attacks against women and children during this time were not brought to the police's attention. How many more were never spoken of to any official body? The unabated violence against women we see today was sanctioned by the Church and state during the witch-hunts. Sturgeon's apology is part of a constellation of legal measures across Europe addressing these atrocities. In January 2022, the regional parliament in Catalonia passed legislation pardoning those executed as witches, with similar legal initiatives underway in Norway and Switzerland, as well as Scotland.

In May 2022, the General Assembly of the Church of Scotland voted unanimously in favour of a motion to issue a formal apology 'concerning the persecutions of persons accused of witchcraft'. Professor Glen Pettigrove argued that an apology would be an invitation for the Church to scrutinise its values, but also a step towards reconciliation with larger sections of the public who feel alienated from the Church because of past injustices. The Reverend Professor Susan Hardman Moore, principal of

Edinburgh's New College, said an apology is about 'setting the record straight by affirming the dignity of the people our fore-runners wrote off'. One could argue that the historic Kirk did more than 'write off' certain people; it played a primary role in killing thousands. I hope that this will be acknowledged in a formal apology.

True memorial is more than the legal gesture of a pardon, apology or a designated heritage location. It is emotional, intel-lectual and spiritual work. Long before the work of a legal pardon or national memorial began, people all over Scotland were remembering the accused on a grassroots level, quietly and without media fanfare, out of love for our shared ancestors. Locally, they tend the folk memorials, leave offerings and update archaic signs. I've seen countless others collaborating to bring this injustice to light – doing the work of witness, often alone and unsupported. People hold community events, and write songs, poems and plays of remembrance. They weep together, privately and secretly. The contributions of artists, writers, storytellers and modern witches shaped this book.

My journeys to the monuments and landscapes associated with the accused have been circuitous, as was the research and its discoveries. Often, because of my disability, I returned to locations multiple times in different seasons. I went back to revise a memory, talking to my past and future selves simultane-ously. In drafting this book, I have repeatedly come back to the stories of the accused and the places they knew. There is wonder in it, and that rarest of emotions – enchantment. My telling of these experiences and women's lives is interlaced and inter-twined. In hindsight, I'd like to think this is deliberate, a distinctly Celtic way of ordering the world in knotted puzzles, a wyrd web.

History isn't just a distant mirror – it's a fractured one. For women and non-binary people, the shards are particularly ill-fitting and sharp. Many pieces are missing or deliberately destroyed. The impulse to wholeness is human. We invent and fill in the blanks, courting ghosts and making do in our reparations. Some consider the epidemic of witch-burning during the seventeenth century a mass hysteria that lasted generations. Others claim it was a systemic extermination of a certain kind of woman and a singular consolidation of power. Medical science supplanted herb lore, Christian customs destroyed ancient, inherited pagan beliefs, and the written word triumphed over oral history. The losers in all this were women – especially older, impoverished women.

Yet fifteen per cent of the accused were men. Those I studied, like the fascinating Andro Man, edged beyond the scope of this work, their experience markedly different from that of the women I was writing about. Their lives are as important and deserve a book of their own. Absent from the historical record is the presence of non-binary people – this omission is one I have reluctantly perpetuated, because I found little evidence to back my conviction that non-binary people also suffered and died. The gender identity of the accused is unknown in many cases, but we must assume that non-binary individuals were part of this picture.

The #MeToo movement inspires me to consider the brave voices – survivors' voices – from this historical time. Might their stories be profoundly relevant to women and non-binary people today? In these accused women, I see myself and so many like me who are marginalised and erased. In the shadow of the #MeToo movement, a culture of toxic masculinity and modern conspiracy theories continues to flourish. Perhaps the witch-hunters, like modern men who persist in victimising women, felt that the hardships they faced were the result of malicious outside forces rather than socio-economic factors and their own culpability. While this terrible period in history is over, the way we remember its victims continues to be shaped by a tradition of misogyny and ignorance.

On 24 June 2022, the Supreme Court of the US overturned Roe v. Wade, which had insured the constitutional right to abortion. Immediately, Christian zealots claimed this as a victory, emboldened and mobilised. Intimidation and outright attacks on women's healthcare centres and LGBTQIA peoples increased. The legal precedent for the catastrophic decision has witch-hunting at its heart. Supreme Court Justice Samuel Alito's argument to overturn Roe v. Wade refers to a treatise from 1673 by a seventeenth-century barrister and judge, Matthew Hale, who condemned women to death at the witch trials of Bury St. Edmunds. When I began writing this book, the misogynist dystopia of four hundred years ago felt remote but frighteningly familiar. After the US Supreme Court ruling, these lessons from long ago are even more urgent.

*

Popular culture has a way of eating things up and spitting them out, and witches are no exception. Witches are trending on social media sites like TikTok and Instagram, with witch-related tags gaining billions of views. New Age products and services are a multi-billion dollar industry. The latest witch fad will run its course, but what grows in its wake? Is there life for the witch after Urban Outfitters' crystal grids, tarot card Kickstarters and Black Philip memes? I look forward to a time when the market exhausts its commodification of the witch and she is free to evolve in new ways. Yet witch tourism remains a source of income for many. Unfortunately, the myth of the witch is stronger and more lucrative than any genuine witness to atrocity.

While the witch-hunts in Scotland were virulent, it was not a uniquely Scottish problem. The witch-hunts in Europe claimed an estimated 60,000 lives. Outside of Scotland, witch tourism is more developed in other parts of the UK and the US. The Lancashire Witches Walk is a memorial to the victims of the Pendle witch trials: the five-mile walk features plaques with stanzas from a poem by Carol Ann Duffy – one line profoundly claims that those killed have 'only future tourists who might grieve'. Undoubtedly, many tourists interested in witches bring a genuine desire for dignified memorial. The Pendle witch trials are also commemorated by a bronze and steel sculpture of Alice Nutter, a woman killed as an accused witch, being led in chains to her death. This lone woman at the moment of her death, captured forever before the gibbet or pyre, gives the illusion that these deaths were singular, anomalous – a personal tragedy rather than a mass atrocity.

Every town has its cottage industries of ghost tours and gruesome historical attractions, and witches are good for their business. When I lived in York, ghost tours made their rounds every night, and guides competed for the tourist pound. Can you imagine the public outcry that would meet any attempt to trivialise the horrors of other atrocities, like the Middle Passage or the Holocaust, as this sort of cartoonish Halloween entertainment? The witch-hunts sought to dehumanise the accused – and they clearly succeeded in the popular imagination. We like to think we've advanced from the candlelit age of superstition, yet the accusation of witchcraft is still so potent it robs its victims of basic human sympathy, even centuries after their persecution, torture and murder at the hands of the state, the mob and their neighbours. Like the sensational Lillias Adie plaques in Torryburn, cynical fictions often serve as a substitute for genuine women's history. The recent Jack the Ripper Museum in East London was cruelly proposed to the council as a Women's History Museum when in fact it celebrates the legend of the serial killer.

Salem, Massachusetts, 'The Witch City', is famed worldwide for its witch tourism. Even the police cars are emblazoned with witches flying on brooms. The town does also have a powerful memorial to the twenty people executed for witchcraft during the Salem witch trials in 1692. A series of granite benches in a low stone wall surround the Old Burying Point. Each bench is inscribed with the names of the accused, and their dates of execution. The designers Maggie Smith and James Cutler were inspired by the Vietnam Memorial. While this memorial creates space for remembrance, the town itself caters to the witch tourist dollar. In October, half a million visitors descend on the city to visit the 'Witch House' and Witch Museum, as well as to peruse the witch-themed shops. These are cautionary tales for those of us who would like to see a national memorial in Scotland – in the wrong hands, they can become a travesty. Perhaps even if the memorial is effective, dark tourism will be an inevitable companion to its power.

A cry for more monuments to women is not the same as a cry for a memorial to those killed during the witch-hunts. A monument is a marker of greatness, perhaps giving shape to a past event. A memorial is a space for grief, bringing dignity to the victims while it reminds us of atrocity. It should be a physical prayer – *never again*.

The stones, hills, mazes and menhirs I've gathered in this book form another map of the dead. The boreholes, unmarked graves, hillocks, mudflats, crossroads, caves and roadside shrines are stand-ins. Often, these memorials are marked the 'last woman burned', as if this could keep history from repeating, like a revenant stone over the grave of the unquiet dead. During the years of witch-hunting in Scotland, real women were rounded up in their thousands. Where is the outrage at the atrocity of mass death? There is no marker for the scope and magnitude of this loss, and these stones with their mistaken signs are not enough. Most memorials to the accused are accidental, vague or shrouded in myth. The best-known, like the Maggie Wall Monument and Janet Horne's Memorial Stone, mark the deaths of unknown or fictional women.

Witch-burnings have become hackneyed metaphors – from the misuse of the term 'witch-hunt' in political punditry, to music videos such as Madonna's 'Dark Ballet' and Jessie Reyez's

'Body Count', both of which feature executions at a pyre. The witch being led in chains to the flames is the celebrated moment, rendered in film and poetry, and cast in bronze. In the popular imagination, public executions of countless women are reduced to the spectacle of a singular woman burning. The machine set up to do the killing, the thousands of men involved, is rarely discussed. In the words of Norwegian witch-trial scholar Liv Helene Willumsen, the machine was 'a powerful apparatus'. The accused always faced a wall of men who held the power of life and death over them. The image of the burning woman is not a potent archetype, transcending suffering through martyrdom; it is obliteration.

A death at the pyre was a beacon of righteousness and terror. In Scotland, those executed for witchcraft were 'burnt to ashes'. The Kirk believed this ensured the accused would forever be outside of God's mercy. Christian cosmology was apocalyptic: at the end of time, Christians would be resurrected, as long as their bodies could be found and pieced together. Even those who died in disgrace could be offered a second chance, unless there was no body left to resurrect. This concept was a source of theological debate from the Middle Ages, but was still very much alive in seventeenth-century Scotland. The accused who died in this way were essentially damned forever.

In every village, town and city in Scotland, there's a plinth devoted to the war dead. Even my tiny local post office has a list of the postal workers who died in the Great War. Was the terror of the witch-hunts, lasting hundreds of years, not a war on women, community and folkways? And yet the dead have no wreaths, no sanctioned hour. This is my war, and I will remember my fallen sisters. Let there be no more ghost tours looking for Bald Agnes, her spirit still shaved and naked from her trials, wandering Holyroodhouse; no more 'witch's skulls' in pubs over the bar. In my dreaming, I wish for every thumb-screw, jougs, and scold's bridle in every museum case and private collection to self-immolate, to erupt in a blue, devouring heat.

I imagine a vast circle of Carlin stones, a poison garden in Nor Loch. The 'Witches Wall' on Castle Hill in Edinburgh is no longer a typo on the Visit Scotland website, but a real place for sorrow and song, a site for *caoineadh*, or lamentation. Pipers will play Karen McCrindle Warren's 'Lament for the Accused' on the hill, in the tolbooths and on each Gallows Green where the accused died.

I call all revenants to their stations, every carlin and Cailleach. Listen. Can you hear the wild keening, the drums of the charge, our advancing tattoo?

Glossary

ben – hill or mountain

blackhouse – traditional house constructed of two layers of unmortared stones packed with peat and earth and roofed with thatch

bodach – old man or a ghost

branks – scold's bridle

Cailleach – the Celtic goddess of winter and the creator-goddess in much Scottish folklore

cantrip – an incantation or spell

carlin – old woman

Carlin stone – prehistoric standing stone or natural stone associated with witches or the Cailleach

clachan – a small village or settlement

dreich – dreary

drystane – dry stone, a type of construction using unmortared stones

Elfhame – fairyland

Fair Folk – a euphemistic name for fairies

haar – a freezing mist from the North Sea

jougs – an iron collar on a chain

Kirk/kirk – church

kirk session – a church court overseen by a minister and local elders, usually landowners

likewake, or lyke wake – the watch over a dead person, often with festivities

Makar – poet

megalith – large standing stones or slabs

menhir – upright/standing stone

muirstane – moor stone

notar – notary

piobaireachd – an ancient, traditional music for the Highland bagpipe, played for formal occasions of lament

spaewives – wise women, diviners or healers (from the Scots word *spae*, meaning to see into the future)

stravaig – to wander aimlessly, to ramble

tolbooth – town hall (tolbooths were originally where taxes were paid, and served as meeting places for local magistrates, but they also doubled as prisons)

wirried – strangled

wyrd – fate, destiny, or prophecy

Notes

INTRODUCTION: PIPE SONG

'ancient and graceful Banff . . .' Carter, Angela. 'My Father's House'. *Shaking A Leg: Collected Journalism and Writings*. Penguin, 1997, p. 15.

'as a woman I have no country . . .' Woolf, Virginia. *Three Guineas*, 1938. gutenberg.net.au.

An estimated 4,000 people were formally accused and over 2,000 were executed. For general statistics, I relied on: Goodare, Julian, Martin, Lauren, Miller, Joyce and Yeoman, Louise. 'The Survey of Scottish Witchcraft'. shca.ed.ac.uk/witches.

He had seen the Interactive Witchcraft Map . . . The Interactive Witchcraft Map is a visual representation of the extensive work of the Survey of Scottish Witchcraft: University of Edinburgh. 'Witches Map'. witches.is.ed.ac.uk/.

'. . . a synonym for woman-hunting'. Christina Larner's pioneering study of the Scottish witch-hunts is in: Larner, Christina. *Enemies of God*. Basil Blackwell, 1983, p. 3.

CHAPTER I: SEAMARK

'I am in compact with the devil . . .' Lillias's interrogation record is in: 'Minutes and Proceedings of the Kirk-Session of Torryburn, in Fifeshire, and the Confession of Lillias Adie'. In Webster, David. *A Collection of Rare and Curious Tracts on Witchcraft and the Second Sight*. Thomas Webster, 1820, gutenberg.org.

'You, witch-wife . . .' Henderson, Lizanne. *Witchcraft and Folk Belief in the Age of Enlightenment*. Palgrave Macmillan, 2016, p. 222.

Methods of guarding against fairy wrath . . . Nineteenth-century folklorists like John Gregorson Campbell and Walter Gregor were an invaluable resource of folk belief demonised during the witch hunts: Gregorson Campbell, John. *The Gaelic Otherworld*. Birlinn Origin, 2019; and: Gregor, Walter. *Notes on the Folk-Lore of the North-East of Scotland*. Publications of the Folklore Society, 1881.

Scholars like Diane Purkiss have argued . . . Diane Purkiss's nuanced exploration of fairy belief and traumatic memory in Scottish witchcraft confessions informed my interpretations: Purkiss, Diane. 'Sounds of Silence: Fairies and Incest in Scottish Witchcraft Stories'. *Languages of Witchcraft: Narrative, Ideology and Meaning in Early Modern Culture*, edited by S. Clark. Macmillan Press, Ltd, 2001, p. 95.

CHAPTER 2: FATAL SISTERS

The stones are now separated . . . The archaeological record for many historic sites in Scotland can be accessed through Historic Scotland's online database, Canmore: Canmore. 'The Witches Stone'. canmore.org.uk.

'You should be women . . .' Shakespeare, William. *Macbeth*. shakespeare.mit.edu.

'Horror covers all the heath . . .' Gray, Thomas. 'Fatal Sisters. An Ode'. Thomas Gray Archive. thomasgray.org.

'. . . hardened them to denie.' Brodie, Alexander. *The Diary of Alexander Brodie of Brodie*. Spalding Club, 1878. archive.org.

. . . a mention of the torture used on Issobell Monro . . . Issobell Monro's ordeals appear in: Maxwell-Stewart, P. G. *An Abundance of Witches*. Tempus, 2005, pp. 170–171; and: Fraser, William. Chiefs of Grant, Charters. Item 320. *Histories of Scottish Families*. National Library of Scotland digital archives.

The agrarian year of early modern *Gàidhealtachd*, or the Gaelic-speaking area of Scotland, turned in quarters . . . For notes on the 'Celtic Year', see: Gregorson Campbell. *The Gaelic Otherworld*, p. 539.

'. . . it was she first made the whistle for calling another through the night . . .' Gregory, Lady Augusta. *Gods and Fighting Men*. J. Murray, 1904. gutenberg.org.

CHAPTER 3: KIRKYARD AND HOLLOW HILL

'Alas, I deserve not to be sitting here . . .' For transcripts of Isobel Gowdie's confessions, I've used Emma Wilby's in-depth study of Isobel: Wilby, Emma. *The Visions of Isobel Gowdie*. Sussex Academic Press, 2013, pp. 37–52; as well as: Pitcairn, Robert. *Criminal Trials in Scotland 1488–1624*, vol. 3, Bannatyne Club, p. 602. digital.nls.uk.

Isobel was one of at least 664 people accused across Scotland between the spring of 1661 and the autumn of 1662. An analysis of the witch-hunts in the terrible years of 1661–2 are found in: Levack, Brian P. 'The Great Scottish Witch Hunt of 1661–1662'. *Journal of British Studies*, vol. 20, no. 1 (Autumn, 1980), pp. 90–108.

Witchcraft scholar Emma Wilby recently found the full confessions . . . Wilby, *The Visions of Isobel Gowdie*, p. 3.

One ballad, 'The Elfin Knight . . .' 'The Elfin Knight' Springthyme Records. springthyme.co.uk.

. . . diarist Dorothy Wordsworth noted that blackhouses looked like 'so many black molehills'. Evocative details of rural Scottish life are found in: Wordsworth, Dorothy. *Recollections of a Tour Made in Scotland A.D. 1803*. J. C. Shairp, 1874. gutenberg.org.

It was abandoned, its tower disintegrating, even in Isobel's day. Inshoch Castle, Canmore. canmore.org.uk.

Montrose was merciless . . . Spalding, John. *Memorialls of the Trubles in Scotland and in England A.D.1624–A.D.1645.* Spalding Club, 1850. digital.nls.org.

. . . the legendary Belgian 'thief of hell' called *Dulle Griet*, or 'Mad Meg'. Winsham, Willow. 'Dulle Griet: The Many Faces of Mad Meg'. *The Witch, the Weird, and the Wonderful.* 13 April 2015. winsham.blogspot.com.

The *seelie wights*, those fairy-ghosts and spirit helpers of my ancestors, are here. For a discussion of fairies as shamanistic helper spirits in Scottish witchcraft lore, see: Goodare, Julian. 'The Cult of the Seely Wights in Scotland'. *Folklore*, vol. 123, no. 2, August 2012. pp. 198–210.

CHAPTER 4: CLIMBING THE LAW

'All kinds of ills that ever may be . . .' For both Agnes Sampson and Gelie Duncan's interrogation record, I used: Pitcairn, *Criminal Trials in Scotland.* vol. 1, pp. 230–241, 245–247. digital.nls.uk.

Gelie Duncan worked for a man named David Seaton. Details of Gelie's life are recounted by Louise Yeoman: Yeoman, Louise. 'Injustice in 16th Century Scotland'. *Witch Hunt.* BBC Radio Scotland. 7 November 2019.

***Newes from Scotland* . . .** is reprinted in: Pitcairn, *Criminal Trials in Scotland*, vol. 1, pp. 213–223.

The Gyre Carling is a legendary giant . . . Jennings, Andrew. 'The Giantess as a Metaphor for Shetland's Cultural History'. *Shima: The International Journal of Research into Island Cultures*, vol. 4, no. 2, 2010, pp. 1–14.

I return to Nan Shepherd's book *The Living Mountain* . . . Shepherd, Nan. *The Living Mountain. The Grampian Quartet.* Canongate Books, 2010.

CHAPTER 5: ATHENA OF THE SALTPANS

This garden was born of a celebratory moment in Prestoungrange, sixteen years ago ... The Prestonpans memorial events are archived on the local historical society website: Prestonpans Historical Society. 'Our Witches Remembered: 10th Anniversary'. prestoungrange.org, 22 November 2013.

... the Baron appealed to Queen Elizabeth II for a royal pardon, and she sent the matter to her ministers ... The Queen's minister's response to the Prestonpans pardon is outlined in: Barons Courts of Prestoungrange & Dolphinstoun. Trinity Session: Elizabeth II. 53. 2004. July–November. prestoungrange.org.

In 1678, the bailie, drummer and other men in Prestonpans violently seized the widow Kathrine or Keddie Liddel ... A record of Keddie's imprisonment is found in: *The register of the Privy Council of Scotland*. 3rd series, vol. 6 (1678/1680), p. 13. babel.hathitrust.org.

By the end of the seventeenth century, most of the male population could sign their names, but female literacy remained significantly lower ... *A History of Everyday Life in Scotland, 1600–1800*. Edinburgh University Press, 2010, p. 167.

Witnesses in the Prestonpans trial records spoke of terrifying night visits, something modern historians attribute to the phenomenon of sleep paralysis. Sleep paralysis as demonic phenomena in early modern Scotland is explored in: Dudley, Margaret and Goodare, Julian. 'Outside In or Inside Out: Sleep Paralysis and Scottish Witchcraft'. *Scottish Witches and Witch-Hunters*, edited by Julian Goodare. Palgrave Macmillan, 2013, pp. 372–423.

Fini's owl mask inspired the denouement of *The Story of O.* McDermon, Daniel. 'Sex, Surrealism and de Sade: The Forgotten Female Artist Leonor Fini'. *New York Times*, 6 November 2018.

'. . . provides a beautiful spectacle at the heart of the development.' 'Neighbours hail artist's tribute to executed villagers'.
Scotsman, 8 December 2011.

'the shades of night are gathering . . .' Hegel, G. W. F. 'Preface'.
Philosophy of Right, translated by S. W. Dyde, 1896.

CHAPTER 6: EDGE OF THE NORTH SEA

'Is thair na mair following me?' The confessions of the accused
from Aberdeen and Aberdeenshire are found in: Spalding
Club, *The Miscellany of the Spalding Club*, vol. 1–5, vol. 1, p.
126.

. . . they did time in the correction house. The role of the correc-
tion house in women's lives is found in: Phillips, Zoe. 'History
of Aberdeen's Infamous House of Correction Revealed'.
Evening Express, 17 May 2020; and: DesBrisay, Gordon.
'Twisted by Definition: Women Under Godly Discipline in
Seventeenth-Century Scottish Towns'. *Twisted Sisters: Women,
Crime and Deviance in Scotland Since 1400*, edited by
Yvonne Galloway Brown and Rona Ferguson. Tuckwell Press,
2002, p. 143.

The witches' ring . . . Open Space Trust. 'The Witches' Ring'.
openspacetrust.org, 27 January 2017.

I saw the needlework listed in the Kirk's Statement of
Significance . . . Open Space Trust. 'Statement of Significance'.
openspacetrust.org.uk.

The German witch-hunting manual *Malleus Maleficarum* or
The Hammer of Witches . . . *Malleus Maleficarum*, trans.
Rev. Montague Summers. J. Rodker, 1928, p. 58. wellcome
collection.org.

CHAPTER 7: JUST PEOPLE

'. . . for the murther [of my stepsister] . . .' The confessions of
the accused in Forfar are transcribed in: Anderson, Joseph,
LL.D. 'The Confessions of the Forfar Witches (1661), from

the Original Documents in the Society's Library'. *Proceedings of the Society of Antiquaries of Scotland*, vol. 22, 1888, pp. 241–262.

The scold's bridle, sometimes called the Forfar bridle ... *Statistical Account for the Parish of Forfar, 1793*, quoted in: Dalyell, John Graham. *The Darker Superstitions of Scotland*. Waugh and Innes, 1834, p. 685.

A Forfar bridle was found 'preserved in the old steeple' of the kirk at Forfar. Wilson, Daniel. *The Archaeology and Prehistoric Annals of Scotland*. Wilson Sutherland and Knox, 1851, p. 693.

'... couldnae say ae thing but she could say twa to it'. Stevenson, Robert Louis. 'Thrawn Janet', 1881.

... who no doubt knew a great deal of Scottish folklore and was a storyteller herself. Robb, David. *Robert Louis Stevenson*. Northcote House Publishers, 2015, p. 18.

'Wear some bright coloured clothes and bring no flowers.' 'Cashley'. Family Announcements. *The Courier*. 17 May 2017.

CHAPTER 8: SPAEWIFE

'For meikle kens she o' book-lore ...' Millar, Alexander Hastie. *Haunted Dundee*. M.C. MacLeod, 1923, p. 15.

'... living picture goes at last to its own herd'. Kirk, Robert. *The Secret Commonwealth of Elves, Fauns and Fairies*. Dover, 2008, p. 22.

'His hour was pursuing him ...' Wilby, *The Visions of Isobel Gowdie*, p. 345.

The first memorial is part of the Dundee Women's Trail. 'Dundee Women's Trail'. dundeewomenstrail.org.uk.

'... the destruction of Presbytery Records ...' Millar, *Haunted Dundee*, p. 18.

'The awesome flames had done their wark ...' Millar, *Haunted Dundee*, p. 15.

'Her father he's caad up the stake ...' Jelks, Maureen. 'Bonnie Susie Cleland'. Springthyme Records. springthyme.co.uk.

... **Alexander Maxwell bemoans the state of the old graves in the Howff** ... Maxwell, Alexander. *The History of Old Dundee*. William Kidd, 1884.

CHAPTER 9: NEVIN STONE

'Like Diana, who in one capacity was denominated Hecate ...' Scott, Sir Walter. *Minstrelsy of the Scottish Border*, vol. 2, 1806. gutenberg.org, p. 216.

Other women accused of witchcraft in nearby places have similar names. The source for the different Kates with similar names executed for witchcraft is: Goodare, *et al.*, 'The Survey of Scottish Witchcraft'.

'... bit of an editor war going on'. 'Talk: Kate_McNiven'. Wikipedia. wikipedia.org.

... **but in the case of Wikipedia, this mystery is also down to gender bias.** 'Who Gets To Be Notable And Who Doesn't: Gender Bias On Wiki'. *All Things Considered*. npr.org, 13 July 2021.

'... cunning consists of casting of a Clew'. Montgomerie, Alexander. 'The flytting betwixt Montgomerie and Polwart', 1629. Early English Books Online Text Creation Partnership. quod.lib.umich.edu.

The legendary mother-witch Nicnevin made mythic tracks all over Scotland and beyond. An exploration of nocturnal goddess figures in Scottish and continental witch trials can be found in: Henderson, Lizanne and Cowan, Edward J. *Scottish Fairy Belief*. John Donald, 2007, p. 136; and: Ginzburg, Carlo. *Ecstasies: Deciphering the Witches' Sabbath*. Hutchinson Radius, 1990, pp. 96–97.

'The Holocaust, or, The Witch of Monzie: a Poem Illustrative of the Cruelties of Superstition'. Blair, George. *Holocaust, or the Witch of Monzie*. Shaw, 1848.

Reverend George Blair was the pastor of the village parish for only a year. University of Dundee Archives. 'Papers relating to the Witch of Monzie'. archiveshub.jisc.ac.uk.

A singular standing stone, the Nevin Stone. The archaeological record of Monzie's Neolithic sites is in: Canmore. 'Monzie'. canmore.org.uk.

'. . . mantled with venerable ivy'. Blair, George. *Holocaust, or the Witch of Monzie.*

CHAPTER 10: POLICE TAPE AND RITUAL LITTER

'The Tinker folk know her as their own.' Jess Smith's lecture 'Storytelling' at the Winter's Last online event. 23 January 2021.

Local residents care for the memorial . . . Holder, Geoff. 'Maggie Wall Witchcraft Monument, Dunning'. spookyisles.com, 17 July 2014.

In 2019, a twenty-two-year-old woman named Annalise Johnstone was violently killed . . . Local coverage of the murder of Annalise Johnstone can be found here: Wilkie, Stephen. 'Death probe cops visit Perthshire witch memorial linked to Ian Brady'. *Express*, 22 May 2018; 'Woman linked to unsolved Perthshire murder seriously injured after alleged attack at home'. *Courier*, 17 February 2021; and 'Perthshire murdered Annalise Johnstone disliked by fellow Travellers because she was gay, High Court hears'. *Daily Record*, 10 May 2019.

When Ian Brady died at a high-security hospital in 2017 . . . Kirk, Tristan. 'Ian Brady's final request to be buried to "witch orgy" soundtrack blocked by judge'. *Evening Standard*, 13 October 2017.

I heard a ghost story from Jess Smith . . . Jimmy Somebody's Maggie Wall ghost story is retold by Jess Smith in: Smith, Jess. *Sookin' Berries*. Birlinn, 2008, pp. 6–9.

Despite historians' claims that Maggie Wall never existed . . . Beachcombing's Bizarre History Blog. 'Maggie Walls and Witch Cobblers'. strangehistory.net, 10 October 2011.

'*Clach air do chàrn.*' Macdonald, T. D. *Gaelic Proverbs and Proverbial Sayings, with English translations.* E. Mackay, 1926, p. 59. National Library of Scotland digital archives.

'In memory of Maggie Wall . . .' McKerracher, Archie. *Perthshire in History and Legend.* John Donald, 2000, p. 210.

CHAPTER 11: HEDGE MAZE

'. . . *I think that ye are not well, and ye are not weil* [right].' I found the confessions from the Crook of Devon in: Begg, R. 'Notice of Trials for Witchcraft at Crook of Devon, Kinross-shire, in 1662'. *Proceedings of the Society of Antiquaries of Scotland*, vol. 22, November 1888, pp. 211–4.

. . . when the accused described their devils, each offered their interrogators a different demonic man. Different devils at the Crook of Devon are detailed in Larner, Christina. *Enemies of God.* Basil Blackwell, 1983, p. 148.

'. . . shrine to rational thought'. 'Witches' maze sends Satan packing'. *Scotsman*, 28 March 2009.

'I have done nothing; is there a God?' McSmith, Andy. 'Toil and trouble: the last witch?'. *Independent*, 29 February 2008.

CHAPTER 12: WALL'S END

'The devill told yow . . .' The records for Bo'ness were found in: *The Scots Magazine*, vol. 34. Sands, Brymer, Murray and Cochran, 1772, pp. 718–20.

. . . according to the Falkirk Local History Society . . . For notes on Carriden House, see: Bailey, Geoff B., 'Carriden House.' Falkirk Local Historical Society. falkirklocalhistory.club.

'In some ways they *are* the dead, or the dead are with them.' Purkiss, 'Sounds of Silence', p. 84.

'beneath the thin diabolical crust . . .' Henderson and Cowan, *Scottish Fairy Belief*, p. 138.

'by means of torture . . .' Federici, Silvia. *Caliban and the Witch.* Autonomedia, 2014, p. 191.

These debates changed . . . Levack, Brian P. 'The Decline
and End of Scottish Witch-Hunting'. *The Scottish Witch-
Hunt in Context*. Manchester University Press, 2008, p.
172.

'Witch Organisation: Dances.' Davidson, Thomas. *Rowan Tree
and Red Thread*. Oliver and Boyd, 1949, p. 17.

They were all widows . . . Henderson, Alistair. 'The Urban
Geography of Witch-Hunting in Scotland'. *Scottish Witches
and Witch-Hunters*, edited by Julian Goodare. Palgrave
Macmillan, 2013, p. 551.

'. . . extracted from imprisoned and tortured witches . . .' Larner,
Enemies of God, p. 190.

'I am thyne and thow art mine.' Henderson, *Witchcraft and Folk
Belief in the Age of Enlightenment*, p. 135.

Elizabeth Scotland was a merchant's widow . . . Details of
Elizabeth Scotland's confessions are from: Goodare, *et al.*,
'The Survey of Scottish Witchcraft'.

Such a place appears in the ballad 'Gil Morice'. 'Gil Morice'.
Child Ballads. contemplator.com.

CHAPTER 13: IN THE MARGINS

'She was going betwixt her own house . . .' Bessie's confessions
are in: Pitcairn, *Criminal Trials in Scotland*, vol. 1, pp. 50–8.

Historian Sir Walter Scott transcribed Bessie's confession . . .
Scott, Sir Walter. *Letters on Demonology and Witchcraft*.
George Routledge and Sons, 1884, p. 277.

**Witchcraft scholar Emma Wilby argues these and other hard-
ships . . .** Wilby, *The Visions of Isobel Gowdie*, p. 241.

. . . a 'crown of the sun', a twenty-shilling piece . . . Murray,
Joan E. L. 'The First Gold Coinage of Mary Queen of Scots'.
The British Numismatic Society. britnumsoc.org.

In the ballad 'Thomas the Rhymer' . . . 'Thomas the Rhymer'.
Tam Lin Balladry. tam-lin.org.

In Dalry, Elfhame is not a magical land but a very real place. The map of the 'Elfhame' cave is archived online at: 'Cleeves Cove'. Scotland Off the Beaten Track. sobt.co.uk.

I have seen this uncanny preacher-man's disguise . . . Alexander Peden's mask. National Museum of Scotland. nms.ac.uk.

CHAPTER 14: RED THREADS

'Dost thou hear this now? Thou turnest thy back to me, when I am telling the truth . . .' The seventeenth-century account of Christian's alleged demonic possession, *Narrative of the Sufferings and Relief of a Young Girl in the West, with Trial of the Seven Witches Condemned to be Executed at Paisley*, is reprinted in: Davidson, *Rowan Tree and Red Thread*, pp. 175–217.

In folk belief, horseshoes deflect ill will . . . Henderson and Cowan, *Scottish Fairy Belief*, p. 88.

Hutchison argued that, just as Christian parents raise Christian children . . . Larner, *Enemies of God*, pp. 165–6.

The seven accused shared an advocate named James Robertson. For James Robertson's arguments regarding natural causes of witchcraft see: Levack, 'The Decline and End of Scottish Witch-Hunting', p. 179.

The Reverend David Brown preached to the doomed . . . Larner, *Enemies of God*, p. 167.

The author of the pamphlet is unknown . . . McLachlan, Hugh and Swales, Kim. 'The Bewitchment of Christian Shaw: A Reassessment of the Famous Paisley Witchcraft Case of 1697'. *Twisted Sisters: Women, Crime and Deviance in Scotland Since 1400*, edited by Yvonne Galloway Brown and Rona Ferguson. Tuckwell Press, 2002, p. 68.

. . . Hugo Arnot laid out his imposter theory . . . Arnot, Hugo, Esq. *A collection and abridgement of celebrated criminal trials in Scotland, from A.D. 1536 to 1784. With historical and critical remarks*. W. Smellie, 1785. wellcomecollection.org.

Modern medical historians pathologise Christian's

behaviour. McDonald, S. W., Thom, A. and Thom, A. 'The Bargarran Witchcraft Trial – A Psychiatric Reassessment.' *Scottish Medical Journal*, vol. 41, no. 5, October 1996, pp. 152–8.

Current research affirms that many people diagnosed with this disorder have a history of childhood sexual trauma. For childhood sexual abuse, trauma, and conversion disorder, see Hailes, Helen P., Yu, Rongqin, Danese, Andrea, Fazel, Seena. 'Long-term outcomes of childhood sexual abuse: an umbrella review.' *The Lancet Psychiatry*, vol. 6, no. 10, October 2019.

Bargarran House stood in ruins in the nineteenth century ... Paisley Local History Society. 'Paisley's Enchanted Threads'. paisleysenchantedthreads.co.uk.

CHAPTER 15: ROADSIDE SHRINE

'Of withered beldames auld and droll, Rigwoody hags would spean a foal.' Burns, Robert. 'Tam o' Shanter'. Scottish Poetry Library. scottishpoetrylibrary.org.uk.

'In Burns's rhymes they travel on/ And won't be lost.' Heaney's tribute to Burns: Heaney, Seamus. 'A Birl for Burns'. Scottish Poetry Library. scottishpoetrylibrary.org.uk.

Burns based his rollicking poem on an anecdote from a farmer ... 'Tam o' Shanter'. Wikipedia. wikipedia.org.

... what poet Liz Lockhead has described as 'sex pest' Burns. Dugdale, John. 'Robert Burns: was the beloved poet a "Weinsteinian sex pest"?'. *Guardian*, 24 January 2018.

... sections of unworked land were left fallow for the *Hynde Knight* or fairy king. On the practice of land left for the fairies or other mysterious land spirits, see: Gregor, *Notes on the Folk-Lore of the North-East of Scotland*, p. 179; and Lyle, Emily. 'The Good Man's Croft'. *Scottish Studies*, vol. 36, 2013, pp. 103–24.

The Reformation orchestrated a complete cultural overhaul,

changing people's relationship to the land and each other. Federici. *Caliban and the Witch*, pp. 69–75.

Rig is part of *rigwoodie*, a derogatory word in Old Scots, meaning tough and bony. Examples and definition of 'rigwoodie': 'Rigwiddie'. Dictionaries of the Scots Language. dsl.ac.uk.

Margaretha Haughwout is an herbalist, permaculture programmer and member of the Coven Intelligence Program . . . Yerba Buena Center for the Arts. 'The Coven Intelligence Program: Which plant would you choose to teach ethics to artificial intelligence?' youtube.com.

Recent work by scholar Julian Goodare has examined evidence of a native shamanistic tradition recorded in Scotland . . . Goodare, 'The Cult of the Seely Wights in Scotland', pp. 198–219.

In 1913, it was almost entirely covered in road scrapings. The archaeological record for the Witches' Stone can be found at: Canmore. 'Witches' Stone, Spott'. canmore.org.uk.

There is no record of Marion's execution. Goodare, *et al.*, 'The Survey of Scottish Witchcraft'; Larner, *A Source-book of Scottish Witchcraft*; and Sinclair, John. *The Old Statistical Account of Scotland*, vol. 5. William Creech, 1893. statac-cscot.edina.ac.uk.

CHAPTER 16: COME THE SHIPWRECK OF THE WORLD

'Come tak me noo, an tak me a . . .' Dennison's version of the Orkney witches charm appears in: MacKenzie, William (Secretary, Crofters' Commission). *Gaelic Incantations, Charms, and Blessings of the Hebrides*. Northern Counties Newspaper and Printing and Publishing Company, Limited, 1895. National Library of Scotland digital archives.

'the loneliest beach between two seas . . .' Stevenson, Robert Louis. 'The Song of the Morrow'. *Fables*. Association for Scottish Literary Studies, 2012.

'. . . most common in such wild partes of the worlde . . .' King James I. *Daemonologie*, 1597. gutenberg.org.

It was against this fraught storm of change . . . For anarchy and rebellion in early modern Orkney, see: Bennett, Martyn. 'James VI and I and the Fringes of the Enlarged Kingdom'. *Renaissance Forum*, vol. 7, 2004.

. . . eighty-one people were accused of witchcraft in Orkney, seventy-three of whom were women. Statistics for the accused in Orkney are from: Goodare, *et al.*, 'The Survey of Scottish Witchcraft'.

In 2020, nine more cases of witchcraft accusation were discovered by Orcadian archivists. Ragnhild Ljosland. 'Launch of New Orkney Antiquarian Journal vol. 9: Commemorating Victims of Orkney Witchcraft Trials'. Orkney Heritage Society, 27 September 2020. youtube.com.

In Timothy Neat's book *The Summer Walkers* . . . Neat, Timothy. *The Summer Walkers*. Birlinn, 2016, pp. 223–4.

'. . . clad in black and the other with a green tartan plaid about him'. Elspeth's confessions are found in: Maitland Club. *Miscellany of the Maitland Club*, vol. 2, part 1, 1840. National Library of Scotland digital archive.

'. . . paradoxically liberating, though told under terrible duress . . .' Purkiss, 'Sounds of Silence', p. 82.

'Mark me not to endless pain . . .' Music from the Orkney memorial is archived online: 'Drive the Cold Winter Away'. Melody: Trad., from Playford's 'Dancing Master', 1650. Arranged by Kate Fletcher and Corwen Broch. Orkney Heritage Society. soundcloud.com.

CHAPTER 17: ROUGH MUSIC

'All I have confessed . . .' Documentation of the proceedings concerning Janet's and Beatrix's ordeals are found in: *Annals of Pittenweem: Being Notes and Extracts from The Ancient*

Records of that Burgh 1526–1703. Lewis Russell, 1867, pp. 109–125.

The families of the accused bore the expense of the executions ... For the financial effect of witchcraft accusation on families of the accused in Pittenweem, see: Larner, *Enemies of God*, p. 115.

... scoring them 'above the breath'. Scott, *Letters on Demonology and Witchcraft*, p. 637.

Janet Cornfoot's daughter hid in their home as her mother was killed ... Another account of Janet's ordeal is in: Webster, D. *A Collection of Rare and Curious Tracts on Witchcraft and the Second Sight*. Thomas Webster, 1820, p. 77. gutenberg.org.

'... rashness in having a hand in the foresaid wroungous imprisonment ...' *Annals of Pittenweem*, p. 125.

Pittenweem is named for the cave ... 'St. Fillan's Cave and Well'. Canmore. canmore.org.uk.

Church lore says ... 'St. Fillan's Cave'. BBC Scotland. bbc.co.uk/Scotland.

One hundred able-bodied seamen died ... Larner, *Enemies of God*, p. 82.

In 2012, some of the locals opposed the suggestion of a memorial to the accused ... 'Pittenweem say "no" to witch memorial'. deadlinenews.co.uk, 13 April 2012.

'May we and those who have cause to pass this way in the days to come ...' Paul, William. 'Pittenweem raises £75,000 for fishermen memorial'. *The National*, 29 September 2019.

CHAPTER 18: A LINGERING, VORACIOUS IMAGE

'The date of the last executions ...' Black, George F. *A Calendar of Cases of Witchcraft in Scotland, 1510–1727*. New York Public Library, 1938, p. 83.

Burt was an English rent-collector and engineer ... Burt, Edward. *Letters from the North of Scotland*. William Paterson, 1888, p. 244.

'In the year 1722, a Sheriff-depute [sic] of Sutherland, Captain David Ross of Littledean . . .' Scott, *Letters on Demonology and Witchcraft*, p. 635.

At the time of Janet Horne's execution, the minister of the parish church was Robert Kirk . . . Henderson and Cowan, *Scottish Fairy Belief*, p. 120.

In Highland folklore that survived into the nineteenth century . . . Gregorson Campbell, *The Gaelic Otherworld*, p. 21.

'. . . like an unextinguished lamp, and going in a circle . . .' Kirk, *The Secret Commonwealth of Elves, Fauns and Fairies*, p. 61.

A person taken by the fairies was a *sithbheire* . . . Gregorson Campbell, *The Gaelic Otherworld*, p. 4.

. . . fairy foundlings were known to reveal themselves unwittingly by their fondness for music and dancing . . . Schoon Eberley, Susan. 'Fairies and the Folklore of Disability: Changelings, Hybrids and the Solitary Fairy'. *Folklore*, 1988, vol. 99, no. 1, 1988, pp. 58–77.

They steal what is known in Gaelic as *toradh* . . . Gregorson Campbell, *The Gaelic Otherworld*, p. 11.

He travelled back and forth between the two states so many times he earned the nickname 'Journey'. Center for Biological Diversity. 'Wolves on the West Coast'. biologicaldiversity.org.

'It is a very beautiful district . . .' Wordsworth. *Recollections of a Tour Made in Scotland A.D. 1803*, p. 138.

According to pitchcare.com . . . Ellingham, Amy. 'Royal Dornoch Pond passes the Sniff Test'. pitchcare.com.

'While hunters celebrated the slaughter of the last wolf . . .' Cowan, Edward J. and Henderson, Lizanne. 'The last of the witches? The survival of Scottish witch belief'. *The Scottish Witch-Hunt in Context*, edited by Julian Goodare. Manchester University Press, 2002, p. 199.

'Do I contradict myself . . .' Whitman, Walt. 'Song of Myself', 1892. poetryfoundation.org.

CHAPTER 19: HOMECOMING

'Scho had freindis in that court . . .' Alisoun's confessions are in: Pitcairn, *Criminal Trials in Scotland*, vol. 1, pp. 161–4.

. . . Alexander Melville, a leader of the Presbyterian Kirk and principal at St Mary's College in St Andrews . . . For James Melville's reconnaissance on Alisoun, see: Parkinson, David J. ' "The Legend of the Bischop of St. Androis Lyfe" and the Survival of Scottish Poetry'. *Early Modern Literary Studies*, vol. 9, no. 1, May 2003.

'This year, in the winter, appeared a terrible Comet . . .' Melville, James. *The Autobiography and Diary of Mr. James Melville*. Wodrow Society, 1843, pp. 58, 137.

An act of parliament that same year outlawed idle folk, including minstrels, songsters and storytellers. Henderson and Cowan, *Scottish Fairy Belief*, p. 115.

'. . . blasphematiounis, rymes or Tragedeis . . .' Parkinson, ' "The Legend of the Bischop of St. Androis Lyfe" and the Survival of Scottish Poetry'.

The gist of the sections of Sempill's poem concerning Alisoun . . . The stanzas of Sempill's *Legend* concerning the bishop's 'trafficking with witches' appear as a footnote to her confessions in: Pitcairn, *Criminal Trials in Scotland*, vol. 1, pp. 161–4.

Rumour claimed the bishop let her get away . . . Parkinson, ' "The Legend of the Bischop of St. Androis Lyfe" and the Survival of Scottish Poetry'.

Pitcairn noted this tithe was a kind of annual 'decimation'. Pitcairn, *Criminal Trials in Scotland*, vol. 1, p. 164.

'Agnes Finnie – accused of witchcraft in 1645 . . .' Edinburgh Dungeon. 'Witches' Judgement'. thedungeons.com.

'. . . takes its name from the hundreds of women and men burned at the stake.' 'Our Story'. thewitchery.com.

EPILOGUE: SIFTING THE ASHES

The hunts in Vardø erupted . . . For a history of witch-hunter John Cunningham in Norway, see: Willumsen, Liv Helene. 'Exporting the Devil across the North Sea: John Cunningham and the Finnmark Witch-Hunt'. *Scottish Witches and Witch-Hunters*, edited by Julian Goodare, Palgrave Macmillan, 2013, pp. 169–219.

. . . a community wreath-laying ceremony planned for Lillias Adie's grave . . . Peebles, Cheryl. 'Torryburn witch Lillias Adie honoured in village of her persecution'. *Courier*, 2 September 2019.

' . . . setting the record straight by affirming the dignity of the people our forerunners wrote off'. Swanson, Ian. 'Church of Scotland General Assembly 2022: Official apology for church's role in persecution of those accused of witchcraft'. *Scotsman*, 25 May 2022. scotsman.com.

Supreme Court Justice Samuel Alito's argument to overturn Roe v. Wade . . . Supreme Court of the United States. *No. 19–1392: Dobbs v Jackson*. 1st Draft. 10 February 2022, p. 17. politico.com.

New Age products and services are a multi-billion dollar industry. Nicole Lenoir-Jourdan. 'How witchcraft became a multi-billion dollar industry', 29 October 2020. theconversation.com.

The witch-hunts in Europe claimed an estimated 60,000 lives. Goodare, *et al*., 'The Survey of Scottish Witchcraft'.

'only future tourists who might grieve . . .' Duffy, Carol Ann. 'The Lancashire Witches'. literarylancasterpoems2.weebly.com.

The recent Jack the Ripper Museum in East London . . . Brooke, Mike. 'Angry women unveil protest billboard in East End facing Jack the Ripper museum'. *East London Advertiser*, 23 May 2016.

In October, half a million visitors descend on the city to visit the 'Witch House' and Witch Museum . . . Hines, Morgan. 'The perfect place to visit this Halloween: Salem, Massachusetts, is "Witch City" '. *USA Today*, 7 October 2019.

Acknowledgements

Shortly before his death, Walter Benjamin wrote in a letter that every word we succeed in publishing 'is a victory wrenched from the powers of darkness'. Thanks to those who blazed a path through obscurity. One bright day in January, my agent Kevin Pocklington pulled me from the slush pile of his inbox, changing everything. Thank you, Kevin, for believing in the work and for being steadfast. My editor Charlotte Humphery brought a perfect mix of passion and grounded clarity to the editing process. Tara O'Sullivan's keen eye was invaluable, as was the help of Holly Knox, Sadie Robinson and Nico Parfitt. Cover designer Natalie Chen and illustrator Iain Macarthur built a beautiful home for these words.

This is a book about outsiders, written by an outsider. Yet, I had my in. Public libraries allowed me access to information, and librarians remain guardians of that marker of civilisation: accessible knowledge. Jane Stewart and others at the local library in Banff were supportive and resourceful in helping me find obscure texts in their collections, even during a pandemic. Thank you to Robbie Mitchell, Lorna Black and other librarians at the National Library of Scotland, and Lucy Gibbon of the Orkney Archives. Your know-how was essential to researching this difficult topic.

The scholarship of Silvia Federici, Emma Wilby, Christina Larner and Lizanne Henderson cleared the way through this dense and troubling history. The Survey of Scottish Witchcraft – the work of Julian Goodare, Lauren Martin, Joyce Miller and Louise Yeoman – has been an invaluable resource, but any errors in interpretation of historical texts are mine alone.

Acknowledgements

There were conversations along the way with folks who shared their knowledge of history, landscape and the mysteries of the publishing world: Geoff Bailey of the Falkirk Historical Society, Helen Callaghan, little_snappers on Instagram, Arthur Ninfield of the Open Space Trust, Pamela Norrie aka Hag O' the Hills, Vikki Paschetto, Jennifer Selwyn, Douglas Spiers, Douglas Stevenson, Kate Stewart, The Taibhsear Collective, Allison Weightman, Dave Warren and Kiefer Duffy – *tapadh leat a charaid*.

My patrons on Patreon saw this project through from its initial field notes to the final book. Their generosity kept the heat on and the cats fed.

Paul Watson published some of this work in his inimitable *Rituals & Declarations*. Other chapters of the book first appeared in other forms in *Cunning Folk*, *Stone*, *Root and Bone*, *A Beautiful Resistance*, *The Bottle Imp* and *Folklore for Resistance*.

Deep gratitude to my ain wee covine, moon-kin and demon-minders: Edith Abeyta, Shel Glaister-Young, Carolee Harrison, Lori Matsumoto, Carolena Nericcio, Judith Stewart and Mike Row, my companion and co-conspirator. This writing was born out of a discussion with Jesse Bullington. He was the first reader for this work, and carried the light through its darkest moments. This book would not exist without his friendship.

A book comes into existence through an alliance of souls. For all the spirits, living and dead, who guided the writing, and to the friends whose memory is part of this work – scholar Wendy America Hester and Petra Mayer, a friend for fifteen years, my sister-in-mayhem and one of the very first supporters of the book. Rest in power, Speedy.